# AN ILLUSTRATED HISTORY OF KINGSTONE

## JAMES F. GALLIMORE

# Introduction

This second edition of **An Illustrated History of Kingstone** follows its first publication, in 1997. The village has not changed greatly in the interim, but during this time information has become more readily available, enabling the writing of a more comprehensive account, and the correction of earlier errors.

Why write a book about the history of Kingstone?
Kingstone seems to be a very ordinary village, but even if that is so, why should ordinary life go unrecorded? Every place has a history!
Those who live in Kingstone, or have some connection or acquaintance with the village will, I hope, find something in this book which interests them.

Beyond this my reasons are personal. Kingstone is a place I know well. It has been the birthplace, home and final resting place for generations of family members, so for me this small village will always have a special significance.
This book is dedicated to my parents, John and Olive Gallimore for their contributions to village life in Kingstone, and to my grandmother, Elsie Gallimore who provided the inspiration for the project.

James F. Gallimore 2018

----------------------------

Second Edition
Published by James F. Gallimore

Copyright © 2018 James F. Gallimore
All rights reserved.

ISBN 978-1544747286


**Acknowledgements:**

The picture on the cover of this book shows Kingstone school, dated 1910-1912.
The photograph, taken from the churchyard also shows, behind the school - left to right, Nene House (end of), the Primitive Methodist Chapel, Manor Farm, Walnut Farm, (part of) the 'Barracks' and the cottages at Church View.
Photograph by Mr. Alfred McCann, of Uttoxeter.
Reproduced by permission of Staffordshire Archives and Heritage Service

**Plate 1** (page 1) Kingston Church, a view from the north, with bridge & cottages. This water colour painting, undated, but c.1830-40 is of Kingstone old church, but also shows the bridge over the Tad brook at the junction of Church Lane and Uttoxeter Road, and the cottages/ Poor Houses, now the site of Kingstone Village Hall and car park.
Reproduced by permission of the Trustees of the William Salt Library, Stafford.

# CONTENTS:

| Chapter | Title | Page |
|---|---|---|
| 1 | The Beginnings of a Village | 7 |
| 2 | Kingstone - Lords and Masters | 9 |
| 3 | Who, Where and When? | 17 |
| 4 | Places and people: | 27 |
|  | A. Kingstone Central | 33 |
|  | B. Woodcock Heath, Leese Hill and the North | 65 |
|  | C. Park Lane to Cuckolds Haven | 71 |
|  | D. Kingstone Wood | 75 |
|  | E. Callowhill, in the deep South | 83 |
|  | F. Blythe Bridge to Wanfield | 87 |
| 5 | Some Kingstone families | 99 |
| 6 | Social Gatherings | 107 |
| 7 | Rambling and Recollection | 117 |
| 8 | Church and Charity | 125 |
|  | Bibliography | 135 |

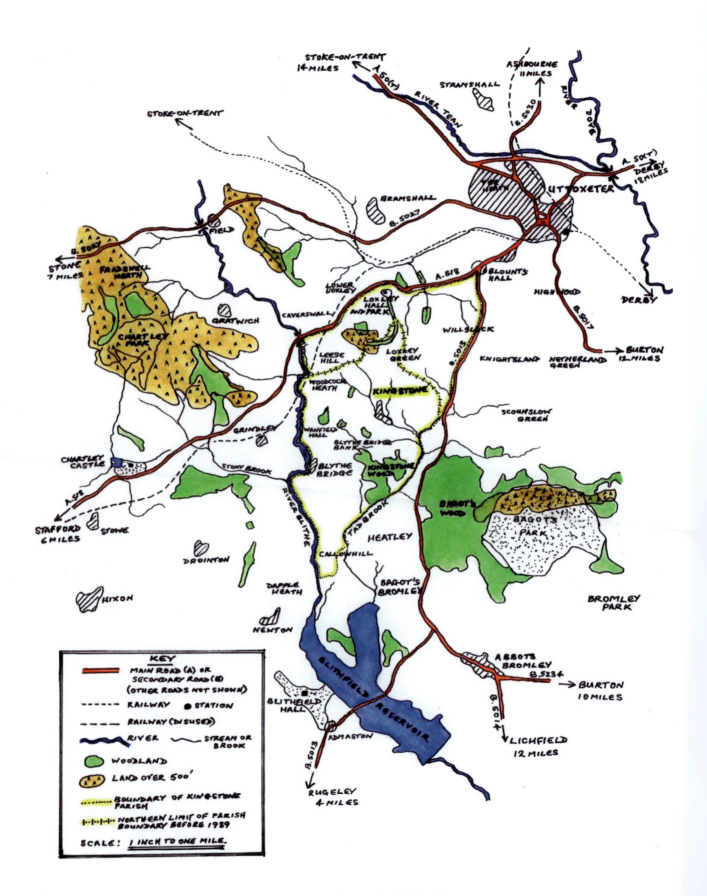

Fig. 1 **KINGSTONE** and surrounding districts
(based on Ordnance Survey map, 1962)

# Ilustrations

[All black and white drawings and later colour photographs are by the author unless otherwise indicated]

| Figure | Property or feature | Page |
|---|---|---|
| 1 | Map of Kingstone & surrounding districts | 4 |
| 2 | Goring Coat of Arms | 11 |
| 3 | 'Tithe Map' of Kingstone 1837 | 26 |
| 4 | 1837 map showing division into zones A-F | 29 |
| 5 | 1717-20 map - Zone A | 30 |
| 6 | 1837 map - Zone A | 31 |
| 7 | 1837 map - enlarged view of part of Zone A | 32 |
| 8 | Proposal for a new church 1803 | 36 |
| 9 | Kingstone church (in 1984) | 39 |
| 10 | Kingstone church chest | 39 |
| 11 | Moss Farm | 40 |
| 12 | Kingstone Hall Farm | 42 |
| 13 | Church View | 44 |
| 14 | The 'Barracks' | 45 |
| 15 | Walnuts Farm | 47 |
| 16 | Dog & Partridge/Shrewsbury Arms | 48 |
| 17 | Manor Farm | 49 |
| 18 | Primitive Methodist Chapel/Shop | 50 |
| 19 | Kingstone School | 51 |
| 20 | Centre of Kingstone showing *Barn Yard* and *Orchard* | 56 |
| 21 | Church Farm | 58 |
| 22 | Mount Pleasant | 60 |
| 23 | Black Pits Farm | 62 |
| 24 | 1717-20 map - Zone B | 64 |
| 25 | 1837 map - Zone B | 64 |
| 26 | Woodcock Heath Farm | 66 |
| 27 | Leese Hill Manor | 68 |
| 28 | 1717-20 map - Zone C | 72 |
| 29 | 1837 map - Zone C | 72 |
| 30 | 1717-20 map - Zone D | 76 |
| 31 | 1837 map - Zone D | 76 |
| 32 | Dowry Farm | 79 |
| 33 | 1717-20 map - Zone E | 82 |
| 34 | 1837 map - Zone E | 82 |
| 35 | Callowhill Hall Farm | 83 |
| 36 | Upper Callowhill Farm | 85 |
| 37 | 1717-20 map - Zone F | 88 |
| 38 | 1837 map - Zone F | 88 |
| 39 | Blythe Bridge Hall Farm | 89 |
| 40 | Blythe Bridge Hall Farm | 89 |
| 41 | Blythe Bridge Hall Farm | 90 |

| 42 | Blythe Bridge Mill | 91 |
| 43 | Blythe Bridge Smithy | 93 |
| 44 | Wanfield Hall | 97 |
| 45 | Manlove Coat of Arms | 98 |
| 46 | Bakewell Family memorials | 104 |
| 47 | Seating plan for Kingstone old church 1636 | 129 |

| Plate | | Page |
| --- | --- | --- |
| 1 | 'Kingston Church', from the north, with bridge & cottages | 1 |
| 2 | Ingestre Hall | 16 |
| 3 | Kingstone village spring | 25 |
| 4 | Kingstone old church (view from the north) | 33 |
| 5 | Kingstone old church (view from the south-east) | 34 |
| 6 | Sherrat tombs | 35 |
| 7 | Font in Kingstone old church | 35 |
| 8 | Kingstone church (Illustrated London News) 1861 | 37 |
| 9 | Kingstone church - circa 1880? | 38 |
| 10 | Stone block in church wall with lettering | 38 |
| 11 | Kingstone School 1901 | 52 |
| 12 | Kingstone School, fancy dress c.1932 | 54 |
| 13 | Kingstone School, fancy dress 1933 | 54 |
| 14 | Kingstone School, fancy dress 1933 | 55 |
| 15 | Potts' Lane | 61 |
| 16 | Former road connecting Potts' Lane with Blythe Bridge Bank | 63 |
| 17 | The well at leese Hill | 65 |
| 18 | Assault at Hollyhays 1892 | 73 |
| 19 | Kingstone Wood | 75 |
| 20 | Kingstone Wood - more than forestry and pheasants | 81 |
| 21 | Sale of Blythe Bridge Estate 1795 | 87 |
| 22 | Tommy Wood | 106 |
| 23 | 'Welcome Home' from the Boer War 1901 | 108 |
| 24 | Dance programme in the Institute | 111 |
| 25 | Kingstone WI party in the Institute 1952 | 112 |
| 26 | Some ladies try their luck | 114 |
| 27 | The 'Queen' and her retinue | 114 |
| 28 | The opening of Kingstone Fete | 115 |
| 29 | Fancy dress parade | 115 |
| 30 | Queen Noreen is crowned | 116 |
| 31 | Elsie Gallimore | 123 |
| 32 | Kingstone old church (water colour) 1857-1861 | 124 |
| 33 | Kingstone Church 1913 | 127 |
| 34 | Gratwich church 1913 | 127 |
| 35 | Kingstone old church - interior (water colour) 1857-1861 | 130 |

| Table | | Page |
| --- | --- | --- |
| 1 | Population of Kingstone 1801-1911 | 20 |
| 2 | A guide to the Tithe Map and Schedule 1838 | 27-28 |
| 3 | Incumbents of Kingstone Church | 126 |

# CHAPTER 1: THE BEGINNINGS OF A VILLAGE

## 'Kingstone'

Various spellings have been used, but no known specific reference reveals the origin of this place name.

    KINGESTON
        KINGESTUN
            KYNGESTON
                KYNGSTON
                    KYNSTON
                        KINSTON
                            KINSON
                                KINGSTON
                                    KINGSTONE   - in modern times

The name of the village has gradually evolved, as indicated above.
The earliest records seem to be for KINGESTON (Pipe Rolls 1166 and Assize Rolls 1227)(9).
KINGSTON - a common place name, usually Old English. *Cyninges -tun*, the king's tun, royal manor or farm (9).
The current name, KING<u>STONE</u> is misleading, its origin having nothing to do with 'stone'!
Staffordshire appears to have been largely passed by in earliest times. Prehistoric sites are known within the county boundary, but these seem to be limited to the northern uplands, which being less forested were more easily habitable. In general, the Romans didn't find much to interest them in Staffordshire, and they probably never got closer to the Kingstone area than Rocester, where they had a settlement on the route of the road which ran east to west between Derby and Newcastle under Lyme. Much of what became Staffordshire would have been densely forested during Roman times, and well-wooded even until recent centuries. The county was also sparsely populated, and even in the Anglo-Saxon period, Staffordshire was divided into only five administrative areas or Hundreds (compared with e.g. Kent which had sixty-eight Hundreds) (8).
The great forest of Needwood is considered to have originally covered the entire area between the rivers Trent, Dove and Blithe, and relatively few settlements were recorded here at the time of the Domesday Book in 1086. Places recorded before Domesday were generally in the valleys of these three rivers, so it seems that the newer settlements gradually developed later in the higher forested terrain between these rivers (28).
Uttoxeter, the nearest town, appears to have developed in the Anglo-Saxon period in a valley at the confluence of the rivers Dove and its tributary, the River Tean.
There are, in England, nearly fifty places called Kingston(e), all derived from *Cyninges-tun* (dating from the Anglo-Saxon period), most of which, including this Staffordshire Kingstone, are not mentioned in the Domesday Book. Their origins are unclear, but in most cases these places have no known significant past or royal associations. Neighbouring habitations which are mentioned in Domesday include Uttoxeter, Gratwich, Bramshall, Loxley, Chartley, Hixon, Drointon, Newton (in Blithfield), Blithfield, Abbot's Bromley and Marchington (7).
In 1086 Kingstone was probably almost entirely wooded and not of sufficient size or worth to be listed as a separate unit in the Domesday Book. The suggestion that it may then have formed part of the neighbouring manor of Loxley (Locheslei) seems to be the most plausible explanation (11). The sizable area of woodland - 1½ leagues (2¼ miles) long x ½ league (¾ mile broad) which was recorded in Domesday as part of Loxley could have accounted for at least part of Kingstone parish. The Domesday manor of Loxley has also been estimated to have been at least 3128 acres, whilst in a more recent period it amounted to only 1735 acres. This leaves at least 1393 acres unaccounted for which could have formed the bulk of the 2009 acres of Kingstone parish (36).
Domesday Loxley is likely to have included the area known as Leese Hill, formerly called 'Loxley Leyes', or 'Kingston Leyes' (page 67), later divided between Kingstone parish and Loxley (in Uttoxeter parish).
The reference in the Domesday Book to 'Bagot' (described in other documents as Lord of Bromley i.e. Bagots Bromley) holding Bramshall, is intriguing (7). A large area of woodland - ½ league (¾ mile) long x 4 leagues (6 miles) broad is recorded for Bramshall. We can only speculate, but this woodland could have formed a

continuous belt from Bramshall to Bagot's Bromley, and included what was later a part of Loxley, or Kingstone. Some of future Kingstone could have been part of Domesday Gratwich, which perhaps then included some of Loxley. Gratwich had a mill, which seems can only have been on the site of Burndhurst Mill, at Lower Loxley. Newton also had a mill, but no other mill is listed which could then have been on the site of Blythe Bridge Mill, in Kingstone parish.

Clearly, at the time of Domesday there would have been, in the Kingstone area, no roads as such. Even today all the local roads are narrow lanes. Footpaths and trackways would have provided the only option for those who needed to travel. Some will have journeyed on horseback, but for most people walking was the only option. Even if Kingstone was not a destination in itself, it may have been on routes which connected other localities. Blythe Bridge (more recently renamed 'The Blythe' to distinguish it from Blythe Bridge near Stoke on Trent) is at a fording place on the River Blithe, and there is a stronger case for some sort of early settlement there.

The river crossing at Blythe Bridge provides a logical point of connection for someone going e.g. from Bramshall to Drointon, Loxley to Blithfield, or Hixon to Marchington. Also, although not mentioned in Domesday, there are places nearby which are of some antiquity, including Callowhill Hall, and Booth (otherwise Bold or Bould).

At Booth (just across the river in Blithfield parish, and about one mile south of Blythe Bridge), Lower Booth Farmhouse is thought to be 15th. century in date, but built on, or next to, the site of a deserted medieval village, dating from at least the 1170s (and now a scheduled monument).

Old footpaths (and who can say how old they are?) survive, or are traceable which suggest that travellers could have found it convenient to pass through what is now the centre of Kingstone village, even as long ago as 1086! An ancient track or fosseway is said to have existed which passed from the north through Uttoxeter Heath, along Picknalls Lane, past Blount's Hall, and then cut across the fields south-west of Popinjay Farm to Loxley Bank Farm. It then continued to Loxley Green and up Fisherwick Lane (unidentified) by Leese Hill, and over the River Blithe to where there were said to have been *'ancient forges near Grindley'* (33). From Leese Hill a track going west can be traced which would have crossed the River Blithe just before Leafields, then linked with the road (now A518) going in the direction of Chartley and Stafford. Alternatively, if the destination was e.g. Newton or Drointon there was the option to go south from Leese Hill and ford the Blithe at Blythe Bridge.

The river crossing at Blythe Bridge could have otherwise been reached by going via Loxley Green, and following a route along the line of what is now Uttoxeter Road, and through the centre of Kingstone.

Present-day roads follow a fairly obvious east-west route which are probably along the line of much older tracks. A medieval traveller, going from e.g. Stafford could have chosen to go through Grindley to cross the river Blithe at Blythe Bridge. His journey to e.g. Derby, logically via Marchington, is likely to have taken him through the centre of what is now Kingstone. [A footpath from Kingstone cuts across the fields to a place called Cuckold's Haven (Fig. 29, Page 72), linking with another footpath leading towards Marchington.]

Mary Queen of Scots may have the made the reverse journey, on being moved from Tutbury to Chartley, in 1585. Routes following a generally north-south path are rather less obvious. Carry Lane, now a little-used track, runs towards Kingstone from Leigh and Field, with the indication that it was once the continuation of another track which passed through Tean and Cheadle from all places north. This was probably a route of some importance in the past. Carry Lane links with Watery Lane (called Park Lane in the past, Fig. 24, page 64) and Leese Hill.

The route south from Leese Hill, through Blithe Bridge leads to Blithfield, and on to Rugeley, whereas 'Watery Lane' would have also provided links with tracks going through Kingstone and Kingstone Wood, leading southwards towards Abbot's Bromley and Lichfield. In tracing these routes we may be able to understand why this place, later called Kingstone, developed where it did.

After the Norman Conquest Needwood became the hunting preserve of the Ferrers family under the name of Needwood Chase. At an early date the river valleys bordering Needwood were cleared of tree cover, to be followed by piecemeal clearances in medieval times. Other areas remained largely forested until the seventeenth century or later (28). The river Blithe forms the western boundary of the parish of Kingstone, while the Tad Brook flows through Kingstone and forms part of the eastern boundary of the parish. A gradual clearing of forest bordering the river Blithe would have opened up an area of rich fertile land to settlers. On a smaller scale, forest clearing in the next valley through which the Tad Brook flowed would also have opened up areas of land for arable cropping and animal grazing. It is here that 'Kingstone -on-Tad' developed, served by the Tad Brook, a tributary of the River Blithe, and also provided with a natural spring which supplied drinking water.

# CHAPTER 2: KINGSTONE - LORDS AND MASTERS

This book is primarily about those people who actually lived in Kingstone, but during much of its history the village has, for the most part, been owned by rich, powerful, landed individuals who lived elsewhere. As these absentee landlords determined what happened locally, the lives of the ordinary man, woman and child in Kingstone were very much in their hands.

**The Gresley Family of Drakelow, Burton upon Trent**

The origin of Kingstone, the identity of its earliest owners, and the reason why it is so named have become blurred by the mists of time, but by the late 12th. century Kingstone was big enough to support a church, said to have been in existence by about 1175. In 1199, the advowson (the right to present a clergyman to the living) was in dispute between William de Greseleia (Gresley), and John de Blithfield (page 125)(36).
By about 1240 the advowson and certain lands in Kingstone had been given to Rocester Abbey by William de Gresley [c.1206 - before 1254] but revenues from this were not granted until 1284.
The dispute over the advowson however provides further information about the Gresley family's link with Kingstone, William de Gresley [c.1151 - after 1220] having stated that his grandfather, William fitz Nigel [c.1090 - c.1166] had certainly owned the church in Kingstone (36).
At the time of Domesday, Nigel de Stafford, a son (or perhaps brother) of Robert de Stafford, a powerful Norman nobleman (who is said to have built Stafford Castle), held manors in Derbyshire, including 'Drachelawe' (Drakelow), as well as holdings in Staffordshire, the nearest place to Kingstone held by him (as tenant to the Bishop of Chester) being Drointon. Robert de Stafford's estates were much more extensive, and these included Gratwich and Bramshall (but not Loxley, which was owned by Earl Roger). However, there is no evidence to suggest that in 1086, either Nigel de Stafford or Robert de Stafford owned or held land which could have included what we now call Kingstone (7).
Nigel de Stafford [before 1065 - before 1124] had a son, William fitz Nigel (son of Nigel), otherwise William de Stafford. William de Stafford later assumed the name Gresley (from Castle Gresley in Derbyshire), becoming William de Gresley [c.1090 - c.1166]. It was this William de Gresley who (as it was claimed, above) had owned the church at Kingstone (and presumably Kingstone itself). The interesting implication is that if William de Stafford alias William fitz Nigel alias William de Gresley owned Kingstone church, then Kingstone and its church would have existed earlier than thought i.e. before William's death in about 1166.
Notable members of the Gresley family included Sir Geoffrey de Gresley Kt. [c.1243 - c.1305] who joined Simon de Montfort and others in rebellion against Henry III in what was known as the Baron's War. Following the Battle of Evesham in 1265, when the King's forces prevailed, he forfeited his lands, but was able to recover his properties in the following year by making large payments. Geoffrey de Gresley was knighted by Edward I, despite having, in earlier times rebelled against the Crown. Sir Geoffrey de Gresley was a man of considerable wealth, and Lord of the Manor for a number of places in addition to Kingstone (36). Interestingly he also, it seems, had the right of gallows (habuit furcam) in several places, including Kingstone. Few other families in England had the right to hang thieves 'caught in the act' (in flagrante delicto).
Sir Geoffrey's son, Sir Peter de Gresley Kt.[(1273 - c. 1310] obtained by royal charter the right of free warren (for game or rabbits) in many places, including Kingstone (36).
Sir William de Gresley [c. 1475 - 1521] held numerous manors, including Kingstone. His Staffordshire estates alone accounted for 3000 acres (36). He was succeeded by his brother, Sir George Gresley [c.1494 - 1548].
Sir William Gresley [c.1525 - 1573] succeeded his father (the above, Sir George), and was succeeded in turn by his own son, Sir Thomas Gresley.
Although when the Gresley family of Drakelow acquired Kingstone is not known, they must have owned the village for well over four centuries, up into the late Elizabethan period.
Sir Thomas Gresley [1552 - 1610], who is thought to have had debts, disposed of a number of his estates which included the manor of Kingstone, as well as land at Callowhill and Loxley. In 1593 he sold Kingstone to (his first cousin) Sir Edward Aston of Tixall, near Stafford (page 10)(36)(39). The property comprised:

*'the manor of Kyngeston, otherwise Kynston, and of 20 messuages, 10 cottages, a mill, 30 gardens, 260 acres of land (presumably arable), 100 acres of meadow, 200 acres of pasture, 200 acres of wood, 300 acres of furze and heath, 100 acres of land covered in water and 90s. of rent in Kyngeston, otherwise Kynston, Callohill otherwise Callowhill and Loxley.'*

[The conveyance names Thomas Gresley's tenants, including Henry Crompton (page 102) who leased the 'water corne mylie' (water corn mill), which must have been Blythe Bridge Mill (page 91)].

The Gresley family continued to live at Drakelow, near Burton upon Trent until the 1930s. Their family home, Drakelow Hall was demolished and later became the site of Drakelow Power Station, itself now demolished. [A relatively recent, and distinguished member of the family was Sir Nigel Gresley, the railway engineer and designer of both of the famous locomotives Mallard and Flying Scotsman.]

## The Aston Family of Tixall Hall, Stafford

The Aston family acquired the manor of Tixall and extensive estates through marriage in the early sixteenth century, and they built a new timber-framed house there in the 1550s. This Tudor mansion was the house in which, for 17 days in 1586, Mary Queen of Scots was held prisoner before making her final journey to Fotheringhay. Sir Walter Aston, son of Sir Edward Aston [c.1551 - 1597] found favour at the court of James I, being made a baronet in 1611, although he had to pay £1065 for it, a huge sum, equivalent to at least £100,000 today! In 1622 he went to Spain as an ambassador to negotiate a marriage between Prince Charles (the future Charles I) and the Infanta (daughter of the King of Spain). The proposal was rejected, but when he was King, Charles I showed his gratitude, giving some financial assistance to Sir Walter who had claimed that his expenses in Spain were ruinous. Sir Walter Aston was later elevated, becoming 1st. Lord Aston of Forfar. Lord Aston, and his later family were ardent Catholics, and consequently lost power and influence. They remained at Tixall Hall until the eighteenth century when the lack of a male heir ended the family line. Sir Walter Aston [c.1584 - 1639], the 1st. Lord Aston, disposed of his Kingstone property. He sold *'many of the tenements to the tenants, and the seignory (lordship), woods and some of the chief farms to Henry Goring, who has his seat there'* (10). An indenture dated 28 May 1625 records that Sir Walter Aston sold the manor of Kingstone together with various messuages to Henry Goring of Grindley, in Stowe parish (39). The above-described context suggests that Sir Walter Aston may have sold his Kingstone estate because of debts incurred while carrying out his mission in Spain a few years earlier. On this evidence the Aston family owned Kingstone for only about 32 years.

[Tixall Hall (not the Elizabethan house, but a later house) was demolished in 1927, but the impressive turreted Elizabethan gatehouse remains.]

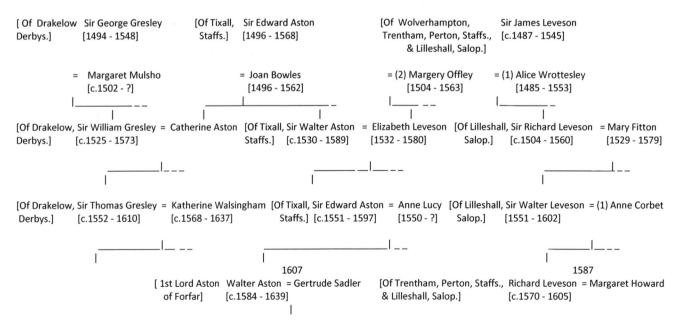

## The Goring Family of Kingstone

Henry Goring [? - 1649] became the first Lord of the Manor of Kingstone who was resident in the village. Although described as being of Grindley (in the parish of Stowe-by-Chartley) before settling in Kingstone, he originated in Sussex.

Henry Goring was a member of a syndicate of five Sussex gentlemen who invested in the developing iron working industry in South Staffordshire in the early years of the seventeenth century. [The Weald in Sussex, in the sixteenth century, had become established as the centre of the English iron industry where there were iron ore deposits, and plentiful woodland from which charcoal could be made, providing the fuel required to process the ore.] By the 1590s the iron industry in Sussex was past its peak, and iron production was becoming well established in other parts of the country, including the Midlands. The five partners are recorded as having purchased a number of Staffordshire furnaces and forges. By 1616 they had already acquired a furnace and forge at Chartley (next to Grindley, and only about three miles from Kingstone) where Henry Goring was manager. Evidence from Stowe parish register indicates that Henry Goring lived at Grindley before Kingstone, and interestingly, Redfern made reference to there having been ancient forges near Grindley (33). A recession in the iron industry in the 1620s forced the closure of some furnaces and forges, and Goring's partners told him to work out the stock at Chartley, but he claimed he was unable to do so as there were incomplete contracts for wood and ironstone. On the expiry of the lease in 1626 Goring took out a new one on his own account, so ending the partnership. The iron industry in Staffordshire seems to have left most of the partners out of pocket but Henry Goring is thought to have done well out of the business (20). The fact that he was able to purchase the manor of Kingstone at about this time seems to support the suggestion that his iron-working venture was prosperous. Henry Goring made other purchases, including Birchwood Park, in Leigh parish (probably in 1640), and at Booth. Callowhill Hall (the former Lovatt property) seems to have been acquired later, in 1646 (page 84).

Henry Goring is said to have been descended from the Goring family of Horsham, Sussex) (10)(39).

He appears to have been a younger brother of George Goring [1585 - 1663] of Sussex, a favourite at the court of James I who was involved in the successful negotiation of the marriage of Prince Charles (later Charles I) to Henrietta Maria of France. George Goring became Baron Goring in 1628 and was created Earl of Norwich by Charles I in 1644, serving as a Royalist commander during the Civil War. [His son, George Goring [1608 - 1657], also a courtier had a greater involvement in the Civil War, becoming Charles I's leading general -'only Goring defeated Cromwell in cavalry actions'. He also had a reputation for his extravagant lifestyle, and is said to have spent his fortune on drinking and gambling.]

Assuming Henry Goring was of the above family (and the Kingstone Gorings claimed the same coat of arms), his Sussex relatives, although high-born, were debt-ridden. Henry Goring chose to seek his fortune elsewhere.

Henry Goring was one of a number of gentlemen of Kingstone who were fined in 1630/31 for not accepting knighthoods from Charles I on the King's coronation in 1625/6 (36). There is also evidence that he and members of his family (unlike their Sussex relatives) were no Royalists. Henry 'Goreing' of Kingston was recorded in a

Fig. 2  **Goring Coat of Arms**:- Argent, a chevron between three annulets, gules.
Claimed by the Gorings of Kingstone (being that of the Goring family of Sussex).

11

Staffordshire list, dated 1647, of Keepers and Justices of the Peace appointed by Parliament, with a note also recording that he was 'still alive and in the service of Parliament in 1645' (36). In 1649 John Goring of Croxton (Croxden) Abbey, Henry's son was one of the commissioners for the county of Staffordshire collecting fines imposed on the estates of Royalists. John Goring is also said to have been a colonel in the service of Parliament, and Henry Goring's son-in-law, Sir Thomas Sanders (of Little Ireton, Derbyshire) was a celebrated Roundhead colonel. On the other hand, Henry Goring's step-daughter, Jane Orrell was married to Symon Degge (later Sir Symon Degge) who supported, and fought for the Royalist cause during the Civil War. Henry Goring married Joyce Orrell, the widow of Thomas Orrell, a Sussex gentleman who died in 1614. Jane Orrell, then a young child presumably moved to Staffordshire with her mother and step-father, and probably later met Symon Degge in Kingstone, becoming his first wife. Elizabeth, the eldest child of Henry and Joyce Goring was baptised at Stowe-by-Chartley in 1615.

Where Henry Goring lived in Kingstone is open to speculation but this could have been Kingstone Old Hall. [From its later description, Kingstone Old Hall would have already existed, being a timber-framed house of the later sixteenth century (page 117). Perhaps it had been built by the Aston family in the style of their residence at Tixall.] Henry and Joyce Goring had at least four children. Through his children's marriages he established useful links with other landed (influential, and wealthy) families.

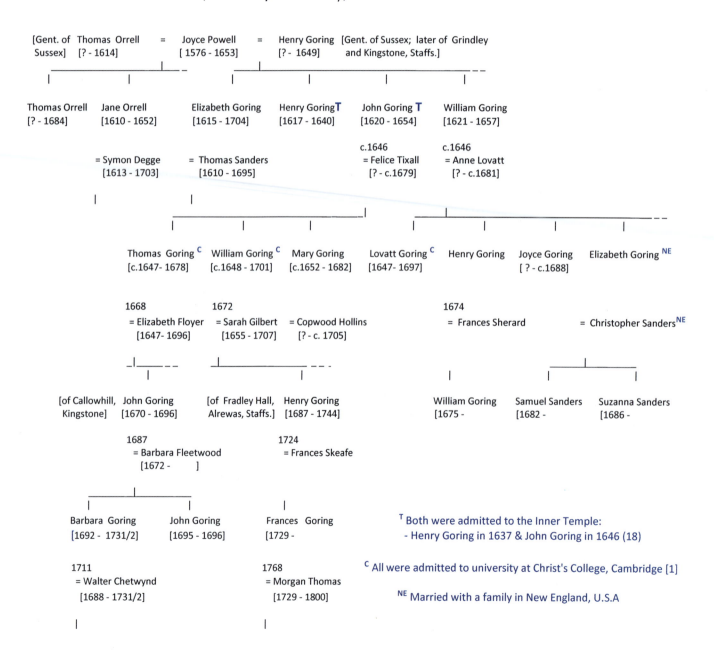

John Goring [1620 - 1654] the eldest surviving son, and Henry Goring's heir, married Felice (or Phelice) Tixall. Leese Hill is said to have become the property of the Gorings partly through the inheritance of Felice Tixall, a co-heiress, one of the four daughters of William Tixall, and by buying the shares in the property of one or more of the three other sisters. Whether the Goring family actually occupied Leese Hill is unknown.
William Tixall's widow is likely to have been still living there until she died in c.1651, but by 1667, Alexander Manlove, who had married Rachel, another of William Tixall's daughters was living at Leese Hill.
Henry Goring's other son, Willam Goring [1621 - 1657] married Anne, co-heiress of Thomas Lovatt of Callowhill. They had their own estate at 'Bold' i.e. Booth (purchased by Henry Goring in 1646), across the other side of the River Blithe, only about ½ mile from Callowhill Hall. William Goring was bequeathed £500 (worth about £40000 today) in his father's will (26).
John Goring did not long outlive his father, and in his will, dated 1654 he referred to his dwelling house as being in Kingston (26). Profits and rents out of his manor of Kingston and of Birchwood Park were to be used for the maintenance of his three young children until the age of seventeen, after which his son Thomas was to inherit the properties.
William Goring, John Goring's younger son was bequeathed land and property in Cheadle, Checkley, and Hollington, and the remaining term in the farm at Blunt's (Blounts) Hall. William Goring [c.1648 - 1701], in 1672, married Sarah Gilbert, an only child and heiress. They lived at Fradley Hall, near Alrewas and produced at least nine children, including Henry Goring (High Sheriff of Staffordshire in 1722) who inherited the property, and apparently extended it - the Hall is said to have had 40 rooms by 1723!
John Goring's daughter, Elizabeth married Copwood Hollins, a wealthy gentleman of Dilhorne Hall.
The Goring inheritance in Kingstone passed to John Goring's elder son and heir, Thomas Goring who was only about seven years old when his father died. Thomas Goring [c.1647 - 1678], (High Sheriff of Staffordshire in 1675) married, in 1668, Elizabeth Floyer, the daughter of a rich barrister of Hints, near Lichfield. Callowhill featured in their marriage settlement (39).
Thomas Goring, in turn died when his son and heir, John Goring was still a child. John Goring [1670 - 1696] married Barbara Fleetwood in 1690. They had a daughter, Barbara, and a son John, baptised at Kingstone on 20th. August 1695. John Goring wrote his will on 22nd. March 1696 and died shortly afterwards, evidently by his own hand; he was buried at Kingstone on 3th. April 1696 (39). John Goring's mother, Elizabeth quickly followed, being buried on 23rd. April, and tragically, John Goring's infant son, John died, and was buried two days later, at Kingstone on 25th. April 1696. John Goring was of Callowhill when he died, being in possession of an estate which seemed to include Callowhill Hall. The reasons for his ill-feeling towards the Chetwynd and Bagot families is unknown, but in his will (26), his dying wish was:
*'if Callowhill ever should be sold I desire neither Mr. Chettwinde (Chetwynd) nor Sir Walter Bagot may ever buy it.'*
John Goring wishes were not granted, as we shall see later!
John Goring's only surviving child and heir was his daughter, Barbara Goring. When still a minor, she married, in 1711, Walter Chetwynd. The Chetwynd family structure was complicated, with several different branches and a number of Chetwynds with the name Walter. Barbara Goring's husband was Walter Chetwynd [1688 - 1732] of Grendon, Warwickshire (MP for Lichfield, who also served in Government as paymaster of pensions), a distant cousin of his contemparary and namesake Walter Chetwynd [1678 - 1736] of Ingestre (and MP for Stafford). If Walter Chetwynd had benefited from the Goring inheritance, it was spent, as in 1731 he was said to be in reduced circumstances, resigning his parliamentary seat to accept the governorship of Barbados (at £2000 per annum). Unfortunately, he died before he could take up the post, leaving his widow Barbara to face his creditors, and she died only about a month later [30]. They were both buried at Grendon.
A document dated 1716 contains the following detail (39):-

*Release of the Manor of Kingstone and Birchwood Park and Callow Hill Estates of Kingstone; cottages and market tolls in Uttoxeter. Parties: Walter Chetwynd of Grendon and Barbara his wife née Goring to John Chetwynd of Meere.*

The document, in summary indicates the transfer (presumably sale) of ownership of the Manor of Kingstone and other property, including Callowhill - the new owner being a Chetwynd!

## The Chetwynd, Talbot and Chetwynd-Talbot Families

The identification of the afore-mentioned *'John Chetwynd of Meere'* (page 13) is key in tracing the further ownership of Kingstone.

The Chetwynd family lived at Ingestre, near Stafford, being formerly 'de Chetwynd' and originating from Chetwynd, just north of Newport, Shropshire. They came into the possession of Ingestre through marriage in the thirteenth century. Ingestre Hall was originally built for Sir Walter Chetwynd in 1613, on the site of the his family's earlier manor house. [Ingestre Hall (page 16) was largely rebuilt following a fire in 1882 but on the original lines.] Walter Chetwynd's son and grandson were both called Walter, the third Walter Chetwynd [1633 - 1692] being known as an antiquary. On his death, without heirs, although he had closer relatives, and because of an entail, his estate passed to his third cousin once removed, John Chetwynd [1651 - 1702] of Rudge, Shropshire and Maer, Staffordshire. [John Chetwynd purchased Maer Hall (about five miles south-west of Newcastle under Lyme) in 1693, a property retained by the family until 1802 when it was sold to Josiah Wedgwood II, son of the famed potter, Josiah Wedgwood I.]

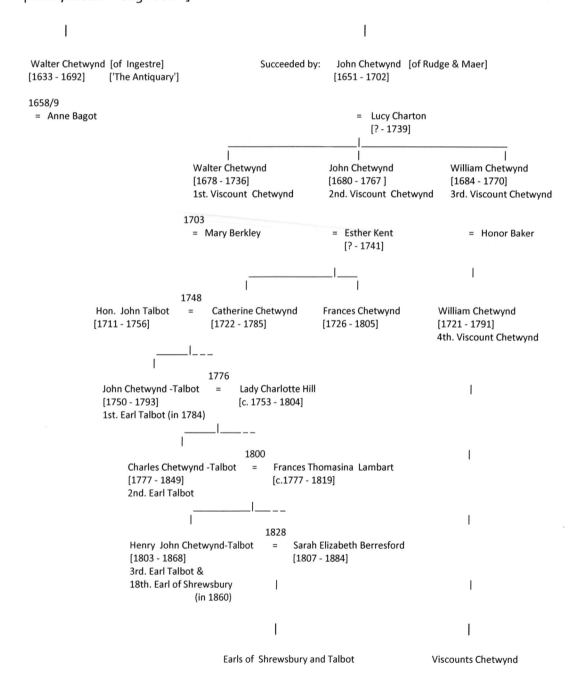

John Chetwynd had three sons, the eldest of whom, another Walter Chetwynd [1678 - 1736], became the 1st. Viscount Chetwynd in 1717, but being without heirs was succeeded by his next brother, John as 2nd. Viscount. This John Chetwynd [1680 - 1767] was '*John Chetwynd of Meere*' (Maer) who became the next owner of Kingstone (or most of it). An early eighteenth century survey of the manor of Kingstone shows that the Honourable John Chetwynd then owned much of the land. This will be examined in more detail in Chapter 2 (39).

John Chetwynd had two daughters but no surviving sons, and the youngest of the three brothers, William Chetwynd [c.1684 - 1770] succeeded him as 3rd. Viscount Chetwynd, with the title later passing to William's descendants. However, the Ingestre estate, including Kingstone (and Gratwich which had long been in the possession of the Chetwynds) was inherited by John's elder daughter Catherine Chetwynd [1722 - 1785] with the younger daughter Frances also receiving a share (39). Catherine Chetwynd, the daughter and heiress of the 2nd. Viscount Chetwynd married the Hon. John Talbot [c.1711 - 1756] in 1748. Their son, known as John Chetwynd-Talbot [1750 - 1793] inherited Ingestre, becoming first, Baron Talbot, then Viscount Ingestre and 1st. Earl Talbot. He was succeeded as 2nd. Earl Talbot by his son Charles Chetwynd-Talbot [1777 - 1849]. The 2nd. Earl Talbot was recorded as lord of the manor and owner of most of Kingstone parish at the time of the Tithe Apportionment in 1838 (24). He also seems to have been noted for his enthusiasm for farming his estates. An interest in agricultural improvement using more scientific methods was a growing trend amongst landowners of the period (42).

Henry John Chetwynd-Talbot [1803 - 1868], 3rd. Earl Talbot (son of the 2nd. Earl) was destined for yet higher rank through his Talbot ancestry.

The 1st. Earl of Shrewsbury, John Talbot [c.1387 - 1453] was apparently born in Shropshire, which would make his title logical. He was a soldier who was heavily involved in defending English conquests of parts of France. He was appointed Constable of France by Henry VI, being in effect the King's Deputy.

The 6th. Earl was assigned, by Queen Elizabeth I the task of ensuring that Mary Queen of Scots was confined, and did not escape imprisonment from her various places of imprisonment which included, locally, Tutbury Castle, and Chartley Manor (next to Chartley Castle).

The 15th. Earl of Shrewsbury was responsible for turning a former hunting lodge at Alton into Alton Towers, and for the creation of gardens which were the wonder of the age. The 16th. Earl, who continued this work was also a leading Catholic, and the patron of the architect Augustus Pugin, best known for his designs for The Houses of Parliament, but also for designing churches, notably the Roman Catholic church at nearby Cheadle. The 16th. Earl employed Pugin in making alterations and additions to Alton Towers. Alton Towers became the family seat of The Earls of Shrewsbury in 1831.

The 17th. Earl died childless in 1856, without an obvious heir. A long and expensive legal case then followed to determine which of various claimants would be his successor.

In 1860, the House of Lords decided that Henry John Chetwynd-Talbot, 3rd. Earl Talbot was the rightful heir to the title '18th. Earl of Shrewsbury', even though his relationship to the 17th. Earl was something of the order of 10th. cousin once removed! [Both he and the 17th. Earl were apparently both descended from Sir Gilbert Talbot, 3rd. son of the 2nd. Earl of Shrewsbury who lived in the time of King Edward III].

It seems that news of Earl Talbot's success, on acquiring the additional title of the Earl of Shrewsbury was met with great celebration locally (33). Formal possession of Alton Towers took place on 14th. April 1860 when a large gathering formed at Blount's Green, just outside Uttoxeter, waiting to be joined, at about 11 am, by the new Earl of Shrewsbury's party making their way from Ingestre. The procession continued into Uttoxeter to be greeted by the ringing of the church bells and with much flag-waving, the town being decorated with wreaths and banners. There was a triumphal arch in front of the town hall where a deputation gave an address and congratulated the Earl. The procession, said to have been over a mile long continued on to Alton Towers where as estimated crowd of between 35000 and 40000 people provided a welcome.

The Earl entertained about 4000 persons at the Towers. During the afternoon, in Uttoxeter, the poor were 'made to enjoy the occasion', said to have been about 500 families, or several thousand people, who were provided with about 600lbs. of beef, 600 loaves, and more than 300 gallons of ale while a band played at the Town Hall, and a cannon, planted on the new Cemetery ground was occasionally discharged (33).

By the early 20th. century the fortunes of many landed families were in decline. Great estates and grand houses were sold. In July 1918 the Earl of Shrewsbury and Talbot's Gratwich, Kingstone and Birchwood Park estates were sold, totalling 2146 acres.

The sale of 883 acres in Kingstone, a substantial part of the parish, included Kingstone Hall Farm and Broomy Leasows Farm, Moss Farm, Dowry Farm, Manor Farm, Church Farm, Woodcock Heath Farm, the Shrewsbury Arms Inn, the village school, the blacksmith's shop and the wheelwright's shop (both in Blythe Bridge), together with Moorfields, The Mosses, other small holdings, cottages and blocks of land. These properties were generally bought by the tenants (39).

In October 1918 the sale took place of the Loxley Park estate comprising over 2934 acres of land (the other main local landowner), again with the former tenants being the purchasers. [Loxley Hall had been the seat of the Kynnersley family since 1327.]

In November 1918 the Earl of Shrewsbury and Talbot sold most of his Alton estate totalling 6745 acres. Alton Towers itself and its contents were sold in 1924.

In recent years the present Earl of Shrewsbury and Talbot lived at Wanfield Hall in Kingstone. It is interesting that he should have chosen to live there. Wanfield once belonged to the Chetwynd family, Walter Chetwynd of Ingestre, having sold the property in 1614.

Plate 2 **Ingestre Hall,** near Great Haywood, Stafford - the home of the Chetwynd family and their successors.

This 17th. century mansion was built in 1613 by Walter Chetwynd, replacing an earlier manor house. [At about the same time Walter Chetwynd sold Wanfield, at Kingstone to Rowland Manlove.]

The house was however renovated and rebuilt in the 19th. century.

In 1960 the then Earl of Shrewsbury and Talbot sold his 1100 acre Ingestre Estate.

Ingestre Hall is now owned by Sandwell Council and used as a residential Arts and Conference Centre.

# CHAPTER 3: WHO, WHERE & WHEN ?

Information about who lived where and when in Kingstone, during times past can be obtained from a variety of sources. Parish registers were ordered to be kept from 1538, but prior to this date there are 'slim pickings' in other documents. These mostly record issues related to taxation, transfers of land and criminal misdemeanours.

## 1. Subsidy Roll of 1327

The Subsidy Roll of 1327 lists every man (sometimes woman) in each town and village and the amount each was taxed (based on a twentieth part of all his moveable goods, with those whose moveable goods did not amount to 10s. being exempt). This Subsidy was granted by the First Parliament of Edward III to meet the expenses of the war with Scotland (36). The Staffordshire list includes 'Kyngeston' i.e. Kingstone, as below:

**Kyngeston**

|  | s. | d. |
|---|---|---|
| De Hugone de Hampton | ij | vj |
| Galfrido Broun | iij |  |
| Ric'o Atteyate | ij | vj |
| Ric'o fil' Hugonis | ij |  |
| Ric'o de Payneslowe | iij |  |
| Ric'o filio Joh'is | xxj |  |
| Joh'e Muryel | ij | viij |
| Ricardo de Gretewych | ij | j |
| Henr' de Melewych | ij | iij |
| Margerita Hewet | iij | iij |
| Joh's filio Joh'is |  | xiij |
| Hugone Gamel | ij |  |
| Wili'mo filio Galfridi | ij |  |
| Summa | xxx.s. | iij.d. |

Although we cannot make any connection between any of the above individuals and those of a later era, the above is of interest as it is the earliest known list of some Kingstone inhabitants. At this time surnames were still evolving and in many cases 'filio' i.e. son of, appears. For example 'Wili'mo filio Galfridi' translates as William, son of Geoffrey. Others take their name from nearby places, including 'de Gretwych' (of Gratwich), 'de Melewych' (of Milwich), 'de Hampton' (of Hampton, in Blithfield parish) and 'de Payneslowe' (of Paynsley, near Draycott in the Moors?). The sums assessed are for e.g. 'Galfrido Broun' (Geoffrey Brown) ij *s.* (three shillings), for 'Joh's filio Joh'is' (John, son of John), xiij.*d.* (eight pence), the sum total for 'Kyngeston' being xxx.*s.* iij.*d.* (thirty shillings and three pence).

## 2. Lists of Families in the Archdeaconry of Stafford 1532-1533

This sixteenth century list of personal names, arranged by family survives for most of the parishes in the archdeaconry of Stafford. The nature and purpose of this record is uncertain since it does not list all inhabitants within a parish, and lists some who were dead as well as the living. The value of the list is in indicating personal names occurring within a given parish at a relatively early date (41).
This record provides us with is the earliest record of individuals identifiable as Kingstone residents.

[Note that only surnames are listed here. The full listing is of 32 family groups, with forenames being given as well as surnames.]

The entry for Kingstone lists the following :

Thomas* Abell, - the vicar or curate

Lovott (Lovatt) ; Tyxsall (Tixall) ; Wright ; Normon (Norman) ; Alsop ; Hyll (Hill) ; Holand (Holland) ; Barton ; Bayle (Bayley) ; Chalner (Challinor?) ; Key ; Rasskyll ; Sountt (Sant?) ; Clerman ; Buttler ; Russell ; Pryce ; Flemynge (Fleming) ; Forde ; Alen (Allen) ; Bott ; Wodcok (Woodcock) ; Clarke ; Hogson (Hodgson) ; Sherott (Sherratt) ; Coop (Cope) ; William (41).

* This seems to be an error; other evidence (page 126) names John Abell.

No other records are known until the following century. Another unusual record, dating from 1636 is of a seating plan for Kingstone church. This is described in Chapter 8, page 129. Thirty years later, householders then living in Kingstone were listed (along with their expected contribution), in a taxation record, as follows.

## 3. Hearth Tax - Kingstone Constablewick 1666

Governments have sought to raise revenue by imposing taxes on e.g. land, servants, game, windows and even hairpowder! The Hearth Tax was levied annually from 1662 - 1689 and is of interest in demonstrating social and financial position. The tax payable was 2 shillings (10p) for each fireplace for dwellings valued at over 20 shillings (£1) a year. Those who were too poor were exempt. Hearth Tax rolls list householders (not owners), including those not charged (36). The following lists thirty two householders in Kingstone who were taxed, and sixteen who were exempt.

| Name of Householder | Hearthes Chargeable |
| --- | --- |
| Mrtrs. Phelice Gorringe (Goring) | Six |
| Mrtrs. Anne Gorringe | Foure |
| Mr. Alexander Maudlee (Manlove) | Three |
| Thomas Steele | Sixe |
| Eliz. Hogkinson | Two |
| Henry Sherratt | Two |
| Richard Twoothe (Tooth) | Seavon |
| Christopher Aberley | One |
| John Martin | One |
| James Trusfeilde (Thurfield?) | Two |
| John Phinmer (Plimmer) | One |
| William Towers | One |
| Widdow Elsmoore | Foore |
| Christopher Hitchcocke | One |
| Thomas Barton | One |
| Godfree Jacson (Jackson) | Three |
| Bettridge Baker | One |
| William Duftloe | One |
| Robert Barton | One |
| John Tompson | One |
| Eliz. Brindley | One |
| John Madeley | One |
| John Holt | Three |
| Richard Hitchcocke | Three |
| Edward Mottram | One |

| | |
|---|---|
| Henry Barkes | Three |
| Thomas Jenkinson | One |
| Walter Brindley | One |
| Dorrothy Smyth | One |
| Tim Pearce (Pierce) | Three |
| William Barton | One |
| Ellinr. Tomkinson | One |

The following are certified for not being Chargeable according to the Act.

| | |
|---|---|
| Eliz. Hodgkinson | Henry Sherratt |
| John Morton | Thomas Barton |
| John Tompson | Edward Mottram |
| Tim. Price | Dorothy Smyth |
| Hum. Gaunt | Richard Roper |
| John Maidley | Amey Crichloe |
| John Mills | Nicholas Mills |
| Sebastian Hollins | Henry Barkes |
| John Hichcockes | |

By William Barton, Constable

Allowed by Edward Bagott }
} Justices of the Peace
John Whitall }

Comment Interesting inclusions for Kingstone are Mistress Phelice (Felice or Felicia) Goring (widow of John) and Mistress Anne Goring (widow of William).
Alexander Maudlee (Manlove) resided at Wanfield Hall (only three hearths ?).
Thomas Steele and Richard Toothe with six and seven hearths respectively were clearly men of means. The inventory associated with the will of Richard Tooth, dated 1666 provides evidence of a large house and a substantial farming operation. He was a yeoman of Blythe Bridge, and the only property fitting the description would seem to be Blythe Bridge Hall (page 87).

## 4. Kingstone Wills

None of the above records tells us about where in Kingstone people lived. Wills are a very valuable source which provide all sorts of information about individuals, their families and associates (24)(26). They also, occasionally tell us, specifically, where the testator or other people lived. The earliest surviving will, made by a Kingstone resident dates from 1534. The content of the wills is beyond the scope of this book, and early Kingstone wills have been expertly studied and transcribed, and some content published elsewhere (46). However, information extracted from the wills of Kingstone people is used where relevant in discussing the properties named in Chapter 4.

## 5. Post Office Directories

Other sources which may list the residents of a town or village, together with a more specific idea of where they lived include Post Office directories, which date from the early nineteenth century. These provide descriptions of the village of Kingstone, and lists of tradesmen, businesses and private residents. The earliest available Staffordshire directory dates from 1818, and gives the following (but quite limited) entry (29).

**Staffordshire Directory 1818 :**     Kingston

        Adams Thomas, gentleman
        Beard J. vict. Dog & Partridge
        Croxton Thomas, farmer
        Hubbard J. bricklayer, &c
        Johnson William, farmer
        Stonier William, corn-miller
        Ward John, farmer
        Wilson Thomas, blacksmith
        Wood William, gentleman
        Wood George, farmer
        Woolley Thomas, tailor

Later directories, notably in 1834 and 1851 were much more comprehensive, and these sources, together with some later directories have also been used (in Chapter 5) in attempting to determine who lived where. Directories excluded most women, as well as all labourers, servants and children.

## 6. Census Returns

All of the above sources, where they exist, have been used in this book, but it was not until the nineteenth century that census returns (completed every ten years between 1841 and 1911) provided detailed information which told us who all the people were, where they lived, and how they spent their lives (4).
Most residents today do not have rural occupations and travel to places of work outside the village; in some cases to distant towns and cities. This transformation in terms of lifestyle has of course taken place in most rural localities. Picture by contrast the rural village scene in the early years of the last century, or certainly in the nineteenth century with a much more self-sufficient community of farmers, farm labourers, and servants, together with a miller, blacksmith, wheelwright, butcher, schoolmaster, vicar, tailor, dressmaker, shoemaker, publican etc. For many, walking would have been their usual means of getting from place to place. For the farming folk an excursion away from the village would usually have been a visit to the Wednesday market at Uttoxeter (using horse-drawn transport). In the present age the motor car is regarded as an essential possession, especially in rural areas; it has certainly had a major effect on village life.
The present population of Kingstone parish is at a level which is the highest in its history. The 2011 census recorded a population of 629 in Kingstone in 259 households.
Population figures for Kingstone show a peak in 1831, followed by a steady decline during the remainder of the nineteenth century (Table 2) (43). In 1818 there were only 67 houses (and 67 families, consisting of 152 males and 183 females i.e. 335 in total ) (43). In 1848 there were also 67 houses (43).

| Table 1 **Kingstone Population** 1801- 1911 ||||
| --- | --- | --- | --- |
| Date | Population | Date | Population |
| 1801 | 276 | 1861 | 312 |
| 1811 | 335 | 1871 | 278 |
| 1821 | 355 | 1881 | 280 |
| 1831 | 368 | 1891 | 252 |
| 1841 | 339 | 1901 | 223 |
| 1851 | 326 | 1911 | 197 |

Census records reveal interesting changes in population structure. At the time of the first census, in 1841 there was little evidence of anyone having a place of work outside Kingstone. Some residents had independent means, and there were of course farmers, and related trades which included - blacksmith, wheelwright and miller as well as a pig dealer, maltster, a wood labourer and sawyer. Other trades included a tailor, dressmaker, shoemakers and two schoolmasters. Most villagers, however worked as agricultural labourers or as servants. Occupations in Kingstone in 1851 were broadly similar to those in 1841, (the shoemakers being now called cordwainers). The village had an additional tailor who was also a grocer, as well as being a dissenting minister. Population numbers were fairly stable, with 326 residents (172 males and 154 females) living in 69 dwellings.

In 1861 most people in Kingstone were similarly employed as in 1851 and there was now a full-time grocer and provisions dealer, and also a stone mason. Some agricultural labourers had more specific roles e.g. carter, drainer, cowman and plough boy.

In 1871, some additional occupations included a retired merchant (living at Wanfield Hall), a cattle dealer, a beer house keeper at Blythe Bridge, and a school mistress who had moved to Kingstone from Derbyshire.

In 1881 further additional roles included a grocer and general labourer who was also a baker, a nurse maid and a certified school teacher who occupied the school house provided. The significant change was that some villagers were now clearly employed outside the village, working on the railway, including a railway labourer, a railway lamp cleaner and a railway signalman. The nearest railway station was at Grindley, on the Uttoxeter to Stafford line, but was within walking distance, being less than two miles from Kingstone. [The Uttoxeter to Staffordshire branch line was constructed in 1867. The line however was underfunded; it operated at a loss and became run down. In 1879 GNR (the Great Northern Railway) took over the line, providing much needed investment and modernisation. It seems likely that this was the point at which some men living in Kingstone were provided with work on the railway.]

In 1891 the railway continued to provide work outside the village, two men being railway platelayers. There were also woodmen, a gamekeeper, a road man, a painter, and a pupil teacher. Significant additions included, for the first time, a resident police constable (living at his 'police office') and a post office run by a resident postmistress. Total population numbers had however showed a steady decline over the decades, having decreased by one third since their peak in 1831. There were now only 252 villagers (136 males and 116 females) living in 52 houses with six houses unoccupied, probably because people were leaving Kingstone to find work and looking for a better life elsewhere.

In 1901 the railway continued to provide work for a labourer, a stoker and two platelayers. Additional occupations within Kingstone included a 'monthly nurse', a bootmaker, a joiner, and there were now three roadmen. A further drop in population suggests that the village was far from being a place where one could live and prosper. My grandmother's written comment (page 119) that school subscriptions from all parents in the village were made by those *'who could afford to give'*, and that *'nobody seemed to have much money'*, seems to be reflective of an impoverished period.

By 1911 there were three railway platelayers, two living at Blythe bridge, one of whom said he worked for GNR, the other living at the post office in Kingstone, his wife being the postmistress. The 'monthly nurse' was now called a midwife, her husband being a tailor. The two roadmen were council employees. The schoolmaster's son was a gent's outfitter (probably in Uttoxeter). There were also two other resident elementary school teachers. A 'clerk working in an agricultural ironworks' will have also been working in Uttoxeter (at Bamford's ironworks). Other Kingstone residents included a gardener, a cattle drover, a gamekeeper, a farm bailiff and two estate labourers. The total population had however showed a further decline.

## 7. Maps and surveys of Kingstone

Where people lived in Kingstone can be most effectively described by maps.

## 7a. Survey map of 1717-1720 [Godson]

The earliest known map is that made by William Godson for a survey of the manor of Kingstone, belonging to the Honourable John Chetwynd Esq.. For some years it appeared that the map was all that survived from this survey until I discovered, in 2017, that the Staffordshire Record Office also held an undated survey of Kingstone which was in fact the schedule which belonged with the map. John Chetwynd's tenants can now be identified, together with the land and other property they held, the field names also being given. All of this provides an interesting comparison with the information given by the 'tithe award' about 120 years later (39). The survey reveals that John Chetwynd owned a substantial part of Kingstone, and his land holding totalled 1000 acres. The map is also interesting in giving the names of neighbouring owners such as Mrs. Manlove of Wanfield and Leese Hill, Mr. 'Kenersley' (Kynnersley) of Loxley Hall, Mr. Degg (Degge), and John Chetwynd's brother, the Right Honourable Walter, Lord Chetwynd. The survey (map and schedule) although undated, must be after 1717, the year in which Walter Chetwynd [1678-1736] (being styled 'Right Honourable') became the 1st. Viscount Chetwynd, his younger brother John Chetwynd [1680-1767] (styled 'Honourable') being the individual identified as *'John Chetwynd of Meere'* who had acquired the former Goring property in 1716.

The survey shows that John Chetwynd owned most of the parish, including Callowhill Hall (contrary to the wishes of John Goring, specified in his will, dated 1696)(26). The map also names Katherine Boulton as an owner of land in Kingstone. Her will is dated 1725, but she died the year before. Mrs Manlove (of 'Lea's Hill Hall') also died in 1724 (being buried at her birthplace of Osmaston, Derbyshire), her will also being dated 1725 (24). However, Godfrey Barks, a yeoman of Kingstone died in 1720 (24). We can therefore date this survey at between 1717 and 1720. John Chetwynd's elder brother, Walter Chetwynd (named on the map as the owner of Gratwich) being newly elevated to Viscount Chetwynd in 1717, commissioned surveys of several of his properties in that year, possibly prompting his brother John Chetwynd to do the same. Having acquired his Kingstone property in 1716 it seems reasonable that John Chetwynd would be keen to examine his recent purchase in detail by commissioning his own survey.

The map shows Callowhill Hall with an extensive range of buildings. 'Windfield' (Wanfield) Hall and 'Leas' (Leese) Hill Hall are both shown as substantial properties, but in other ownership. Particular points of interest include the tiny 'island' of land in the road close to Church Cottage, and the well at Leese Hill crossroads (both of which still exist), the moat near Moss Farm, and the pool at Black Pits with the through-road behind. Musty (Moisty) Lane is shown, and also Moss Lane (both now gone). Large areas of common land then existed on Blythe Bridge Bank and along the road by Wanfield Hall and Woodcock Heath Farm.

Few roadside cottages appear, but this is to be expected since many will have been built later on strips of land which were encroachments on to the common land (as the 1837 'tithe award' map reveals) (24).

Most of the land shown on the Godson map is shaded in a way which suggests the pattern of medieval arable strip farming. Areas not shaded in this way, including the low- lying land alongside the Tad Brook and by the River Blythe are likely to have been used as meadow or pasture. It was the practice in medieval times for each villager to be allocated numerous 'lands' or strips (1/3 of an acre on average) scattered within the two or three large open cultivated areas or 'fields' in each village, so that each family had good and poor soil. Groups of strips running parallel (running down a slope to assist drainage) were known as 'furlongs' (units of area, not of length). Such furlongs (then unhedged) were given names which we now refer to as 'field' names (15). In Midland counties such as Staffordshire the ploughing of strips produced a 'ridge and furrow' pattern which may still be detectable in land which today is under grass. Meadow or pasture could be similarly divided with villagers being allocated strips on which they could grow their own hay crop. After the hay was taken off the land became open as common pasture. The Godson map shows such an area of land, south of the village centre, and next to the Tad Brook. The *'Town Meadow'* was divided into strips or portions, each called a *'dole'*. The schedule reveals that occupiers of several different properties were allocated one or more *'dole'* in the *'Town Meadow'*. Whether, by this date the grazing was still communal is not known.

Typically, each medieval open 'field' could extend to several hundred acres. Land belonging to Woodcock Heath included a block of six fields all with *'Old Field'* in their name e.g. *Nearer Old Field, Further Old Field, Middle Old Field* which together with the adjoining woodland called *Old Field Coppy* formed a unit of over 30 acres. This land may have been part of one of Kingstone's medieval open fields. Similarly land belonging to Kingstone Hall Farm, to the south of Kingstone Wood included a block of six fields all with *'Srouls'* in their name e.g. *Great Srouls, Upper Srouls*. If the 12 acre woodland called *Srouls Coppy* is added, this made up a 47 acre unit. [Lands in Kingstone called *'Shroulds'* are mentioned in earlier documents dating back to between 1616 and 1715 (39).]

Names given to the fields in John Chetwynd's manor of Kingston are of interest. Some are non-specific e.g. grassland referred to as *meadow, pasture or leasow*, and there were *crofts* and *closes* suggesting small enclosed pieces of land, usually near to the homestead. *Broomy piece, Rushey Yearnsley* (Callowhill Hall) and *Gossey Meadow* (Kingstone Hall) all indicate land prone to weed infestation with broom, rushes and gorse, respectively. There were several small plots of land called *Hempland* suggesting that hemp was grown, an important crop with a number of uses but particularly used in rope making. The type of crop grown is also indicated in *Barley Croft* and *Bean Field* (Woodcock Heath). *Brickhill Leasow* and a pool called *Brickhill poole* (just west of Abbott's Wood) suggest a brick making site. Several fields were called *Marlpit Leasow*. Marl, a lime-rich clay was dug out to to add nutrients to lighter soils and improve their water holding capacity. The resulting marl pits - of which a number are shown on the map became small ponds, providing drinking water for livestock. *Stocking Field* (Callowhill Hall, page 83) is thought to suggest former woodland. A *holme* is a flat piece of low-lying ground by river of stream, which is exactly the case as in *Sweet Holmes* (Kingstone Hall) for land alongside the Tad Brook. *Holme* may otherwise refer to holly, very common in hedges locally. A *sich*, in *Blakeley sich* (Blythe Bridge bank) (pages 60, 67) refers to slow-flowing water in a drain or ditch. A *balk,* as in *Staulk Baulk* (at 'Birches Corner') suggests a medieval 'land' or strip which has been grassed over as a permanent right of way (16). *Two Butts on the Comon* (Blythe Bridge), probably means an abutting strip of land, rather than a place for archery practise. *Dovehouse Close* may suggest a former dovecote (Callowhill Hall). *Gaunt's Ground* (east of Wanfield Hall) recalls the name of an old Kingstone family. The same may be true for *Morris Leasow* (near Broomy Leasows) and *Pratts Leasow* (on 'Moss Lane'). Five fields, west of Moss Farm had *Ash Croft* in their name, next to woodland called *Ashton Coppy* (later called *Ashcroft Coppice*). The origin of the names *Berry Field*, and *Leech Field* (both Callowhill Hall), *Sir Hugh* (south of Moss Farm), *Cockey Nook* (near Broomy Leasows) remain open to speculation. The origin of the names *Nearer Piss Brook* and *Further Piss Brook* for two fields (shown at the western corner of the crossroads at the end of the lane marked as Park Lane) can be deduced. The lane itself has been called Piss Brook Lane. There is no brook here, but the area seems poorly drained and today the lane is called Watery Lane!

**[The Godson map is too large to be reproduced here in its entirety. Areas (zones) of the Godson map are however reproduced in the Chapter 4 where specific properties in Kingstone are identified and discussed.]**

## 7b. The 'Tithe Map' of 1837 [Lofthouse] and the 1838 apportionment

The 1837 Tithe map is inevitably large (size A1 equivalent) and cannot be fully reproduced here, but a scaled down version (size A4 equivalent) is illustrated [Fig. 3] to provide a general idea of the extent of the parish.

**[Areas (zones) of this map are reproduced in the Chapter 4 in a larger format enabling specific properties in Kingstone parish to be identified and discussed.]**

This most informative of maps, produced by Lofthouse in 1837 was used in the 1838 *Apportionment of the rent-charge in lieu of tithes* (24) (Fig. 3, page 26). Traditionally one tenth of the agricultural production of any holding was due to be paid to support the priest of the parish. The Tithe Commutation Act of 1836 resulted in the conversion to monetary payment (24). For Kingstone the total charge for the parish was set at £126 in 1838 (24). For each parish three statutory copies were made of the 'tithe award'; the parish copy being retained by the church (Kingstone's copy, encased in a metal cylindrical tube with the title 'Kingston Churchwardens' being kept in the church chest).
In 1838 the parish of Kingstone consisted of about 2010 acres including 605 acres of arable, 1125 acres of pasture or meadow, 251 acres of woodland (not subject to tithe) and 24 acres of roads (24).
The 'tithe award' is full of useful detail; it gives names of owners and occupiers, and provides information about 'field' sizes and names, identified by numbered references on the associated map.
Information is also revealed about how the land was used, whether it was meadow or pasture, or used for arable crops. The type of standing crop is given for Kingstone, the arable crops included oats, wheat, barley, rye, potatoes, beans, peas, turnips, cabbage, vetches and flax. Broomy Leasows Farm was largely arable and grew most of these crops. The other farms were about one third arable or fallow, while Manor Farm and Church

Farm were largely down to grass, indicating that livestock rearing and dairying was the main focus there.
In 1838 most of the land (1258 acres) was owned by Earl Talbot (ancestor of the Earl of Shrewsbury and Talbot) the other major landowners (having over 100 acres) being Richard Corbett Lawrence of Leese Hill and Thomas Sneyd Kynnersley of Loxley Hall. If we look at individual properties a number of roadside cottages and gardens are seen to be occupying former common land. Land involved in this ribbon development is named as encroachment, common or enclosure. A particular holding was also often in a number of well-separated parts e.g. Anne Bentley (living with hard-won self-sufficiency) occupied land belonging to Earl Talbot which was only 3 acres in total, but this was in seven small portions scattered along the roadside from the top of Blythe Bridge bank, past Wanfield Hall up to Woodcock Heath. Thomas Wilson, the blacksmith at Blythe Bridge, apart from the smithy, house and garden had six other small pieces of land, in total under two acres, some down to grass but he was also growing wheat and potatoes.

Some of the larger properties also had their field areas well spread (as was also true at the time of the earlier, Godson survey). Manor Farm had land near Broomy Leasows, and Church Farm had land to the north of the Shrewsbury Arms known as the Barn Ground. Each of these farms also had land on the far side of Kingstone Wood and an allocation in the *'In Town Meadows'* (the field divided into strips) near Moss Farm.

Some of the field names were the same as, or similar to those given in the Godson survey e.g. *Shrouds (Srouls)*, *Stockings*, *Dove House*, *Sweet Holmes*, *Berry Field*, *Cocksey Nook*, *Stalk Balk*, *Piss Brook Piece*, *Morris's Leasow* and *Gaunt's Ground* were still in use in 1838. The two-acre field called *Cocksey Nook {302}*, called *Cookey Nook* in the Godson survey was probably the close *'Cook hey'* mentioned by Arthur Needham of Kingston in his will dated 1570/1 (24). It may even have been the parcel of land called *Le Cochayes* which was transferred to John Osbern of Kingston in a document dating from the year 1331 (39)!

The Godson survey only gave the names of fields which belonged to John Chetwynd, whereas the 1838 'tithe award' recorded field names for the whole of Kingstone parish. Inevitably some of the fields will may have undergone a change of name, become divided up or otherwise joined with others to form larger units.
For example, *Abbot's Wood Gate* (the field by the gate into Abbot's Wood) and *Middle Brick house piece* were formerly called, respectively, *Upper and Lower Brick Hill Leasows*. Three small fields bordering the road and lying east of *Ashcrofts Coppice* were called *Ashcrofts* having formerly been one field called *Upper Brook Orchard*. *Near Sir Hughes* was the name now given to the seven acre field directly south of Moss Farm, combining (from the Godson survey) the field formerly *Sir Hugh* with *Moats Meadow* (containing a moat). *Barks Ground* (Blythe Bridge Hall) recalls the surname Barks, an old Kingstone family, but what can be made of *Big Stoopers* (Manor Farm), *Crutchley's Croft* (Broomy Leasow Farm), *Gallows Tree* (Watery Lane), *War field*, and *Devil's Bank* (Leese Hill), *Madam Aimes (Anns?) Piece*, and *Rileys* (Blythe Bridge Hall), and *Wet Reins* (Moss Farm)?

## 7c. Survey of 1801

A further survey of the Manor of Kingston, together with Gratwich and Birchwood Park was carried out for Earl Talbot in 1801 by the surveyor, Samuel Botham (39). [Samuel Botham was also the father of the Uttoxeter poet, Mary Howitt, whose best-known work was *The Spider and the Fly*.]

This survey schedule lists the Earl's tenants and the land (with acreages) that they held, and records the field names. Other owners and their land holdings are similarly recorded. [Note that In a few cases the name of the tenant or proprietor has been crossed out and replaced by another. This is thought to represent later necessary alteration rather than error in the original survey.] The names of the properties are not recorded in the schedule, and although there is a surviving accompanying map (not reproduced in this book) with properties marked, only some of these are named on this map. The map also lacks the reference numbers for the field names, so that the individual fields held by tenants and other individuals cannot be identified from the listing in the schedule.
Fortunately, by comparing the set of named fields held by an individual, with that given in the 1838 in lieu of tithe apportionment, together with the accompanying 1837 map, it is possible in many cases to identify the property concerned, and therefore the person who held the land in 1801.

The 1801 survey map, despite its lack of detail, does enable us to see whether a property then existed on a particular site in 1801, in comparison with the 1717-1720 Godson map and the 1837 'tithe map'. This information has been added, for comparative purposes to Table 2 (page 27 & 28) and reveals that for the great majority of cottages, houses and farms recorded in 1838, a property had existed on the same site in 1801. Information from the 1801 survey has been included in the account describing each property in Kingstone in Chapter 4.

## 7d. Ordnance Survey maps

Ordnance Survey maps, such as those dated 1882, 1890, 1901, 1923 all provide useful information, illustrating changes which have occurred and the extent to which the landscape is unchanged. Reference to these maps is made later in some instances.

## 8. Sale Catalogues

When the two great estates, The Shrewsbury & Talbot Estate, and the Loxley Estate of the Kynnersley family, which between them owned most of Kingstone, were both sold in 1918, the name of each tenant and other details relating to each property were usefully recorded in a sale catalogue. Each sale catalogue was accompanied by a map which showed the distribution of land allocated to each property (39).
Farms formerly on the Shrewsbury Estate such as Church Farm, Manor Farm, Moss Farm and Kingstone Hall Farm with Broomy Leasows all had fairly neat blocks of land attached and close to the homestead (which was not necessarily so 80 years earlier) (24).

## 9. Kingstone and development in the 20th century

Main water and electricity were laid on in Kingstone in the late 1930s. In 1933 an application was made to the rural district council for four council houses to be built in Kingstone; there was said to be a shortage, with 'some of the existing houses being very dilapidated, and almost all farm controlled' (2). It was however not until the end of the Second World War that the housing stock was increased with the building of 14 council houses on Uttoxeter Road in 1946-47, with another 14 council houses at Blythe Bridge in the mid 1950s.
As farming became more mechanised there were fewer jobs working on the land. In any event many villagers sought a better or alternative future by choosing to live and work elsewhere. While farming continued to be important its character changed. In the middle of the century there were still five farms producing milk in the centre of Kingstone; now there are none.
Kingstone has increased considerably in size with an influx of new houses, constructed mostly in the 1960s and 1970s. In many cases this has been at the expense of the older properties, but mostly using 'green field' sites. Housing infill has occurred on Uttoxeter Road, Blythe Bridge Road and Church Lane. The new developments of Stonier Drive, Whitehall Close and Church Close are relatively small scale, compared with the unimaginatively-named 'The Meadows' consisting of about sixty houses. These new developments have transformed Kingstone. Most of the occupants of the new houses will have been new to the area and engaged in employment outside Kingstone, but will have contributed to a much-needed rejuvenation of the village.

Plate 3  **Kingstone Spring** - the source of fresh water for the village before 1936 (now disrupted as a result of housing development nearby).

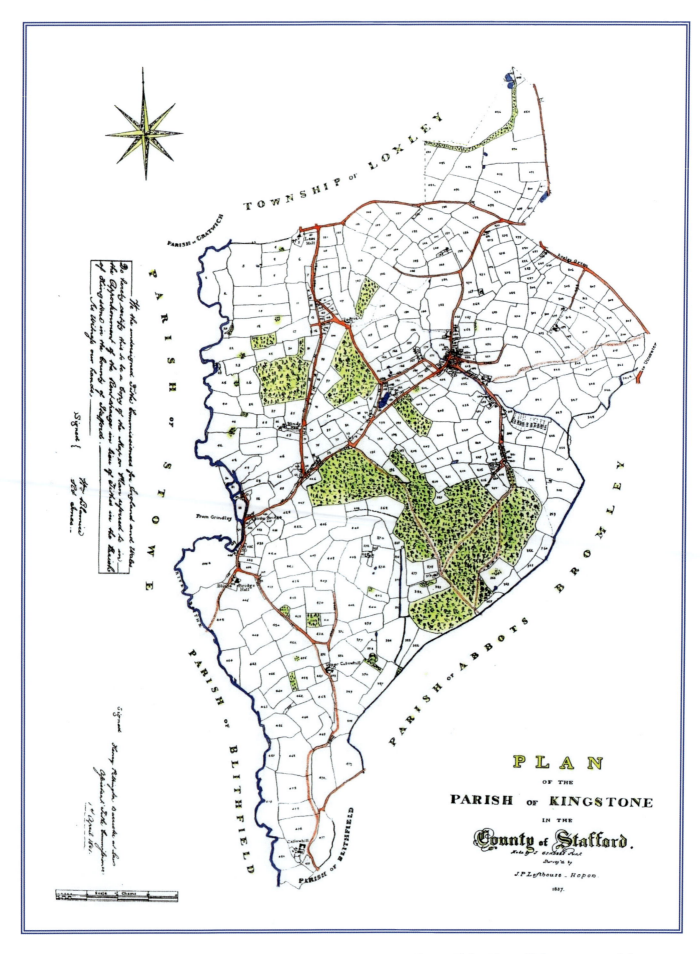

Fig. 3 **Tithe Map of Kingstone parish** 1837

# CHAPTER 4: PLACES AND PEOPLE

In this chapter, individuals properties which exist, or used to exist in Kingstone are identified and discussed, and their occupants at various times also identified, where possible.

The 'tithe map' of 1837 used in the 1838 apportionment of the rent-charge in lieu of tithes was accompanied by a schedule which described all parts of the parish by making reference to numbered areas on the map e.g. 248 for Kingstone Hall Farm. The following table is used to list individual properties discussed in this chapter, together with the relevant reference number given on the map, identified in **BLUE** e.g. Kingstone Hall **{248}**. To provide the necessary detail needed to locate these properties on the map, larger scale reproductions of the 'tithe map' are also given here, divided into six areas or zones A - F. These zones are indicated in Fig. 4, page 29. In the account which follows these same numbers have been used to show the location of the properties discussed on the map of each zone.

For comparative purposes, areas or zones of the earlier 'Godson' map which are equivalent to those used for the 1837 'Lofthouse' map have also been illustrated. Properties present at this time have been identified using numbers in **RED**, given in the following account as e.g. **{3}** for Kingstone Hall Farm.

Table 2 A GUIDE TO THE 'TITHE MAP' AND SCHEDULE [properties existing in 1801 are shown as *]

| Reference | Identification of property | Reference | Identification of property |
|---|---|---|---|
| 5 | Leese Hill Manor Farm* | 139 | Hollydene (Old Town)* |
| 16 | house, Woodcock Heath (demolished) | 155 | Manor Farm* |
| 36 | Wanfield Hall* | 167 | Mount Pleasant/Cherry Trees, Potts' Lane* |
| 52 | Blythe Bridge Mill* | 173 | house, near Nene House (demolished) |
| 55 | Smithy, Blythe Bridge* | 174 | Nene House |
| 64 | house, Blythe Bridge bank (demolished)* | 184 | Ashcroft Farm, Blythe Bridge Road* |
| 66 | 'Yew Tree Cottage', Blythe Bridge Bank | 186 | two houses, Potts' Lane (demolished)* |
| 67 | house and malt-house, Blythe Bridge bank 'Malthouse'* | 187 | house, Potts' Lane (demolished)* |
| 68 | house, Blythe Bridge bank (demolished) | 223 | The Mosses* |
| 79 | 'Woodside Cottage', Blythe Bridge bank* | 232 | Moss Farm* |
| 84 | Blackpits Farm, Blythe Bridge Road* | 234 | house, next to Moss Farm (demolished)* |
| 101 | 'Rosevale', Woodcock Heath | 237 | The old church (demolished)* |
| 109 | house, Woodcock Heath (demolished) | 239 | Church Farm* |
| 111 | 'Magpie Hall', Woodcock Heath (demolished) | 240 | Poor House (demolished)* |
| 115 | Woodcock Heath Farm* | 241 | Barley Mow public house (demolished)* |
| 132 | Galleytree Cottage/Rose Cottage | 244 | Church Cottage* |

27

| | | | |
|---|---|---|---|
| 246 | The Villa (demolished)* | 298 | Broomy Leasows Farm (demolished)* |
| 247 | two houses, near Kingstone Hall (demolished) | 344 | two houses, opposite Moss Farm (demolished)* |
| 247a | house, near Kingstone Hall (demolished) | 346 | house, below Moss Farm (demolished) |
| 248 | Kingstone Hall Farm* | 373 | Dowry Farm* |
| 253 | two houses, Church View (demolished)* | 379 | Moorfields (demolished)* |
| 253a | house, Church View (demolished)* | 394 | Upper Callowhill Farm* |
| 257 | two houses, 'Barracks' (demolished)* | 418 | house, Blythe Bridge (demolished)* |
| 258 | four houses, 'Barracks'(demolished)* | 431 | Butcher's/Wheelwright's, Blythe Bridge* |
| 259 | house and school (demolished) | 437 | The Blythe Inn, Blythe Bridge* |
| 261 | Walnuts Farm/Walnut House* | 439 | house, Blythe Bridge* |
| 265 | Dog and Partridge Inn (later Shrewsbury Arms)* | 445 | Blythe Bridge Hall (demolished)* |
| 276 | Rose Cottage / 'Monkey Tree House'* | 478 | Callowhill Hall Farm* |
| 284 | Hollyhays Farm* | | |

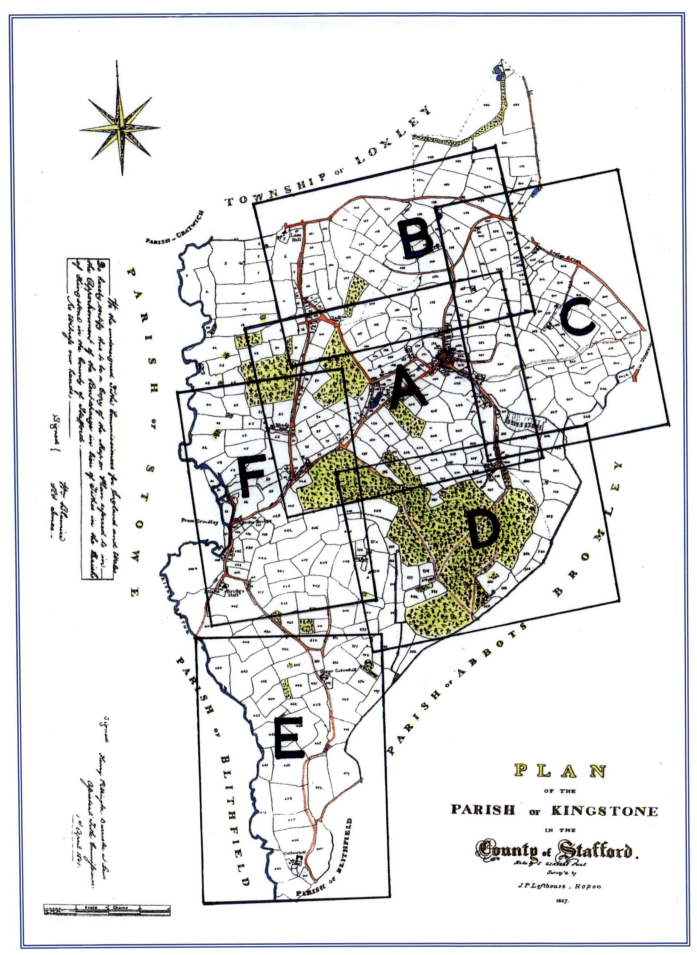

Fig. 4 **Map of Kingstone parish** 1837 - showing zones A - F.

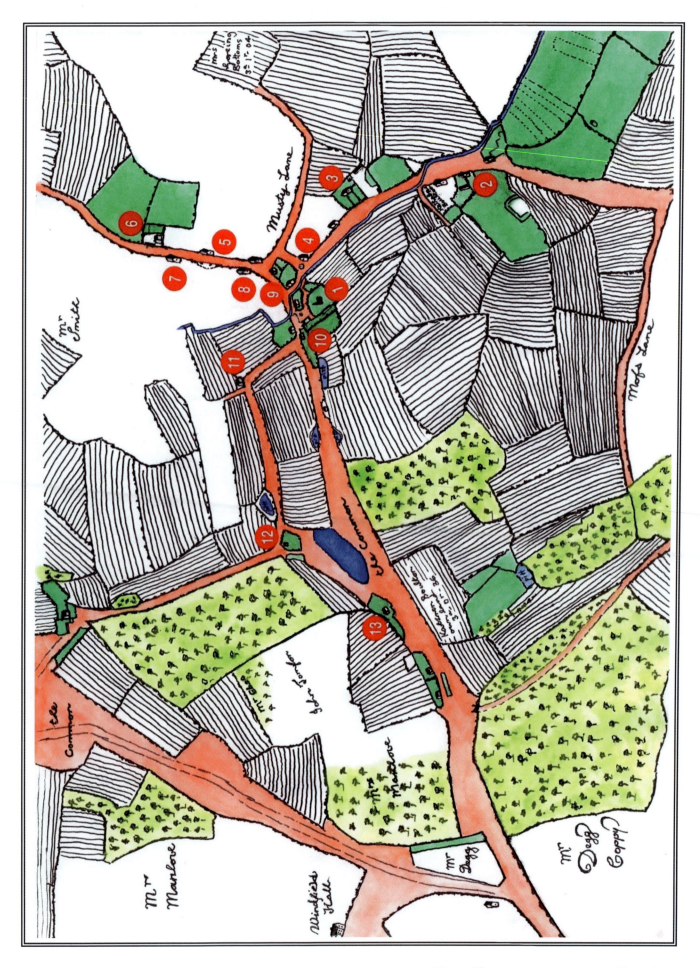

Fig. 5 <u>Kingstone map</u> 1717-20 **Zone A**

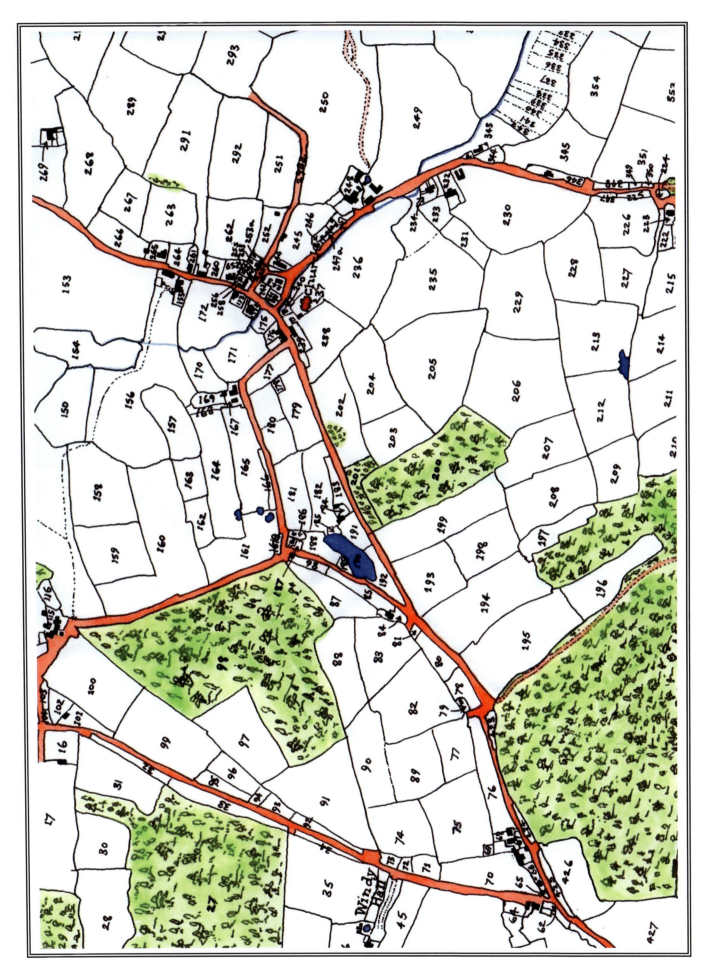

Fig. 6 **Kingstone map** 1837 **Zone A**

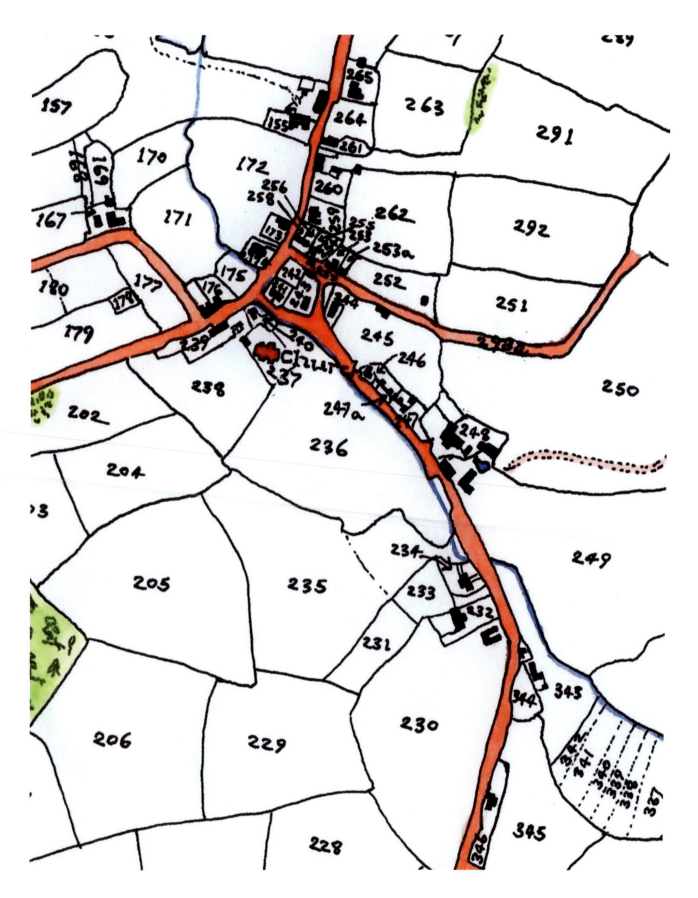

Fig. 7 **Kingstone village centre** - from the 'tithe map' of 1837.
[An enlarged view of part of **Zone A**]

# Central Kingstone [Zone A]

Notable features of the Godson map include the large areas of common land which then existed on Blythe Bridge Road. This land was later encroached upon and enclosed as we see in the 1837 'tithe award' map. Another point of interest shown on the Godson map is the tiny 'island' of land which still exists (with a single tree planted upon it) in the road close to the lych gate, at the main entrance to the present church.
Both maps also show the 'black pool' at Black Pits (which existed until the late 20th. century) and the through-road (now surviving mostly as a track) running behind the pool, and providing a link between Blythe Bridge Bank and Potts' Lane. Musty (Moisty) Lane which is shown has now gone. Properties (or more recent dwellings on the same site) detectable at this Godson period include the old church, Church Farm, Church Cottage, Manor Farm, the old school, Mount Pleasant, the Dog & Partridge (later the Shrewsbury Arms), the Barley Mow (site of the present school), Kingstone Hall Farm and Moss Farm (with the nearby field divided into strips called *'In Town Meadows'*). The Godson map shows the moated site near Moss Farm (still visible today), which was perhaps a place of some importance in the medieval period.

## KINGSTONE CHURCH

The church dates only from 1861. It replaces an ancient church with a tower {237} {1}, which, being in a poor state of repair, was taken down in 1860.
The old church was described as a small, stone structure of the fourteenth century consisting of a chancel, nave and embattled low square western tower. The tower, being constructed of 'common brick', was said to have been of recent date when the church was demolished. This church also apparently retained part of a rood screen (29).

Plate 4 **Kingstone Old Church** (a view from the north - from Redfern)

Sir Symon Degge Kt., judge of West Wales, and an eminent antiquary, was buried here in a chapel he erected on the north side of the church (29)(33). Memorials commemorating Sir Symon and members of his family now lie flat in the churchyard, probably near to the site of the former chapel (pages 101-103).
We are indebted to Redfern (33) for the above drawing of the exterior of the old church (Plate 4).

33

After many centuries of use the old church was said to have been become very dilapidated by the time it was taken down, being described as 'unsightly both externally and internally'. The walls and floor were recorded as being very damp, and the pews 'irregularly arranged and inconvenient' (2).

Kingstone was to have a new church, a very superior building, and at almost no cost to the parish, but the last service held in the old church on 16th. September 1860 was an emotional occasion with many of the parishioners having feelings of regret and sadness (2).

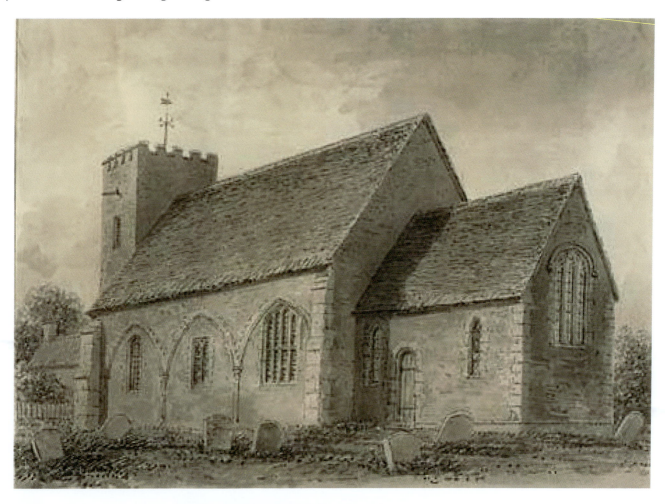

Plate 5 **Kingstone Old Church** (a view from the south east) 1839
Reproduced by permission of the Trustees of the William Salt Library, Stafford.

The exact site of the old church has not been established. A geophysical survey, conducted in 2005 was unable to pinpoint the site of the old church (36). There may however be little to find as the walls of the new church were partly built using materials from the old church (page 36)(2).

Plate 4 (page 33) shows the access to the old church from a path which seems to be on much the same foot print as the path which now leads to the present church from the gate near the Village Hall. Another view of the old church (Plate 5) provides a guide. Many gravestones were moved to the southern boundary of the churchyard in the mid twentieth century, but there are gravestones still in situ, some of which date back to the middle of the eighteenth century, and these memorials also provide an indication as to where this church was formerly located.

Some of the old gravestones bear signs of deliberate damage done in times past. Pitt, writing in 1817, recorded that *'there are no remarkable monuments in the church-yard, but such is the mischievous, and it might be added, the devilish disposition of boys, that they have recently defaced several of the inscriptions on the tomb-stones'* (31).

There are, however, in the middle of the old churchyard, are two very distinctive chest tombs, each covered by a heavy slab (Plate 6, page 35). These date from the seventeenth and early eighteenth century. One carries the name of Margaret Sherrat who died in 1706, with partly-readable inscriptions on the two inward-facing panels, as given below:

The other tomb is that of William Sherratt Margaret Sherratt's husband, who was buried at Kingstone on the 20th. August 1687. William Sherratt's will (with inventory) dated 1687, reveals that he was a prosperous yeoman of Kingstone. Where he actually lived in Kingstone is unknown but his house must have been a substantial dwelling (24).

| HERE LYETH BU RED THE BODY OF MARGARET SHERR AT THE WIFE OF | WILL'M SHERRAT DEPARTED Y LIFE ..... AP Y BEING AGED .... YEARS ANNO Dº 1706 |

Plate 6  **Sherratt tombs** in Kingstone churchyard

The Degge family memorial tablets (page 103) are sited nearby, just to the west of these two tombs. Also, now placed next to these tombs is what is believed to be the font from the old church. It was found in the boundary hedge next to Church Farm some years ago when the Village Hall car park was being constructed.
A painting of the old church font exists (Plate 7, opposite).

Plate 7  **Font in Kingstone old church**  1839
Reproduced by permission of the Trustees of the William Salt Library, Stafford.

Descriptions of the interior of the old church survive.
Some information about the internal layout exists (this being before the Degge chapel was built) in a seating plan of 1636 (Fig. 47, page 129). William Pitt, in 1817 had described the church interior as plain, with pews of oak (31). Some detail is also given in a painting of the church interior (Plate 35, page 130), completed over two hundred years later, shortly before the church was demolished.
A description of the interior of the old church was also provided by a visitor who reported his observations in a newspaper article in 1870 (page 117).

The dilapidated state of the old church led, in 1803, to the minister (John Hilditch) and the inhabitants of Kingstone parish petitioning for its replacement. The existing church was described as *'a very ancient structure and is in a ruinous state and is much decayed in every part'*.

The estimated cost of taking down the old church and rebuilding according to the plan presented was £1337 - 6s - 9d.
The estimate included taking down the old church, laying foundations, new stonework, a good oak roof with Westmorland slate, stone floors, boards for pews and gallery, in addition to plastering, plumbers work and glaziers work for the windows.
The plan was for a classical style building, a sketch of the proposal (southern aspect) is given opposite (Fig. 8).
The entrance was to be at the west end between a pair of towers, surmounted by domes. The floor plan (not shown here) proposed two rows of pews placed centrally within the nave, looking towards a raised central pulpit near the chancel, the pulpit being reached by steps from the chancel. A gallery was also proposed on north and south sides of the nave (39).

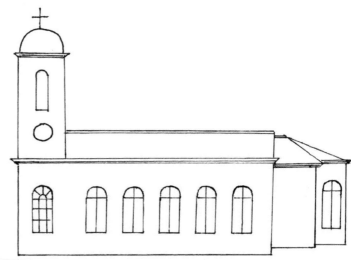

Fig. 8 **Proposal for a new church at Kingstone**
(view from the south)

Nearly sixty years were to pass before a new church was built, by which time fashions had changed and the present church constructed in the favoured Gothic style.

The church which exists today is positioned some distance to the east of the site of the old church in what was formerly a field belonging to Church Farm.
The church was consecrated on 21st. October 1861, an event which was reported in the *Staffordshire Advertiser* (11th. November 1861), and also in the *Illustrated London News* (Plate 8, page 37)(2). The new church was described as having been built in the Early English style consisting of a nave, 60 feet long by 22 feet wide; a chancel 25 feet long by 16 feet wide; a south aisle and a vestry; with a tower and a spire on the north side containing three bells. An arcade of five arches divided the nave from the aisle. The seats were made of stained, varnished deal, and the open-timbered roof rested upon carved stone corbels. The walls were built partly with the materials from the old church, and partly with new stone from the Hollington quarries*. The pulpit and font were made of the same stone and said to be richly carved. Minton tiles were used to pave the floors, those within the rail being of a distinct design. Under the vestry a vault had been constructed to house a heating apparatus by Messrs. Haden of Ironbridge. The church was designed to accommodate 300 persons, including children. The architect was Mr. Brandon of Berkeley Square, London, the builder Mr. Evans of Ellastone and the stone carver Mr. Ford of Alton.
[*Another source states that the church was built of brick with a facing of Hollington sandstone (43)].
The whole cost of building the church was about £2000, and it was erected largely at the expense of the Earl of

Shrewsbury and Talbot (then patron and owner of much of the village).
On the day of the consecration a procession formed near the schoolroom (the Old School? page 46), headed by the churchwardens, and Mr. Pickering the schoolmaster. The following party included 22 clergymen, the Bishop of Lichfield, the Bishop of Oxford (who gave the sermon) and the Earl of Shrewsbury. The whole assembly moved off slowly, passing over the brook, then up the slope of the newly formed churchyard, to enter the church for the consecration service (2).

A detailed description of the siting of the new church was given as follows:

*'The site of the new erection has been selected with great judgement - not where the old building stood, but on the piece of ground adjoining it on the eastern side; so that the old and new burial grounds are included by one fence. Six or seven noble yew trees, full-grown stand at each end of the new church, and on the southern side. On the north side the ground slopes gently down to a clear running brook, which forms a boundary between it and the public road. The slope has been carefully levelled, and when this is covered with verdure, with the church standing at the top of a little knoll, embosomed in yew trees, lifting its modest spire to heaven, with its door and porch open to view, and a spacious pathway leading to it from the road, as perfect a picture of a village church will be presented as is to be found in the county of Stafford'* (2).

Plate 8 **Kingstone Church**
[Illustrated London News - December 28th 1861] (17).

DEC. 28, 1861.]

ST. JOHN'S CHURCH, KINGSTONE, STAFFORDSHIRE.

THE new church erected to replace the former parish church is situated four miles from Uttoxeter, and was consecrated by the Bishop of Lichfield on Oct. 21. The old church had become dilapidated and insecure, and, consequently, the Earl of Shrewsbury and Talbot (in whose gift is the living) was induced to build a new church on an adjoining site, from designs supplied by Mr. D. Brandon, of London. The style of architecture selected for this building is of the Early English period. In plan it has a nave, polygonal chancel, south aisle, and vestry, under which is a crypt for warming the church; and at the east end of the aisle is a tower to contain five bells and a spire. The church is designed to contain three hundred sittings. The walls are constructed of stone from the Hollington quarries. The pulpit and font which

ST. JOHN'S CHURCH, KINGSTONE, STAFFORDSHIRE.

are of a very ornate character, are also executed in the same stone. The floor is paved with Minton's tiles, of varied designs and colour. The open timber roofs rest on elaborately-carved corbels, which, together with the enriched carving of the chancel arch, has been most effectively executed. The seats are of pine, stained and varnished, and are all open and free. The work was begun about twelve months back, and has been very creditably executed by Mr. Evans, of Ellastone, in Derbyshire. The church has been built at the expense of the Earl of Shrewsbury and Talbot, aided by grants from the Lichfield Diocesan Society and the Incorporated Society for Building Churches, and some private subscriptions. The picturesque design of the edifice, which is placed on the slope of a hill, groups well with the surrounding trees and scenery.

A double row of shaped yew trees line the main path up to the present church. These yew trees probably date from the mid 1870s; a faded old photograph (Plate 9, below) shows these yew trees as recently-planted saplings, with the gravestone of Henry Cottrell (buried in 1878) in view on this photograph.

Various later additions to the church include stained glass windows which were placed in the chancel in memory of Alfred Johnson (1905) of The Villa (page 43), and of Louisa and John Stonier (1929), of Kingstone Hall. [ A stained glass window has been fitted at the west end of the nave in recent years.] The church also contains a brass lectern which was presented by William Bathew of Wanfield Hall in 1911. The corbels (on which the the roof timbers rest) and the altar rail were painted in the 1960s by Mrs. W. E. Upton, wife of the then vicar. The lych gate, now at the bottom of the main path was added in 1929. It was presented by Kingstone Womens Institute, and replaced a pair of old swing gates which were in a dilapidated condition (Plate 33, page 127) (2).

Plate 9 __Kingstone Church__ - circa 1880?

A plaque in the church vestry records that the clock (which has a diameter of four feet) was presented to the church by the past and present scholars of Kingstone School, and dedicated on the 4th. July 1932. Apparently, the installation of a clock in the church tower was the idea of Mrs. Beech, the schoolmistress of Kingstone School (who no doubt wished to 'encourage' her pupils to get to school on time) and she, together with the school children set up a fund to raise the money needed to pay for the clock (2).

The newspaper report of the consecration of Kingstone church in 1861 made reference to the fact that the walls of the present Kingstone church were built partly using material from the old church (2). Could any of this material be visible? Certainly the walls of the present church show a good deal of variability.
I wonder also how many Kingstone people who think they know their church, have seen the intriguing lettering on a stone block (as illustrated below) set into the back (south) wall of the church. Could this have come from the old church, and what does it mean?

Plate 10 __Stone block in church wall with inverted lettering__ as it actually appears (*left*); and with the 'corrected' view of the same stone block (*right*).

38

Fig. 9 **Kingstone Church** (in 1984)

Kingstone church contains items of interest removed from the old church - these include the bell frame and bells, both of which are of considerable age. The smaller bells were cast in the early sixteenth century by William Culverden of London. The first treble has inscribed upon it SANCTE JACOB ORA PRO NOBIS (Pray for us St. James); the second treble SANCTE LEONARDE ORA PRO NOBIS (Pray for us St. Leonard). The tenor, inscribed GOD SAVE THE QUEENE 1595, was by Edward Newcombe of Leicester, but being badly damaged has been recast. The three bells cover the period of the Reformation and their inscriptions reflect this (40). Lynam, in his celebrated book about Staffordshire bells, provides illustrations which show the decoration and inscriptions of the church bells at Kingstone (25).

Ellen Wright of Kingstone, in her will, dated 1543 allocated *to the mendying of the bellys at kynston xx$^s$* i.e. the sum of twenty shillings, towards the repair of the church bells (24).

Lastly of particular interest, positioned in front of the pews and in the nave near the pulpit is an iron-bound wooden chest inscribed with the name of the donor and dated 1608 (Fig. 10).

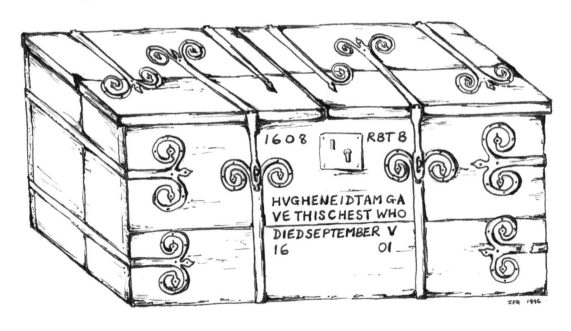

Fig. 10 **Kingstone Church chest**

This chest, without doubt, has been removed from the old church. We are indebted to Mr. Peter Woolley of Kingstone for his extensive research into the wills of past residents of Kingstone, and thereby his identification of the donor of this chest. Hugh Netam (Needham) of Kingstone, in his will dated 1601 left :-

*40/- to the parishioners of Kingstone - part of it for a sufficient chest to be placed in the church at Kingstone and to be inployed unto the use of the said parishioners and further I will that my name be cutte or ingraved upon the said chest* (24)(46).

The chest records the death of 'Hughe Neidtam' as September 5th 1601. The inscribed initials and date suggest that the chest was made in 1608. RBT B may have been the person who made the chest, or churchwarden (possibly Robert Barton, a yeoman of Kingstone, who died leaving a will in 1637).

**MOSS FARM { 232} {2}** The present farmhouse is of red brick but may clothe a more ancient interior (Fig. 11). A house existed on the site of this property at the time of the Godson survey. Simon Tompson was then the tenant of what was a small farm of 29½ acres. This property, like many more in Kingstone was then owned by John Chetwynd (39). The 1801 survey reveals that Moss Farm, was then a 70 acre farm, owned by John Chetwynd's descendant, Earl Talbot, and with John Willart as tenant. (John Willart died in 1814; his name is scored out in the survey schedule and substituted by the name Jas. Fernyhough, who was presumably his successor.) By 1838 'Moss House Farm' had been reduced to 54 acres with John Shaw as the Earl's tenant (24).

Fig. 11 **Moss Farm**

Thomas Johnson (previously of Moorfields), described as a farmer with 60 acres in 1851, and 71 acres in 1861, was probably living at Moss Farm; he died in 1864. From 1865 Alfred Johnson, a son of Thomas Johnson farmed at 'Moss House Farm' which had increased in size to 85 acres by 1871 (39)(4). Alfred Johnson and his family were still living here in 1891. George Johnson (son of Alfred Johnson's elder brother, Joseph Johnson) was farming at the Moss Farm by 1901, and still farming here in 1911 with his two sons (4).
In 1918 Moss Farm was sold in the Shrewsbury Estate sale and purchased by the then tenant, George Johnson. The farm was almost 78 acres; the 'tidying-up' by the Estate to allocate land more logically to the nearest farm having resulted in all of the *In Town Meadows* becoming part of Moss Farm (39). The Johnson

family appears to have continued to live at Moss Farm for some years after. Thomas Johnson, son of George Johnson, was described as being of Moss Farm when he died in 1937 (2).

To the east of Moss Farm, and on the other side of the lane, the *In Town Meadows* are shown on both the 1837 'tithe map', and the earlier Godson map. This meadow or pasture, south of the Tad contained traces of medieval strip farming. The Godson survey only reveals which of John Chetwynd's tenants held these strips, called *'doles'*. Simon Tompson held one strip, as did John Boulton (page 47), while John Barton (below) and Thomas 'Croxdon' (page 51) each had two strips. In 1838 the allocation of strips in this area was fully described and divided amongst more distant farms including Manor Farm with four strips, Walnuts Farm with two strips, Broomy Leasows Farm with two strips and Church Farm with four strips (24).

The Godson survey reveals that a single house then existed opposite Moss Farm, next to the *In Town Meadows* (and in Wood Lane i.e. the lane continuous with Church Lane between Moss Farm and Kingstone Wood). John Barton, a tanner, was the tenant here. He had a scattered holding of 42½ acres, some of which would later be absorbed into Moss Farm, including the field directly south of the house at Moss Farm, then called *Moats Meadow*, together with the moat it contained (36).

In 1838, on the site where earlier, John Barton had his house, two cottages {344} (owned by Earl Talbot) then existed. One was occupied by Thomas Fernyhough and the other by Thomas Shenton (24) (39). Thomas Fernyhough and Thomas Shenton, both agricultural labourers were still living in Kingstone in 1841. These cottages were probably occupied, in 1871, by John Potts and James Wood, both labourers, with John Potts still living here, in Wood Lane, in 1881 (4) (39). These cottages had gone by 1901.

On the same side, but further down the lane, between Moss Farm and Kingstone Wood there was another cottage. In 1838, and in 1841 this cottage {346} (also owned by Earl Talbot) was occupied by Joseph Bond, a labourer (24)(4). Thomas Fernyhough, an agricultural labourer, son of the above Thomas, had moved here with his wife and son by 1861.

At Uttoxeter petty sessions, in 1856 Thomas Fernyhough (senior) of Kingstone brought charges of assault and wilful damage against the brothers William Elsmore and John Elsmore (sons of John Elsmore of Blythe bridge Bank). It was however reported that Fernyhough *'showed unmistakeable signs of being drunk'*. The case was dismissed and he was ordered to pay costs (2).

Thomas Fernyhough (junior) was still in residence in 1891 with his wife, Mary Ann who was described as a dressmaker. Their son, also called Thomas was a painter, and lived with them. By 1901 Thomas Fernyhough, described as a roadman, was a widower, living at 'The Cottage' with his son Thomas (4).

In December 1902 Thomas Fernyhough wrote to his landlord's agent to say, with regret, that after 40 to 50 years he felt compelled to leave the cottage because *'it is in such a dreadful condition that it really is not fit for anyone to live in. The chimney and the end of the house have fallen in and the rain comes into every room; so that I have no comfort in any part of the house. For the sake of my own health I must seek a warmer abode this winter'* (39). [In Elsie's Story, page 121, this family were living in a 'pretty thatched cottage' - not so pretty after all!] The cottage had gone by the time of the 1923 Ordnance Survey map but damson trees existed in the hedgerow for many years indicating its former location.

In 1838, a house {234}, owned by Earl Talbot, existed on a ¼ acre plot of land directly north of the farmstead at Moss Farm, with Thomas Cope as tenant. In 1871, Mary Johnson was the tenant, and in 1882 Charles Beard, a 'wood labourer' lived here, where he also had a workshop (39). He was probably still here in 1891, then described as a woodman (4). William Sherratt, the tailor (page 44) was the tenant of this cottage in 1904 (39).

At the time of the Godson survey this plot, and the house upon it were owned by Katherine Boulton, by then an elderly widow. Katherine Boulton owned land elsewhere in Kingstone but was also tenant of about 32 acres. Her rented holding included land which would later become part of Church Farm. In particular, Katherine Boulton was tenant of a narrow strip of land running along the churchyard boundary on the south side of the church. In the Godson survey this piece of land was called *Barn Yard*. The survey map shows that a substantial long building then occupied this plot. Could this have been the village tithe barn?

The terms 'moss', and 'mosses' in the name of the nearby property suggests wet or boggy ground, perhaps with bog moss (Sphagnum) in the area of Kingstone Wood.

**KINGSTONE HALL FARM {248} {3}** This property was the 'star lot' in the Shrewsbury Estate sale in 1918, the sale details then making reference to a <u>modern</u> farmhouse (Fig. 12)(39). Redfern's short description of Kingstone Hall as *'a timber house covered by plaster'* is intriguing, as it suggests there was a house on this site of a much earlier date (30). Another source gave a more informative description, and in 1870, wrote - *'Kingstone Old Hall is an interesting specimen of the half-timbered, many-gabled style of the sixteenth century'.*
I can't help feeling we have lost a gem! The present house is however of some character, its appearance suggesting a house of late-Victorian construction in the then-fashionable half-timbered Tudor style. Perhaps this design was an attempt to reflect the type of house it replaced, a house which had truly belonged to the Tudor age. The farm buildings (converted into housing in recent years) probably also date from the late nineteenth century. If we speculate who might have lived at Kingstone Hall in centuries past, it seems likely that Henry Goring (page 11) who moved from Sussex to purchase the manor of Kingstone in 1625, would have lived in a fine house such as 'The Hall' described above. By the time of the Godson survey, Kingstone Hall, like much of the village was owned by John Chetwynd, with occupants living here as tenants of the Chetwynds and their successors, the Chetwynd-Talbots up until 1918. Thomas Launder was tenant of this farm which consisted of 123½ acres at the time of the Godson survey.

The 1801 survey of Uttoxeter reveals that George Wood was then Earl Talbot's tenant at Kingstone Hall Farm (39). The 'traveller' (page 117), who in 1870 described Kingstone, wrote that Kingstone Hall was occupied by the family of Wood for several generations. Evidence can be found in Kingstone churchyard on gravestones which record the death of Lydia Wood of Kingstone Hall (who died in 1829 aged 72) and her husband George Wood (who died 1830 aged 74, he also sharing a grave with his mother, Mary). The gravestone of George Wood's father, John Wood is also nearby. A family by the name of Sharratt lived at Kingstone Hall during the 1830s; Sampson Sharratt (son of William Sharratt) of Kingstone Hall married Ann, the widow of William Elsmore of Chartley, at Stowe in 1838, but had a farm dispersal sale at Kingstone Hall in March 1839 (2).

In 1838 Kingstone Hall Farm (at nearly 182 acres) was the largest farm in the village and parish (as it is today) and owned by Earl Talbot with Clement Cotterell as tenant (24). [Clement Cotterell had previously been farming at Birchwood Park, in Leigh parish, which was also owned by Earl Talbot.] Clement Cotterell died in 1859 and his wife, Hannah then became tenant. The Cotterell family held the farm for many years, Samuel Cotterell having succeeded his mother by 1876 (29). The acreage of the farm has varied widely. It comprised 180 acres (similar to 1838) in 1861, but had increased to 249 acres by 1871 as it then included mostly of the land of Broomy Leasows Farm. Kingstone Hall had a similar acreage in 1881, but in 1885 Samuel Cotterill was required to release the Broomy Leasows land.

By 1891 the Cotterell family had moved away and John Holland and his family were in residence at Kingstone Hall, being still here in 1901 (4).

In a tragic accident, in 1893, John Holland shot and killed Thomas Johnson, the 72 year-old former gamekeeper, when out with other farmers on a deer hunt in Kingstone Wood. Thomas Johnson's brother, Alfred Johnson was amongst the shooting party (2). The Holland family left in 1903.

Fig. 12 **Kingstone Hall Farm**

By 1912 John Stonier (son of Richard Stonier, the schoolmaster and farmer) was tenant of Kingstone Hall and also the adjoining Broomy Leasows Farm (28). He purchased the 272 acre joint holding in the 1918 Shrewsbury Estate sale for £9100 (39). By 1928 Ernest Stonier, son of John, was the owner and occupier (29). He died in 1933, leaving in his will money for the 'Stonier Bequest (page 117-118), and with his death the Stonier connection with Kingstone came to an end (his younger brother, Richard Stonier having moved away to a farm at Hanbury Park Farm, near Tutbury). Stonier Drive, in Kingstone is now the only visible evidence of the Stonier family's former significant presence in the village. Thomas Bettson (brother of Alfred Bettson of Woodcock Heath Farm) succeeded Ernest Stonier at Kingstone Hall Farm, and his descendants still live there today.

**The VILLA** The Godson map shows that a single house existed on a site next to the road between Church Cottage and Kingstone Hall (39). The 1801 survey map shows a cluster of buildings, probably where, in 1801, James Bakewell (page 105) owned three houses and a malt-house on a croft of about 1½ acres.
The 1837 'tithe map' shows a different arrangement, except for one house {246} (nearest the village centre). This house, later known as 'The Villa' was occupied, in 1838 by Samuel Durose, a bricklayer and builder (24). He owned this house as well as Church Cottage and two of the cottages in Church View. Samuel Durose had (jointly, with his brother George) inherited this property in 1820 from his father, William Durose, a farmer of Lower Loxley, as well as the land called *Barley Croft* (then occupied by William Adams).
Samuel Durose, in his will dated 1842, referred to the two acre plot of land, he owned behind The Villa and Church Cottage, called *Ferny Croft and Paddock* (on which old people's bungalows have been built, and also bisected by Stonier Drive) as well another piece of land (along what was then Moisty Lane) called *Barley Croft* (now part of the playing fields) (24). Samuel Durose of Kingstone bequeathed all his property, except for Church Cottage (page 44), to his wife Mary during her lifetime, after which it was to be sold, and the proceeds divided between their children (24). Mary Durose died in May 1842, just 8 days after her husband and the property was offered for sale by auction, in several lots, in September of the same year. This is probably when Thomas Byrd acquired the land which featured in the Byrd Charity (pages 133-134). If so, he would have purchased The Villa and Church Cottage at the same time, but perhaps not the two houses which Samuel Durose had owned in Church View, which were sold as a different lot (2).
Thomas Spooner, formerly of Church View, a farmer of five acres was probably living at The Villa in 1851, although he was described as a shopkeeper when he had an auction sale on his premises in 1856 (2)(4).
A house with three closes of land (*Ferneys Croft and Paddock*, *Barley Croft* and *Broomy Croft*), totalling seven acres, offered for sale in 1891, together with the adjoining cottage occupied by John Fradley (i.e. Church Cottage), and in the occupation of Francis Frederick Sherratt, is thought to have been The Villa.
The cottage in Church View occupied by Police Constable Steele featured at the same auction (2).
By 1901 Alfred Johnson (formerly of Moss Farm) lived at The Villa, and after his death in 1904 his widow, Patience Johnson, continued to live here. Mrs. Johnson was at The Villa (a property with 10 rooms) in 1911 (4).
In 1928 Charles Noakes, who worked for Ernest Stonier at Kingstone Hall, was living at The Villa (29).

By 1838, three cottages had replaced the existing buildings on the site between The Villa and Kingstone Hall. One of the three cottages was then occupied by Thomas Croxton, junior (son of Thomas Croxton of the 'Barley Mow'), living in his own house {247a}. Richard Willart and Elizabeth Wood were tenants living in a pair of cottages {247} owned by Richard Reynolds, a farmer of Mount Pleasant (page 61)(24).
Earlier this century the three cottages were occupied by Mrs. Beard, Tom West and 'Gunner' Johnson (who is said to have invented a gun at the time of the Great War).
A distant view of The Villa and these three cottages (all now demolished) is given on Plate 12 (page 54).

**CHURCH COTTAGE** {244} {4} This is one of the few remaining older houses in the village centre, although very much altered and enlarged. A house which existed here at the time of the Godson survey, may also have been the house on a one acre plot called *Fernycroft*, owned by James Bakewell in 1801 (page 105) (39).
In 1838 this cottage was owned by Samuel Durose (who lived nearby at 'The Villa'), but occupied by Thomas

Beard (24). Samuel Durose bequeathed this cottage to his daughter, Ellen Durose (who married Arthur Gilbert in 1843) but it seems to have been sold in 1842 with the rest of Samuel Durose's former property. Mr. and Mrs. Fradley were living here by 1891, and still in residence in their small cottage, which had only had two rooms, in 1911 (4). They somehow had space for a small sweet shop. Jemima Fradley cleaned the church and also kept the church key (see Elsie's story, page 122). John Fradley, (uncle to his neighbour, Edward Fradley) worked as a labourer but (according to my father, John Gallimore) was also known locally as 'Doctor Tank' being a provider of 'cures' for animal illnesses!

Close to Church Cottage is a small 'island' in the road surmounted by a tree; this tiny piece of land has been there a long time - it is shown on the Godson map of Kingstone, dated between 1717 and 1720. Also nearby, a short distance down the lane to Kingstone Wood, and below the small bridge to the church which crosses the brook, is the site of the spring which supplied the village with fresh water (page 25).

**CHURCH VIEW** (demolished) This row of three cottages (Fig. 13), on the roadside, just north of the central 'island' did look directly across to the present church (although the view towards the old church, being more to the west would have been less direct).

There was a house or houses here in 1801, and in 1838 two cottages in Church View {253} were owned by Samuel Durose, one without a tenant (but later, by 1841, occupied by John Durose, son of Samuel Durose), and the other occupied by Thomas Spooner, junior, a shopkeeper. These two cottages were adverted for sale in 1842, following the death of Samuel Durose (2). The third cottage {253a}, at the eastern end of Church View was owned and occupied by Thomas Durose (half-brother of Samuel Durose), a schoolmaster. In 1820 he had inherited the property from his father William Durose (24).

In 1838 Thomas Durose also had a plot of almost one acre of land (called *Broomycroft*) adjoining his house on its eastern side; now at the southern end of the development called 'The Meadows' (24).

Two cottages 'opposite the church, near the new school and adjoining Kingstone Hall' (in the occupation of Arthur Johnson and Eli Fradley) were advertised for sale in 1877. This advertisement may have described the two houses in Church View which Samuel Durose owned until 1842.

By 1891 the house formerly owned by Thomas Durose had become the 'Police Office', with Frank Steele as Kingstone's resident policeman (4). This cottage, occupied by Police Constable Steele was advertised for sale in 1891 (page 42). Alexander Fisher was the Police Constable living at the the 'Police Station' in 1901, followed by Police Constable Samuel George Cadwallader who had taken over by 1911 (4). In 1918 the death of Constable Cadwallader (aged 37) in an upstairs room in this small low cottage presented difficulties because of the awkward twisting stairs. He was extracted through an upstairs window to be placed on a farm dray, an event witnessed by my father. Constable Cadwallader was evidently much respected; he was buried in Kingstone churchyard with a headstone erected by public subscription (13).

Fig. 13 **Church View**

By 1891, and early in the 20th. century the middle cottage in Church View was occupied by Joseph Sherratt, the tailor who could be seen working in front of the large shop window. His son William followed him in the same trade, being still here in 1912 (29). William Sherratt's wife, Louisa became the local midwife (see Elsie's Story, page 121). 'Granny' Sherratt therefore became well known in the community. She also kept careful records over many years of all the babies she delivered in the area.

The last house in the row ('Barracks' end) was the Post Office which was kept by Harriett Clews in 1891 (4). She had retired to a house at The Barracks by 1901 and Edward and Sarah Fradley lived at the Post Office. In 1911, Sarah Fradley (also, page 46) was recorded as the sub-postmistress here, while Edward Fradley was a railway platelayer (4)(29). Edward Fradley, a son of Sarah and John Fradley died in 1918, a WWI casualty. Church View was demolished in the 1970s to make way for the houses which now occupy the site.

**The `BARRACKS'/SCHOOL VIEW** (demolished) The Godson map reveals that a house then stood on this roadside corner (Fi5. 5, page 30)(39).Two rows (one facing the road, the other end-on to the road), each of three houses, and known as 'The Barracks' (Fig. 14, below) formerly stood in the centre of the village on this corner site, and they had replaced this single house by 1801.

Their implied use as a barracks seems unlikely, the somewhat forbidding appearance of these tall-looking red-brick properties (one row being raised up on the side of the bank) may have been why they acquired the nickname of the 'Barracks'. 'School View' is obviously a more recent name as there was no school on the present site when these houses were built, probably in the late eighteenth century.

In 1838 there were six houses {257} and {258}, all owned by John Beard, and occupied by Joseph Fernyhough, Richard Shenton, James Ward, Richard Ward, all agricultural labourers, and Anne Wood, widow, with one house unoccupied (24). It is difficult to be specific about the later occupacy of these houses.

In February 1876, in an auction sale advertised to take place at the Shrewsbury Arms in Kingstone, there were two lots, the first of three cottages , all unoccupied, the second of two houses and a blacksmith's shop, in the respective occupations of John Babb, Joseph Shenton and John Wilson (blacksmith of Loxley Green).

A reference in the advertisement to the will of George Beard, who had died in 1859 (and had inherited these houses from his father, John Beard) suggests that the advertised houses were those known as The Barracks. Evidently not then sold, the properties were advertised later in the same year when it was then said that Arthur Ainsworth was an occupant, and that there had recently been a village shop in one of the houses (2).

There are various census references to shops in Kingstone and the central position of these properties would have provided a suitable location, although less so for blacksmith's shop.

Charles Bunting advertised a house and shop with bakehouse to let in Kingstone in 1877, which was possibly sited here (2). He may have been the purchaser of the cottages as in the 1891 census these properties were then called Bunting's Buildings, this name being explained by the fact that they were owned by Charles Bunting. He was the father of A. C. Bunting, who became owner of the Uttoxeter brewery in the 1890s. Charles Bunting died in 1891, and all six houses were sold as part of his estate in August of the same year (2)(4).

Charles Bunting's tenants, in 1891, included John Potts, an agricultural labourer, and his wife Elizabeth, living in the row of three houses which faced the School, the other houses in this row being unoccupied. Jane Slater, a widow was living with her son Thomas, an agricultural labourer as the only occupants in the other row of houses.

In 1901, Elizabeth Potts, by then a widow was still living at The Barracks, the other householders being Ann Wilson and Elizabeth Smith, also widows, as well as Harriet Clews (retired post mistress), and George Stevenson, a general labourer (4).

Fig. 14 **The Barracks**

All six houses were advertised for sale in 1909, then in the occupation of Messrs. Johnson, Fradley, Fradley, Stevenson, Deville and Harvey (2).

In later years (c. 1920s/30s) the householders in the row of houses facing the School were Thomas Wilson (of the blacksmith family), Frederick West and Thomas Wood, the village sexton (page 106). Occupants living in the row end-on to the road included Mrs. Wheat, and Mrs. Cadwallader, the widow of Kingstone's police constable who had moved from Church View.

The Barracks houses were demolished in the 1970s when the present houses built on the site.

**The OLD SCHOOL** An intriguing reference to earlier educational provision occurs within the will of Hugh Netam (Needham) of Kingstone (referred to earlier (page 40) in relation to the church chest). In his will Hugh Needham (died 1601) left *'to every scoller* (scholar) *that shall fortune to qooe* (go) *to scowle* (school) at *Kingston at the daye of my funerall 2d'* (24).

I have no knowledge of any other reference to a school in Kingstone until the early nineteenth century. A house and school {259} (owned by Richard Stonier) existed, by 1838 on a site where the middle of one of three bungalows now stands on land south of 'The Walnuts' (below) (24). The earliest map {5}, shows a house on this site, but this cannot have been the same building as the plot was vacant in 1801 (39).

In describing the old school building to my own father, Alfred Bettson of Kingstone had said that at the end of the shop there was a large room which had been a schoolroom. The property was also thought to have been of some age, described by my grandmother (page 121) as having had old lead lattice-paned windows. She also recalled that it had been *'used as a school in my father's time'* (her father having been John Bettson who was born in 1862). In about 1946 this former school was demolished and a bungalow was built on the site.

In the censuses of 1841 and 1851 Richard Stonier and Thomas Durose were both described as schoolmasters at Kingstone, but by 1861 Thomas Durose had died, and Richard Stonier was expanding his farming enterprise (4). Benjamin Johnson (living with his father, a farmer in Kingstone) was now listed as a schoolmaster, as well as Thomas Pickering who originated in Gateshead, County Durham, who presumably lived at the house with the adjoining old school. In 1870 the school was described as a Parochial School, supported chiefly by the Earl of Shrewsbury, and partly by subscriptions, with Louisa Boole was schoolmistress at Kingstone (29). She would probably have lived in the house and also worked in the schoolroom used earlier by Richard Stonier, but her teaching career will have been brief as in 1871 she married John Stonier and became a farmer's wife.

In about 1900 Joseph Campion, a boot and shoe maker, lived and worked in the former school building. His customers had to be patient as he would sometimes spend the whole day at the Shrewsbury Arms, which was open all day at this period (page 121).

The 1901 Ordnance Survey map, records this building as a 'technical school'. During the 1890s urban and rural councils were awarded grants by Staffordshire County Council for the provision of technical instruction. Classes were given in the villages in e.g. horticulture, cookery, bee-keeping, gardening, and dairying. Classes provided at Kingstone included home nursing, dresscutting and woodwork (2). Presumably the old school was used for such instruction at this period. However, the 1923 map marks this building as the site of the Post Office. Sarah Fradley, postmistress, seems to have moved here from Church View (page 44), the building having served as a shop and Post Office up to about 1946. When Sarah Fradley died in 1931 she had been postmistress at Kingstone for 39 years (2). Sarah Fradley's daughter, Harriet Fradley succeeded her mother.

The Post Office and shop later moved to the old smithy in Blythe Bridge (page 92).

**WALNUTS FARM** {261} This tall red brick house of the late eighteenth century (a listed building) (Fig. 15) stands end on to the top of Chapel Bank (the bank, on Uttoxeter Road, leading out of Kingstone towards Uttoxeter). In 1838 this was a farm of about 35 acres owned by William Wood of Kingstone. In the 1801 Survey It had been owned by William Wood (who is likely to have been the father of the above William Wood) (39).

In 1838 the farm was occupied by Richard Stonier, variously described as schoolmaster, parish clerk, engraver and farmer (29). [William Wood was the bachelor uncle of Patience Stonier, née Wood, wife of Richard Stonier.] As a schoolmaster, but also a farmer, in 1851 he farmed 50 acres. In 1861, Richard Stonier's eldest son, William

Stonier farmed 36 acres at what was probably Walnuts Farm while Richard Stonier farmed 111 acres at Church Farm, with his deceased wife's uncle, William Wood also living with the family. Thomas Stonier, Richard Stonier's second son appears to have been at Walnuts Farm in 1871, whilst also being tenant of Manor Farm nearby. It appears fron the census that Richard Stonier (and his youngest son, John) had returned to live at 'The Walnuts' by 1881 as they had the same 64 acre holding as Thomas Stonier had ten years earlier. Richard Stonier died in 1885 and by 1891 William Blackshaw was farming at 'Walnut Tree House'. He seems to have been still here in 1901 and 1911 (4). At the time of the Shrewsbury Estate sale in 1918, the map accompanying the sale catalogue indicates that Miss Blackshaw owned this property. Mrs. James Wood, a farmer, was probably living at 'The Walnuts' in 1928 (29). According to my father, Mrs. Wood tied string to the legs of her hens so that they did not wander off and go across the road to Manor Farm!

There had been two walnut trees behind the house in a small field between the farmhouse and the Shrewsbury Arms (developed for housing in more recent years). A pear tree also stood in this field and my father revealed that children who passed by on their way to school would help themselves to its fruit. I imagine the guilty parties included my father and his brothers and sisters as they walked from Wall Heath Farm at Willslock!

Fig. 15 **Walnuts Farm**

**THE SHREWSBURY ARMS/DOG & PARTRIDGE** {265} {6} Before 'The Birches' was built this distinctive old building (Fig. 16) was the last property in the village before Hollydene (page 70). This property, or an earlier one on the same site was recorded, in the early eighteenth century, as being owned by John Chetwynd, with John Boulton (son of Katherine Boulton) as tenant (39). This was however then a substantial farm of 83 acres, and included land which would later be part of Church Farm.

In 1818 John Beard, victualler, ran the public house here, then known as the 'Dog and Partridge' (page 20)(24). [John Beard was recorded in the 1801 survey as a tenant of Earl Talbot and with 28 acres of land; this probably included the inn and some of the adjacent land.] In 1838, Earl Talbot was the owner of the Dog and Partridge and John Beard was still here as his tenant. Almost 7 acres of land were then included. By 1851 the Dog and Partridge was run by John Beard's son, George Beard, described as a victualler and wheelwright (29).

Earl Talbot succeeded to the additional title of Earl of Shrewsbury in 1860 (33), and the change of name of this public house to the 'Shrewsbury Arms' (by 1870) would seem to be linked to this event. George Beard died in 1858, and his widow, Harriet, then married William Ainsworth. In 1859 William Ainsworth was running the pub. (39), and, like George Beard, he was also a wheelwright, as well as a farmer on a small scale, farming the same holding of about 7 acres (29). William Ainsworth was in trouble in 1865, being fined at Uttoxeter for attempting (a second time) to take fish from the Tad Brook (2). William Ainsworth was still in charge at the Shrewsbury Arms in 1871, but by 1880 he had moved to the Mosses (page 78), and George Finnemore had taken over, and together with the former Croxton holding (see page 51), he now farmed 14½ acres of land (39). Michael John Deaville was the tenant in 1883 with only about ¼ acre which would have comprised just the inn, garden and stables (39). Stretton's Derby Brewery Ltd. were tenants in 1886, but by 1891 the tenant was William Poole, who also farmed at Barn Farm ( page 59)(39). Charles Green was the publican as well as a farmer here in 1901, followed by George Woodings who was the tenant of both Barn Farm and The Shrewsbury Arms in 1905 (4)(39).

In 1910 Charles Bunting Ltd, brewers of Uttoxeter, were tenants of just the inn, garden and stables, but when the Shrewsbury Arms was put up for sale by the Shrewsbury Estate in 1918 it was advertised together with The Barn Ground (page 59), and described as an inn and farm with almost 38 acres (39). It was sold for £1700. In later years the pub. was run by George Woolliscroft in 1912, and Edward Lovatt was the host by 1928 (29). The Shrewsbury Arms, or, as it used to be called, The Dog and Partridge, has long been a gathering place for social activities, including May Day celebrations [See 'A Ramble Round Kingstone' - Chapter 7, page 117]. The Kingstone Friendly Society or Club each year in June held their annual dinner at the Shrewsbury Arms,

Fig. 16 **The Shrewsbury Arms**

following by a service in the church. Sporting activities and various entertainments took place in the field behind the pub. with dancing in the evening. The Shrewsbury Arms was also the location for the annual Kingstone Show which took place in the field {268} belonging to the pub. known as the Barn Ground. [More detail about both Kingstone Friendly Society and Kingstone Show is given in Chapter 6, page 110.]

**MANOR FARM** {155} {7} Probably the oldest property in the village, this was described in the 1918 Shrewsbury Estate sale details as having a 'commodious Early English half-timbered farmhouse'(39). The house is painted black and white according to common practice (Fig. 17, page 49). When Manor Farm was sold (for £1550) at the 1918 sale it was a small dairy holding of about 31 acres (39).
The Godson survey map recorded a house on this site but it was not then owned by John Chetwynd.
In 1801 Thomas Adams owned this farm of about 70 acres. The 1818 Staffordshire Directory (page 20) lists Thomas Adams as a gentleman of Kingstone, and this farm was still owned by Thomas Adams in 1838. The Adams family had lived in Kingstone, Thomas Adams having baptised his son, also called Thomas at Kingstone in 1797. His mother Mary Adams, and brother, William Adams were also buried at Kingstone in 1810 and 1816 respectively. By the time of the 1841 census Thomas Adams had moved away and was living with his son, a park keeper at Burbage in Wiltshire. Thomas Adams, then 85 years old, was still living with his son in Wiltshire in 1851. They may have still owned Manor Farm at this time. Thomas Adams, a yeoman of Loxley died leaving a will dated 1798 (24). He was the father of the above-mentioned Thomas Adams, senior and of his brother William. The freehold messuage, lands and premises where he and his son Thomas lived were

bequeathed to his son Thomas, and in making provision for his widow (Mary) he stipulated that:

*'Also I give unto my said dear wife the priviledge use and enjoyment of the street parlour and chamber over it next the street, and the dairy next the street, being part of my messuage house in Kinston aforesaid now in my son Thomas Adams's possession and for her my said wife to enjoy during the term of her natural Life and one half of the garden on that side towards the church.'*

The above description indicates that this Thomas Adams lived in Kingstone, the property in which he lived, being clearly the existing house of Manor Farm (with the dairy which is now converted into a separate house). Thomas Adams bequeathed another dwelling house he owned in Kingstone to his son Thomas, then occupied by Joshua Preston. This is very likely to have been the house which stood at the bottom of the bank below the Manor Farm. This house {173} was owned by Thomas Adams in 1838 and with John Pakeman, as tenant (24). The Godson map indicates that a house {8} existed on this site over a hundred years earlier (39). In 1884 this house was owned by the Shrewsbury estate when Joseph Fernyhough took over the tenancy of this property from his grandfather, also called Joseph Fernyhough, a labourer who had lived there at least as far back as 1861. Further tenants were John Johnson, from 1885 to 1889, then finally William Wood. After he left in 1890 the cottage was pulled down (39).

Mary Williams was the tenant of Manor Farm in 1838, and she was still here in 1851 and 1861 (24)(4). Mary Williams was the widow of John Williams, a butcher and farmer who had died in 1835. Manor Farm had 62 acres in 1838, much of it in small portions scattered around the village (including four of the *In Town Meadows* near Moss Farm) (24). Mary Williams had three servants to help her to run the farm in 1861, including the 18 year old,

Fig. 17 **Manor Farm**

Thomas Stonier, a son of Richard Stonier. The farm was advertised for sale by auction at the Cross Keys Inn, Uttoxeter in 1868, with Thomas Stonier as tenant, Mary Williams having retired (2). It was presumably at this time that the Shrewsbury estate bought the farm as they were recorded as the owners in 1871. The farm in 1871 was only about 34 acres as some of the land had been redistributed to Moss Farm and Kingstone Hall Farm (39). According to the 1871 census, Thomas Stonier farmed 64 acres, the apparent discrepancy being probably because he also farmed at Walnuts Farm. Thomas Stonier had married Lydia Shaw, Mary Williams's niece at Kingstone in 1864. Mary Williams died in 1872, and Thomas and Lydia Stonier had moved to Cheadle by 1881. The 1881 census reveals that Richard Stonier (and his son John) were then also farming 64 acres which probably included the land of Manor Farm in addition to their own land at the Walnuts Farm. By 1883 Joseph Cotton Locker was tenant of this farm, then 31 acres (39). James and George Woodings were tenants from 1897 to 1910, or later (39). Arthur Derry was at Manor Farm in 1928 (29). Manor Farm is clearly a place of some age and importance in Kingstone, and further research may yield more information, but at present I cannot explain the title 'Manor'.

**PRIMITIVE METHODIST CHAPEL / SHOP** The small chapel (Fig. 18, page 50) was built on the roadside next to Nene House.

By Act of Parliament, meeting houses i.e. places intended to be used for religious worship by Protestant Dissenters were required to be registered. Locally, this meant the completion of a certificate obtained from the Bishop of Lichfield. Such a certificate for Kingstone refers to *'the Primitive Methodist Chapel and premises, situate at Kingstone in the parish of Kingstone and now in the holding of Jeremiah Gilbert P.M. Minister.'*

Jeremiah Gilbert, a noted Primitive Methodist minister, then at Burton upon Trent, registered his intention to use the chapel by a certificate dated the 8th. November 1841. This is an earlier date than that given in the 1851 Staffordshire Directory which states that this chapel was built in 1849 (29).

Primitive Methodist preachers travelled around and visited chapels according to a pre-planned timetable. Surviving circuit plans for 1834 and 1838 indicate that Kingstone was then on the Burton on Trent circuit (32). Two earlier certificates exist, although there is no evidence that these were through petitions for registration by the Primitive Methodists. In 1823, James Allen of Uttoxeter (thought to have been a Wesleyan preacher) certified his intention to use, for worship, a tenement in Kingstone, then in the possession of a John Cresswell, a labourer, but this was at Black Pits (page 61). In 1813, Edward Ward of Kingston gave notice of his intention to use his own house in Kingston as a place for religious worship by an *'Assembly or Congregation of Protestants'* (24). A gravestone in the churchyard (13) is inscribed to the memory of the Rev. James Crompton, Primitive Methodist Minister, who died in 1863, and to his wife Pamala. He was born in Lancashire, and his work took him to many places, but there is no indication that he spent any time in Kingstone. His connection with Kingstone is

Fig. 18 **Kingstone Post Office and Stores (Former Primitive Methodist Chapel)** - in 1983

through his wife, who he married at Weston-on-Trent, near Stafford in 1843. She was formerly Pamala Ward, daughter of John and Mary Ward of Church Farm, Kingstone. The building has long since ceased to be used as a chapel. It was empty for a period but for many years up to the recent past it served as village shop and Post Office (Fig. 18). Prior to this the shop and Post Office, (run by Sarah Fradley, and then her daughter Harriet) was sited at the former school on land below 'The Walnuts' until this was demolished in about 1946, Sarah Fradley having run the Post Office at Church View in an earlier period (pages 43 & 46). [In the 1950s the nearest shop was in the former blacksmith's shop at Blythe Bridge.] This small building has gone through a number of transformations, which included at one time the removal of its front porch for road widening.

The property now belongs to the owner of Nene House. The chapel appears to have been built within the same plot of land where in 1838 a house {173} stood which belonged to Thomas Adams of Manor Farm, with John Pakeman, an agricultural labourer as his tenant (24).

**KINGSTONE SCHOOL/TALBOT FIRST SCHOOL /THE BARLEY MOW** The present school (Fig. 19) occupies the green or central 'island' in the middle of the village which in 1838 was divided into three parts (a pattern which partly remains today). [The whole site is enclosed or 'encased' by railings (formerly wooden fencing), and this may be the origin of the term 'The Cases', the local name for this boundary.]
Earl Talbot owned a beer house or public house called 'The Barley Mow' which occupied the site of the present school {241}, and this may be the same building which is marked on the earlier Godson map {9} (24)(39). Thomas Croxton, senr. was the Earl's tenant at the Barley Mow in 1838, and also tenant of an orchard {243} owned by the Earl which made up the western half of the 'island'.
John Beard was William Perkin's tenant of a small croft {242} opposite the 'Barracks' houses (page 45) which he himself owned (24). The Godson map appears to show that a house then existed on this croft.
The Godson survey reveals that an earlier Thomas 'Croxden' (Croxton) had been John Chetwynd's tenant of the house which then existed on the Barley Mow/Kingstone School site. He farmed about nine acres of land, most of which was along the western side of the road between Potts' Lane and Black Pits. Remarkably, this was much the same block of land which formed the holding of the later Thomas Croxton (his son, or more probably grandson) in 1838. This later Thomas Croxton was born in Kingstone in 1758 and was presumably the same Thomas Croxton who was tenant of the same nine acres in 1801 as in 1838, and also recorded as a farmer of Kingstone in the 1818 Directory (page 20)(29). He was 91 years of age when he died in 1850. In 1834, Henry Elsmore, elder brother of John Elsmore, maltster of Blythe Bridge Bank (page 95), kept the beer house, and seems likely to have been supplied with malt by his brother. The beer house continued to be family-run, Henry Elsmore having married Hannah, a daughter of Thomas Croxton, in 1824. Richard Croxton, the brother of Hannah Elsmore was at the beer house in 1851, but he moved to Ingestre in the same year. Richard's son, Henry Croxton was keeper of the beer house in 1861, and also in 1871 when his holding was ten acres (and

Fig. 19 **Kingstone School**

probably the same block of land farmed by his grandfather, Thomas Croxton) (4). In 1868, Henry Croxton was fined 5s with costs for keeping his beerhouse open after 10 pm (2). Henry Croxton later moved to Stafford where he died in 1874, thus ending the Croxton family connection with Kingstone which can be traced back in Kingstone parish registers to at least 1697. George Finnemore was tenant of the former nine acre Croxton family holding in 1872 before the plot with the beer house was separated from the rest to build the School (39). The present school was formerly opened as the new National School on 13th. November 1877 with lessons beginning on the following Monday 19th. November (2) (21). The Education Act of 1870 had demanded that all children should receive an education up to the age of 10 years, and the 1880 Act raised the school leaving

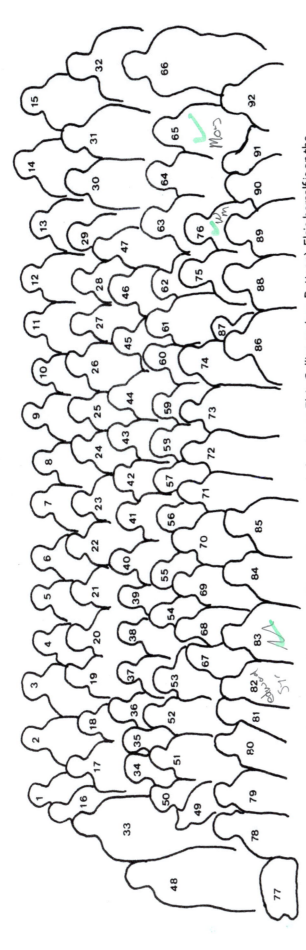

**Kingstone Village School - 1901** The above photograph (Plate 11) was a copy belonging to Elsie Gallimore (nee Bettson). Elsie herself is on the photograph together with her sister and one of her brothers. The photograph also shows Mr. Taylor (schoolmaster) and Mrs. Taylor (schoolmistress) together with their sons Cyril and Basil, and the family's two dogs. Elsie Gallimore supplied the names as given below:

TOP ROW (Boys) [1] Tom. Holland; [2] George Deville ; [3] Sam. Mellor ; [4] Tom. Beard ; [5] Charles Deville ; [6] Richard Wilson; [7] David Steele ; [8] Cyril Taylor; [9] Frank Shaw ; [10] Tom. Green; [11] Fred. West; [12] John Mellor ; [13] Luke Mellor ; [14] William Steele ; [15] Richard Stonier.
SECOND ROW (Boys) [16] Will. Emery; [17] Sam. Emery; [18] Ernal Emery; [19] Geoffrey Deville ; [20] Tom. West ; [21] Richard Titterton ; [22] Ben. Shaw ; [23] Basil Taylor; [24] Ernald Titterton ; [25] Will. Smith ; [26] Stanley Ridout ; [27] Arthur West ; [28] Percy Wilson ; [29] George Mellor ; [30] Ernest Johnson ; [31] Rowland Deville ; [32] Miss Batch (teacher).
THIRD ROW (Girls) [33] Mr. Taylor (schoolmaster); [34] Daisy Warren; [35] Elizabeth Smith ; [36] Alice Whitehall ; [37] Ada Gadsby ; [38] Lucy Warren; [39] Harriet Buxton; [40] Maria Campion ; [41] Elsie Bettson; [42] Annie Sherratt ; [43] Georgina Smith ; [44] Dorothy Warren ; [45] Florence Holland ; [46] May Sherratt ; [47] Tillah Titterton. FOURTH ROW (Girls) [48] Mrs. Taylor (schoolmistress) ; [49] Taylor family dog; [50] Sarah Wood; [51] Mary Johnson ; [52] Laura Elsmore ; [53] Gertie Brandrick; [54] Maud Cotterill ; [55] Nellie Cotterill ; [56] Hilda Cotterill ; [57] Martha Cotterill ; [58] ---------; [59] Nellie Warren ; [60] May Brummel ; [61] Harriet Bettson;
[62] Sallie Holland ; [63] Daisy Sherratt ; [64] Edith Steele ; [65] Mary Fradley ; [66] Miss Mary Jackson (pupil teacher
FIFTH ROW (Small girls) [67] Hilda Martin; [68] Lizzie Gadsby ; [69] Nellie Ridout ; [70] Mabel Brandrick ; [71] ---------; [72] ---------; [73] May Warren
[74] B ---------- Brummel.         (Boys) [75] Charles Whitehall ; [76] William Fradley. [77] Taylor family dog ; [78] Claud Sherratt ; [79] Jack Beard ; [80] Alfred Bettson ; [81] Reg. Whittaker ; [82] Edward Fradley ;
FRONT ROW (Small boys - 5 years old) [77] Taylor family dog ; [78] Claud Sherratt ; [79] Jack Beard ; [80] Alfred Bettson ; [81] Reg. Whittaker ; [82] Edward Fradley ;
[83] Sidney Martin ; [84] Jack Cotterill ; [85] John Warren ; [86] Frank Martin ; [87] ---------; [88] Ernest Whitehall ; [89] Edwin Steele ; [90] ---------
[91] ---------; [92] Sam. Wood.

53

Plate 12 **Children of Kingstone School**, a more informal group in fancy dress c.1932
Note: to the left, the tree (as present) on the small island in the road opposite the recently completed lych gate, a view of The Villa (centre), and beyond, the row of cottages further down Church Lane / Wood Lane.
*Left to right:*
Gladys Whittaker, Malbon Jones, Hetty Gallimore, Mabel Derry, Margaret Whittaker, Daisy Whittaker, Peggy Moss, Edie Sargeant, Joyce Martin, E. Derry, Joyce Lovatt.  *Seated:* Ernest Gallimore, Margaret Wilson.

Plate 13 **Children of Kingstone School**, another group in fancy dress 1934
Note: 'The Barracks' in the background
*Left to right:*
Eric Bettson (Scarlet Runner), Mary Cotton, Nellie Fradley, Edna Richardson, Doris Whittaker, Winnie Whittaker, Margaret Whittaker, Queenie Cotton, Bernard Jackson, Ernest Gallimore (Scarlet Runner).

Plate 14 **Children of Kingstone School**, another group in fancy dress 1934
Note: 'The Barracks' in the background
*Left to right:*
T. Bebbington, Malbon Jones, Lucy Whittaker, ? , Laura Bebbington, Gladys Whittaker, Peggy Moss (Humpty Dumpty), Joyce Lovatt, Nola Bettson, ? , Cyril Bettson, Eric Somerville (Simple Simon), Jackie Horobin, Eric Bebbington.

age to 13 years.
By 1881, William John Hobbis was the schoolteacher, but was judged to be unsatisfactory and removed in 1886, being replaced by Mr. Taylor (21). In 1891 Richard Taylor, the schoolmaster, and wife Amelia, the schoolmistress were living at 'School House', the same house which they called Nene House (4). The present school was enlarged in 1894 and again in 1907 to accommodate 108 children. In 1912 the average attendance was 86 (29). Richard Taylor was the schoolmaster for a period of many years, with Mrs.Taylor teaching the infants (Plate 11, page 52).
In 1918 Kingstone School was advertised for sale as part of the Shrewsbury Estate, being then let on lease to Staffordshire County Council at one guinea per annum. The School then contained a cloak room, a large school room 39ft. 6in. x 17ft. and a large school room 22ft. 6in. x 18ft., two playing fields, lavatories, and a garden (occupied by Mr. Taylor, the Schoolmaster and Mrs. Eliza West). After Mr. Taylor's death, Mrs. Ethel Beech was appointed headmistress. She lived in 'The Bungalow' which was built off the Blythe Bridge Road, just south of Church Farm. ('Beech's Bungalow' was later occupied by Miss. Deville).
Plates 13 & 14 (pages 54-55) show children in fancy dress for nursery rhyme plays organised by Mrs. Beech. Mrs. Beech retired in 1935 and was succeeded by Miss. Guntripp, headmistress of Kingstone school until 1954 (2).

Kingstone School, being a gathering place for large number of children was inevitably where childhood illnesses were likely to occur, with a number of disease outbreaks having been recorded in the past.
The school was closed during February and March in 1900 due to scarlet fever (2)
In July 1918 a whooping cough outbreak closed the school, the same disease resulting in the school being closed for two weeks in October 1937 (2). The most serious incident was in January 1929 when there were

cases of diptheria in Kingstone. This prompted action by the surveyor of the rural district council who reported on the matter of unsatisfactory sanitary arrangements at Kingstone School. He had ordered the school to be thoroughly disinfected, for privies to be emptied, drains cleaned and for the cesspit in the school yard to be emptied. It was commented that the cesspit should never have been in the school yard '*as it soon filled up and backed up the gullies outside the school*' ! The fact that there was no water supply at the school was pointed out, the water used by the children being obtained from a pipe which discharged into the brook, and was liable to contamination (2).
[This water supply was the spring which the village depended on for drinking water until about 1936.]

**NENE HOUSE {174}** Now converted to form a single dwelling, this is one of the few remaining older properties in the village centre. It did not exist in 1801, but had been constructed by about 1825. The history of this house can be traced through an indenture, dated 1825 whereby Elizabeth Johnson, the widow of John Johnson, a timber merchant of Stoke-on-Trent agreed to sell some plots of land in Kingstone to William Perkin, a timber merchant of Uttoxeter (39). One plot of land called *the Barn Yard* had been the site of a property divided into four dwellings, but more recently this had been divided into seven small dwellings (the document names the then occupants)! The indenture also recorded that this tenement had lately been pulled down and three dwellings had since been erected on this plot. Also included in the sale agreement was a plot of land called *the Orchard* (and again the occupants were named). It was further revealed that Elizabeth Johnson was the daughter of Nathaniel Brindley, apparently a potter of Stoke-on-Trent, but formerly of Kingston. The Brindley family were long been established in Kingston, Nathaniel Brindley having been descended from Roger Brindley of Kingstone who died leaving a will in 1613 (24).

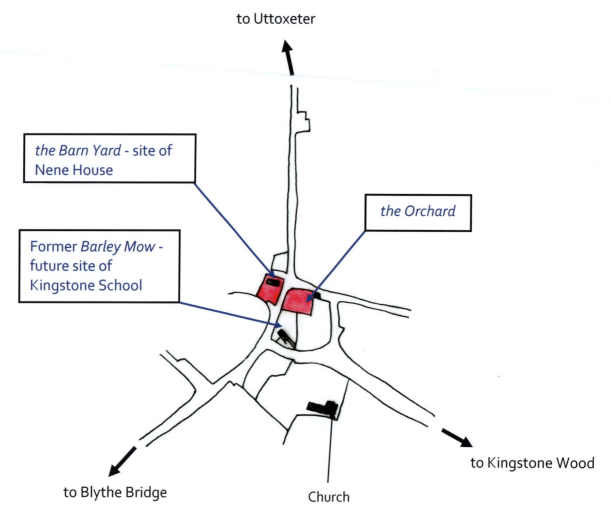

Fig. 20 **Barn Yard** (plot on which Nene House was built), **and Orchard** (used as garden) - former Brindley property in centre of Kingstone village, in about 1874 .
[Also shown is the site used for Kingstone School.]

The *Barn Yard* was amongst property in Kingston left by Simon Brindley of Kingstone (grandfather of Nathaniel Brindley) in his will dated 1742 (24). [Elizabeth Johnson of Stoke-on-Trent was clearly a woman of some status; in her own will, dated 1829 she named two distinguished men as executors, Josiah Spode II and Herbert Minton, both heads of their respective leading pottery firms.]

In 1838 the three cottages (built on the *Barn Yard* plot) owned by William Perkin, were occupied by John Day, a shoemaker, Thomas Barlow and Thomas Fradley (24). In the same year William Perkin advertised the three cottages for sale, his tenants then being Thomas Barlow, Thomas Cope and ...... Shaw (2). Thomas Fradley, an agricultural labourer, and later a farmer, and John Day, a shoemaker both later lived in the 'Black Pits' area. It is not clear who later lived in these cottages until 1874 when it was revealed in an indenture that the owner was then Samuel Ginders of Ingestre, who was also land agent to the Earl of Shrewsbury. Samuel Ginders agreed to sell to the Earl the three dwelling houses with the shoemakers shop adjoining, sited on the piece of land formerly known as the *Barn Yard*. The indenture records that the premises were formerly occupied by Thomas Barlow, John Day and Thomas Fradley (as in 1838), but currently occupied by Adam Fradley and John Fradley with two being vacant (presumably one house, and the shoemakers shop used by John Day).

Samuel Ginders also agreed to sell the the piece of land called the *Orchard* {242}, formerly occupied by John Beard (in 1838), but then held by William Ainsworth. A plan was provided with the indenture, as in Fig. 20 (page 56). The Earl of Shrewsbury and Talbot already owned the other two plots of land adjoining the *Orchard* i.e.the former Barley Mow site {241} and other plot, an orchard {243}. The three plots collectively formed the 'island' site in the centre of Kingstone village, all of which is now occupied by Kingstone School.

The acquisition of the *Barn Yard* site and the three cottages upon it conveniently provided accommodation for a schoolmaster employed at the newly-built school. In 1881, William Hobbis, a 'certified school teacher' was living with his family at 'School House'. However, in a letter dated 9th. May 1882, the schoolmaster Mr. Hobbis expressed his dissatisfaction with the accommodation. He requested repairs to the cottage as soon as possible, complaining that *'in its present state it is of little use as a dwelling house'*.

Early this century there were two properties with Mrs. Eliza West at the far (field) end; she cleaned the school and church. [Born in Kingstone, Eliza Fradley, the daughter of John and Jemima Fradley, she was the widow of Frederick West, an alabaster miner of Draycott in the Clay.] Richard Taylor the schoolmaster with his wife and two sons lived in the near (roadside) end, which was the School House (39). Richard Taylor bought the (then four-bedroomed) school house he lived in, together with the cottage (Nene Cottage) occupied by Mrs. West for £335 when it was sold by the Shrewsbury estate in 1918 (39).

The Taylor family called their home Nene House (after the River Nene near Wisbech - where they originated). Richard Taylor died in 1927 and his (and his wife's) gravestone, which is just outside the church porch is very appropriately in the shape of an open book.

**POOR HOUSE /VILLAGE INSTITUTE /VILLAGE HALL** The present Village Hall, built in 1971, is on the site of the old Village Institute which in turn was on land given by Bernard Bettson in 1921, in memory of his wife (2). The Institute had been an old wooden WW1 army hut, bought for £60 and fetched on a horse-drawn wagon from Brocton army camp. However, this site has an earlier history. The Godson map shows a house, occupied by John Jenkinson (as a tenant of John Chetwynd) on a small island of land at this point, bounded by the Tad brook, the Kingstone to Blythe Bridge road and a lane around the church yard perimeter (39). This churchyard boundary seems similar today, being at a much higher level than the ground on which the Village Hall is built. John Jenkinson farmed about 18 acres of land, including the *Brickhill Leasows* (page 23) which ran alongside the track through *Abbot's Wood* (from the gate on Blythe Bridge Bank), and in 1838 had become fields {195} and {196}. [Part of the field {194} (Fig. 6, page 31) had been the *Brickhill poole* in the Godson survey (Fig. 5, page 30), then apparently open water, although on the Godson map appears as pasture or meadow (coloured green) (24)]. The Overseers of the Poor owned a property in Kingstone in 1801 which was almost certainly this property which they owned in 1838. At this time there were three houses {240}, occupied by John Bentley, John Potts and Dorothy Woolliscroft (24). Redfern's drawing of Kingstone old church (Plate 4, page 33) shows parts of the old cottages on this site, and Plate 1 (page 1) also shows a cottage or cottages. In 1841 John Potts was a wheelwright living here with his wife and four other family members. John Bentley was an agricultural

labourer, and he also had five members of his family living with him (4). Dorothy Woolliscroft, an elderly widow, and her daughter Ellen, occupied other house. In 1851 the wheelwright John Potts and his wife still lived here, but their unmarried 27 year old twin daughters lived with them, and were 'receiving alms' (4). Ellen Buxton was also in his household and 'receiving alms'; she was blind, and the daughter, before marriage, of the now deceased Dorothy Woolliscroft. Another house was occupied by Thomas Wood (the former sawyer of Blythe Bridge), aged 73, a pauper and 'receiving alms'; he was living with an unmarried daughter, aged 43, a son aged 32 without occupation and a grandson aged nine. By 1861 the only reference to provision for the poor was for Sarah Felthouse, an 84 year old widow, 'receiving parochial relief', and living with her 53 year old son, a labourer (4). By this time, however, these houses for the poor had been sold. Ownership of (the then) two cottages was transferred by conveyance, dated 16th. February 1859, from the Guardians of the Poor of the Uttoxeter Union, Richard Stonier and Thomas Spooner, the churchwardens, and also Richard Croxton and John Finnemore, to the Earl of Shrewsbury and Talbot, for the sum of £62 [39]. The cottages *'lately used for the reception of the poor'*, were then said to have been unoccupied (the former residents having died or presumably moved away), and the decision was made to dispose of this provision under the terms of the 1835 'Poor Act'. John Potts had died in 1854 but his wife was still in Kingstone in 1861; she had re-married, and her two daughters lived with her and her second husband, James Wood. Ellen Buxton had died in 1856, and John Bentley and his wife, Mary were living in Abbot's Bromley by 1861. It is not known when the 'Poor House' cottages were demolished, but they certainly do not appear on the Ordnance Survey map of 1882.
The plot of land appears to have then been vacant until the Institute was built on or near the site.

**CHURCH FARM** {239} Although a house {10} owned by John Chetwynd existed on the same site as the present farm house in the early eighteenth century, there was then no Church Farm. William Browne lived in the house, and the only land attached to this roadside property was a plot of about ¼ acre, called *Barn Croft* on the opposite side of the road, on the Pott's Lane corner. The Godson map shows a building (presumably a barn, as no house is recorded) occupying this piece of land where a farm building on the site has recently been at converted into a house). The present rather sombre red brick house (Fig. 21), positioned on the roadside at the bottom of the hill leading towards Blythe Bridge is however of a later date. Thomas Ward was Earl Talbot's tenant in 1801 when the farm consisted of about 106 acres. The farm was a substantial holding of 161 acres in 1838, owned by Earl Talbot, and with John Ward (son of Thomas) as tenant (24).
John Ward, of Church Farm seems to have been a particular target for thieves. For example, at Stafford Assizes in 1829, James Capewell and John Mellor were indicted for stealing six sheep belonging to John Ward of Kingstone. The sheep had been driven to an inn at Derby where Capewell sold them (the sheep being later recovered by John Ward). Mellor, who had been paid by Capewell to help drive the sheep was acquitted, but Capewell, being found guilty was given a death sentence, commuted by the judge to transportation (2).

Fig. 21 **Church Farm**

Fowl stealing was a common offence at this period, but the penalty for what we would now consider a minor misdemeanour could be severe. Amongst those committed to the County Gaol in 1830 were Joseph Beard and William Morris charged with stealing one fowl, the property of ..... Ward of Kingstone; three fowls the property of Samuel Durant of Top Moore, and five fowls the property of ..... Wood of Birchen Bower. Also in 1830, at the Courts in session at Stafford, Joseph Beard and William Morris who were charged with stealing one fowl, the property of John Ward of Kingstone. There were two other indictments, charging them with fowl-stealing at two separate premises on the same evening. The prisoners pleaded guilty, alleging *'their being fresh in liquor'* as an excuse; but were told by the Court that one crime could not be justified by another. They were to be imprisoned for one month for each offence making three in all (2).

In January 1844, Earl Talbot, when reporting on expenditure for the County police force, said that he himself had contributed £5 - 6s - 3d for a constable to be stationed at Ingestre and Kingstone, with beneficial effect. He stated that *'since that time, every individual was employed in that district, which had not been the case for some time, and that depredations and fowl-stealing had diminished.'* However, William Upton of Kingstone, who succeeded the Ward family at Church Farm, was the victim of fowl stealing twice within the following three months (2).

By 1841, Mary Ward, widow of John Ward, farmed at 'Church House', but she moved away to live with one of her sons. William Upton, who farmed 108 acres, was the tenant recorded at Church Farm in 1851 (4).

William Upton was the victim of further criminal activity. At Stafford Quarter sessions in 1855 the case of Simeon Ball was considered. He was charged with stealing two pigs from William Upton of Kingstone, and sentenced to four months imprisonment (2).

Richard Stonier farmed 111 acres in 1861, and 115 acres in 1871 as tenant of Church Farm, a reduced acreage as some of the land more remote from the farm had been redistributed to other farms since 1838. Church Farm was further reduced in size in 1880 when the block of land to the north of the Shrewsbury Arms was used to create a new farm, Barn Farm (below) (39). Consequently, in 1881 when Charles Deville became the tenant of Church Farm, it was a farm of only 65 acres (39). John Bettson (son of John Bettson of Woodcock Heath Farm) was at Church Farm by 1891 (4). John Bettson's daughter Elsie (later Elsie Gallimore) gave an interesting account of her childhood at Church Farm, looking after calves, lambs, pigs and poultry, and her mother manufacturing butter, cheese, pork pies, black pudding and sausages (Chapter 7, page 120).

By 1912 Richard Bettson (a brother of John Bettson) was at Church Farm (29), but Robert Derry was the tenant in 1918 and he purchased the farm, for £2150, when it was sold by the Shrewsbury Estate (39). Church Farm was then only about 67 acres as some land had been more logically parcelled up with adjacent properties e.g. the *Barn Ground* was sold with the Shrewsbury Arms next to it. In 1918 Church Farm comprised *'a substantially built farm house containing sitting room, houseplace, back kitchen, dairy, cellar, two bedrooms, two attics and two cheese rooms'*. There were no en-suites then! Cheese production was more important, and typically farm houses in the Uttoxeter area, including those on the neighbouring Loxley estate had rooms devoted to cheese storage. Robert Derry who owned the field which is situated behind and at the eastern end of the present churchyard, had said (or so my father told me) that his field had *'thirteen yews (ewes) and never had lambs!'* Regrettably all of these have been felled (some stumps remain) except one tree which was then just outside the church yard boundary. This tree is now within the present churchyard following its extension eastwards in recent years.


**BARN FARM/STALK BANK FARM {269}** The 1838 'tithe award' makes reference to a 'barn and rickyard' on this small plot of land, to the north of what was then the Dog and Partridge Inn (later Shrewsbury Arms), but then part of Church Farm with John Ward as tenant. In 1918 the same plot of land was part of a block of land called the *'Barn Ground'* advertised for sale together with the Shrewsbury Arms, and described, then, similarly as *Barn Ground buildings and Stackyard*. Surprisingly, for a short intervening period of about thirty years there was also a dwelling house here. Evidently the decision was made to separate this block of almost fifty acres from Church Farm to form a new unit with John Stonier, the youngest son of Richard Stonier (formerly of Church Farm) becoming the new tenant in 1880, although with John Stonier, at least initially, still living at Walnuts Farm in 1881. According to the 1891 census John Stonier then occupied 'Stalk Bank Farm' which appears to be this property, logically given this name as it included a field called next to Uttoxeter Road called *Stalk Bank* (or *Balk*) {144}, as well as another field {152} (with the same name) next to it which was owned by John Stonier (and on which the property called 'The Birches' was later built, page 71). William Poole (also tenant of the Shrewsbury Arms (page 47) was tenant of this property in 1892, called Barn Farm for the first time, and also for the first time a homestead, rather than just a barn {269} was recorded (39). John Stonier was again recorded as tenant of the same holding of nearly fifty acres in 1897, presumably in addition to being tenant of Broomy Leasows Farm. George and Miss. Woodings were the tenants of Barn Farm in 1905, then 56 acres. George Woodings was also tenant of the Shrewsbury Arms and their holding included the various small crofts next to the pub. which were traditionally rented with it, as well as several pieces of garden next to and within the 'island' site, alongside the School in the village centre. [George Woodings was a son of James and Eliza Woodings who lived at Hollyhays (page 73)]. Whether any of these tenants actually occupied the homestead at Barn Farm, or had labourers in residence is unknown.

**MOUNT PLEASANT/CHERRY TREES** The Godson survey indicates that a house {11} owned by John Chetwynd then existed here on Potts' Lane (39). Pott's Lane is not named on the Godson map but almost certainly takes its name from the family of Potts (or Pott), long associated with Kingstone.
John Pott of Kingstone and William Norman of Caverswall, both yeomen were tasked with making an inventory of the goods of the deceased Ralph Browne of Kingstone in 1601 (24). A place for J. Pott was also included on the 1636 seating plan for Kingstone church. He is likely to have been the same John Pott of Kingston referred to in the marriage allegation for his son and heir apparent, Humphrey Pott, in 1632 (36)(39). John Pott of Leese hill was also named as his son-in-law by John Emsworth, of Leese Hill in his will dated 1664 (page 68).
Humphrey Pott, at his death was living at Leafields, in Stowe parish, but only about a half mile west of Leese Hill. In his will, dated 1684, he left his messuage and land at Leafields to his six sons, including crofts of land that *'joyne'* (join) *the 'hiway'* (highway) *that leadeth to Leese Hill'* (24). Leese Hill is linked (going east) to Kingstone by the 'highway' or lane which is now called Potts' Lane but the reference in this will (in which Kingstone is not mentioned) must describe a route going <u>west</u> (but continuous with Potts' Lane) which once existed, but became a mere footpath (page 8). The lane going west from Leese Hill towards Leafields and linking with the main Uttoxeter to Stafford road (now the A518) is shown on the 1798 Yates map of Staffordshire.
[Interestingly, Kingstone's long-serving curate John Hilditch, who died in office in 1820 lived at Leafields and no doubt travelled from Leafields via Leese Hill and Potts' Lane on his way to church in Kingstone.]
Later documents reveal that Humphrey Pott's sons, William Pott, a wheelwright and Humphrey Pott, a forgeman were still living at Leafields in 1705 (6). [Perhaps this Humphrey Pott worked at the Chartley forge which had been managed by Henry Goring in about 1616 (page 11).]
Humphrey Potts, senior was mentioned in a document dated 1709 concerning a lease of land which included the same crofts named by (his father?) Humphrey Pott in his will in 1684 (6).
Humphrey Pott 'the younger', (probably a son of the above Humphrey Potts, senior) and his wife Ann had several children, baptised at Kingstone between 1705 and 1723. He is the earliest-known definite link with Mount Pleasant as he was living here at the time of the Godson survey; a tenant of about nine acres. This included about five acres on Blythe Bridge Bank, divided into three fields called *Blakeley sich* (pages 23 & 67) (39).

Fig. 22 <u>**Mount Pleasant**</u> (now <u>**Cherry Trees**</u>)

[The tithe map (Fig. 6 page 31) shows the three fields {87}, {83} and {82} which were formerly called *nearer*, *middle* and *further Blakeley sich* in the Godson survey (Fig. 5, page 30).]

The 1801 survey indicates that John Pott, the presumed descendant (grandson?) of Humphrey Pott, was then living here at Mount Pleasant, as a tenant of Earl Talbot, with a holding of 11 acres. John Potts, a wheelwright (born in 1745 at Stowe, the son of John Potts, a wheelwright) was recorded (in a cropping book for the Earl's estate, dated 1814/15) as living at Mount Pleasant. His son, also called John Potts, baptised at Kingstone in 1777, and later described as a wheelwright or carpenter may have lived at Mount Pleasant, but by 1838 he and his family were living in the Poor House (pages 57-58) (4).

John Potts, senior died in 1814. In the 1814/15 cropping book his name is scored through and replaced by that of Richard Reynolds (39). He was in possession of the same land holding that Richard Reynolds had at Mount Pleasant in 1838. In 1838 Richard Reynolds (assumed to be the same Richard Reynolds), an agricultural labourer, was recorded as the Earl's tenant at this small farm of about 12 acres {167} (29)(24). Richard Reynolds appears to have still been living at Mount Pleasant in 1841, and also in 1851 when, at the advanced age of 80, he was described as a farmer of 11 acres.

[Confusingly, the name Mount Pleasant has also been used for Rose Cottage {276}, the property near 'Old Town', north of Kingstone village centre (page 70).] It is unclear who later occupied this property in Pott's Lane, until 1871 when Edward Wilson, the former blacksmith at Blythe Bridge smithy was

Plate 15 **Potts' Lane**, an old leafy lane with steep-sided banks (looking south towards Mount Pleasant and the centre of Kingstone).

recorded as a farmer living in Potts' Lane. Edward Wilson was still at Mount Pleasant in 1901 (now clearly identified as this property (Fig. 22, page 60) in Potts' Lane) (4). By 1912 William Sargeant had established his butcher's business at Mount Pleasant in Potts' Lane and was able to purchase this property (a dwelling with 15 acres) in the 1918 Shrewsbury Estate sale for £750 (29)(39). He was still here in 1928 (29).

My grandmother described the house and cowshed as being thatched before William Sargeant moved into the property. The Sargeant family butchery business continues today in Bramshall and Uttoxeter.

**BLACKPITS, Blythe Bridge Road** Further towards Kingstone, a road (which survives today as a track for most of its length - Plate 15, above) once linked the road and common land on Blythe Bridge Road with Potts' Lane, going past the 'Black Pool' or 'Black Pit' (an area of open water which was almost one acre in size in 1838) (24). In the early eighteenth century there was a small island of land at the Potts' Lane junction where one house {12} then existed, occupied as a tenant by Richard Bull (39). At least two houses existed here in 1801, and three cottages owned by Earl Talbot were in the equivalent area in 1838, a pair of houses {186} of which one was unoccupied, with the other tenant being John Fernyhough, while John Taylor lived in the third house {187} (24).

[John Taylor was living at Black Pits when his son George was baptised at Kingstone in 1816.]

In 1841, John Taylor, an agricultural labourer, and Elizabeth 'Fearny' (Fernyhough), wife of John Fernyhough, were probably living in the same houses. Other householders then living in the area known as 'Black pit' included George Webb and William Johnson (4). All were agricultural labourers except for Edward Woolley, a tailor who also lived at 'Black pit'. [Edward Woolley was baptised at Kingstone in 1813, the son of Thomas Woolley, a tailor of Black Pits.]

In March 1843 Thomas Taylor (a son of John Taylor) was indicted for breaking into the house of William Johnson and stealing two loaves of bread and a cheese. Mary Johnson, who had discovered that the items had gone missing while she was out, said (in mitigation) that Taylor was their neighbour's son, that his mother was dead and she believed his father was not kind to him. She had given him some bread and cheese in the morning and some ham and potatoes at dinner. She found one loaf and a cheese in a hedge the next morning. George Beard, (the innkeeper, page 47) who was also then constable of Kingstone, took the accused into custody. Thomas Taylor was found guilty of larceny and sentenced to one month's imprisonment (2).

In 1851 Sarah Martin, Martha Taylor, a tailor's wife, and Edward Wilson, the blacksmith lived at 'Black pits', with one house vacant (4). Martha Taylor was the wife of Samuel Taylor, a journeyman tailor, away from home. Samuel Taylor was a son of John Taylor (and an elder brother of Thomas Taylor), and is likely to have lived in the house where their father had been tenant. In 1861 Sarah Martin and Martha Taylor were still at Black Pits, but by now Thomas Fradley, an agricultural labourer and John Day, a cordwainer were also living here with their families. In 1869 the Taylor family faced another problem when Samuel Taylor, the fourteen year old son of Samuel and Martha Taylor was charged with the theft of a gun from Michael 'Critchlow' (Crutchley) of Kingstone. Samuel Taylor, the boy's father, appealed for his son to be sent to a reformatory, but was not willing to pay for the cost of his maintenance there. The boy was sentenced to one month's imprisonment with six strokes from a birch rod (2). By 1871 the Taylor family had left the area, to be replaced by James Collier, a bricklayer, the other residents being the same. John Day, a cordwainer (shoemaker) was tenant of one of the cottages {187} at the Potts' Lane junction, with James Collier being the likely occupant of the other cottage (4).

At the time of the Godson map a house {13} existed near the south-west end of the 'Black Pool'. A house was also marked on this site in 1801, and where, in 1838, Earl Talbot owned a house {84} with about two acres, Edward Woolley (the tailor, above) being the tenant (39) (24).

By 1851, and until at least 1871 Sarah Martin, a widow lived here, then a cottage with 3 acres of land (4).

By 1882 this property (Fig. 23) was called Blackpit's Cottage. John Martin (son of Sarah), a labourer was tenant but in 1885 he took one of the other cottages {187} in lieu, where Joseph Fernyhough, junior had been the previous tenant (39).

Ann Deaville was the tenant of this house {84} with about 10 acres of land in 1890. Her holding included land on which the cottages {186} and {187} had stood, but were now demolished (39).

When it was sold by the Shrewsbury Estate in 1918 this was a smallholding with ten acres of land let to George Hollins. It then had a 'modern' house (39). The holding included part of the 'pond' i.e. the *'Black Pit'* or *'Black Pool'*.
The property, by now called Blackpitts Farm was sold for £580.
In more recent times Mavis Doughty, recalled her earlier life living and working at Blackpits, a basic property

Fig. 23 **Blackpits Farm** (demolished in 2017 and replaced by a new house)

with no electricity, when she first arrived there in 1950 (21).

Common land along the length of the road to Blythe Bridge had been encroached by 1801, and at the other (north-east) end of the *'Black Pool'* a house {184} (with one acre) had been built (39).
In 1838, William Cheswell Johnson was Earl Talbot's tenant occupying this property, which is sited opposite the piece of woodland {200} called Ashcroft Wood (24).
Thomas Fradley, first recorded as living in the Black Pits area in 1861, a farmer with a holding of ten acres in 1871, and still resident in 1881, was a later tenant here, at Ashcroft Farm, the name by which it is still known (4).
Frederick Francis Sherratt was tenant here between 1891 and 1899, followed by William Peill from 1900 to 1903, and William Brandrick who was the tenant in 1903 (39).
When sold by the Shrewsbury Estate in 1918, this property (like Blackpits Farm) had been expanded to form a smallholding of about ten acres, and included the other part of the 'pond'. This property, then let to George Hollins (but sub-let to Mr. Bettson), was sold to Arthur Gallimore for £530 (39).

The *'Black Pool'* is no more, being filled in during the latter part of the last century, but part of its outline can still be traced within the boundary of a grassy field.

Plate 16  **Former old road** connecting Potts' Lane with Blythe Bridge Bank,
now a track - a view looking south-west towards Black Pits Farm.

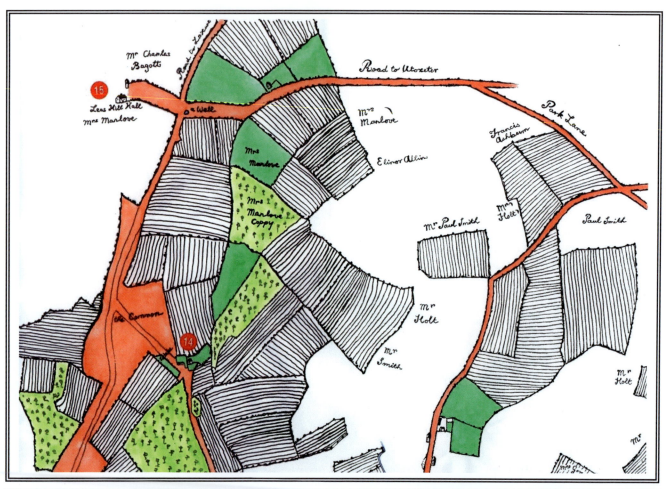

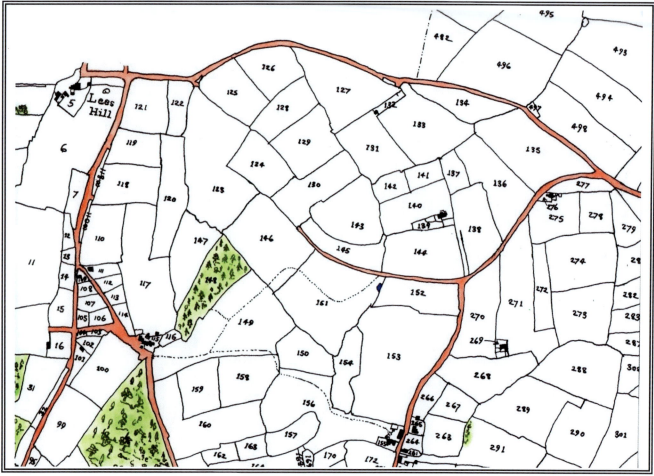

64   Fig. 24 **Kingstone map** 1717-20 (above) & Fig. 25 **Kingstone map** 1837 (below) **Zone B**

# Woodcock Heath, Leese Hill and the North [Zone B]

The earliest available map of the area is the Godson map of 1717-1720 (39). This map (opposite) shows only three properties at Leese Hill. 'Leas Hill Hall' {15} (Leese Hill Manor House) is shown as a substantial residence, with another house (on the site of Upper Leese Hill Farm) next to, and directly to the north of this property. Another house is shown just to the east of the Leese Hill Manor House, on the north side of the 'road to utoxeter' or Park Lane (now called Watery Lane). This house on Park Lane, with about 24 acres of land (on the site of the present Leese Hill Farm) was then owned by John Chetwynd, with Elizabeth 'Griffing' (Griffin) as his tenant. The Griffin family continued to be tenants at Leese Hill. Thomas and Catherine Griffin were living at Leese Hill between 1809 and 1819 when some of their children were baptised at Kingstone. Thomas Griffin was farming at Broomy Leasows in the 1820s (page 74), but returned to Leese Hill (Leese Hill Farm), probably in 1823 after his father Thomas Griffin died, being there by 1841, and still present in 1851 (4). Leese Hill Farm (as opposed to Upper Leese Hill Farm, opposite the Manor), was in Uttoxeter parish. Later a part of the Loxley estate, it was sold in 1918, and purchased by my grandfather, Samuel Gallimore (39). The well shown on the Godson map (Fig. 24, page 64) at Leese Hill crossroads, still in existence in the field corner (Plate 17, below), is sturdily built using stone blocks.

Woodcock Heath Farm is also marked {14}, on the map, next to ' the common' i.e. the area of common land. By 1801 this common land at Woodcock Heath was all that remained in Kingstone parish, but by 1838 it had been enclosed and a number of cottages had been built on the encroached land (24)(39).

Plate 17 The **well at Leese Hill** crossroads

**WOODCOCK HEATH FARM** Continuing along Potts' Lane from Kingstone bring us to Woodcock Heath. 'Woodcock' may be a personal name; a sixteenth century record (page 18) lists a family of that surname living in Kingstone parish (41). Robert Hitchcock, in his will dated 1719 was recorded as being a husbandman of 'Woodcocks Heath' (24). Interestly, the area of woodland, called *Hitchcock's Rough* (*Oldfield Coppy* in the Godson survey) still exists, running north-west of Woodcock Heath Farm {115} . A farm then existed at Woodcock Heath, and on the present site, at the time of the Godson map {14}, being in the ownership of John Chetwynd (39). South of the farm was the area of woodland called *Johnny Field Coppice* {98}.

65

The 1801 Survey of Kingstone reveals that John Felthouse then farmed 111 acres here as Earl Talbot's tenant (39). In 1834 Woodcock Heath Farm was still farmed by John Felthouse (29), and in 1838 he was recorded as the tenant of 139 acres, the property belonging to Earl Talbot (24). John Felthouse married Jane Wilson (daughter of Thomas Wilson, the blacksmith of Blythe Bridge) and by 1841 they were living at Stafford, and later moved to Worcestershire (4). James Allen, the tenant here in 1841, was probably not the James Allen mentioned earlier (page 50); he had links to Blithfield where he was buried in 1850.

Fig. 26 **Woodcock Heath Farm**

In 1841 John Bettson was farming at Drointon (in Colwich parish) but by 1851 he had taken the tenancy at Woodcock Heath Farm (4)(29). His son, John Bettson had succeeded as tenant by 1870, and lived here until he died in 1896 (29). Eleanor Bettson, widow of the second John Bettson ran the farm together with her younger sons Richard and Thomas until she died in 1901. Her eldest son, John who had been at Church Farm during this time then moved to Woodcock Heath Farm in 1902, and remained here until he died in 1912 (4). Woodcock Heath farmhouse and buildings are of old red brick, but the farmhouse was unfortunately covered in 'stone' cladding towards the end of the last century (Fig. 26).
The farm was sold (for £4500) in the 1918 Shrewsbury Estate sale to the tenant Mrs. Bettson (widow of the third John Bettson). This *'desirable agricultural and dairy farm'* then consisted of nearly 169 acres (39). By 1928 Alfred Bettson had taken over the farm from his mother (29). The farm was later sold by Alfred Bettson, so ending the long connection between the Bettson family and Woodcock Heath.

The Godson map shows that there was a large area of common land to the west of Woodcock Heath Farm (39). The 1801 survey map shows no other properties in the area, but by 1838 this common land had been enclosed with many small plots of land or encroachments, and with several houses or cottages built upon them, all with between a half and one acre of land. Earl Talbot owned three of these properties.
In a house {101} situated at the northern end of the lane going past Wanfield Hall, the tenant in 1838 was George Grimes (24). The 1851 census records Ann Grimes, an agricultural labourer, as the householder; her husband was not at home (4). Jesse Ainsworth, a wheelwright, was tenant here in 1871. This property (today called Rosevale) was advertised for sale in The Shrewsbury Estate sale in 1918 as a small holding, then let to Martha Whitehall. It had almost five acres but divided into nine small crofts, closes or gardens. Joseph Whitehall, a roadman and agricultural labourer was living with his family at Woodcock Heath in 1901. He died in 1908 and his widow, Martha was still here in 1911 where she farmed in a small way. My father recalled that when it was the time of year for young lambs to have their tails docked he was sent on an errand (as a boy in the 1920s) to take the lambs tails to Mrs. Whitehall at

Woodcock Heath, so that she could use them to make lambs tail pie! Thomas J. Whitehall, a son of Joseph and Martha Whitehall died in 1918 whilst serving in WW1. Another son, Charlie, known as 'Driver' Whitehall,was so called because he drove a steam traction engine used to power a threshing machine. He later lived at The Villa (page 43) and went round the local farms to thresh the corn during the months after the harvest.
One of the pieces of land attached to 'Rosevale' in the 1918 sale was a garden with an old cottage, the cottage otherwise called Magpie Hall (39)! In 1838 Magpie Hall was the cottage {111}, where Edward Wood, an agricultural labourer lived with his family. He died in 1859, but his widow Sarah Wood was still here in 1861 (4).
Michael Crutchley, a wheelwright (and son of Michael Crutchley, the gamekeeper, page 77 ), was the tenant in 1871. In 1869 at Uttoxeter, in the case of Johnson v. Crutchley, the plaintiff, a farmer of Blythe Bridge brought an action against the defendant (Michael Crutchley), a wheelwright to recover £5 for an assault. The plaintiff (Joseph Johnson) had been sitting in the Barley Mow public-house when he heard someone call out his name. He turned his head and allegedly received a severe blow to the eye from the defendant, Crutchley, resulting in a black eye. It was suggested that Johnson may have provoked Crutchley, with bad language being used prior to the assault, but the verdict was given to Johnson with £3 damages (2).This cottage was called Magpie Cottage in 1891 when William Smith, an agricultural labourer lived here (4). William Sherratt, a tailor, and his wife Louisa moved to this cottage from Willslock, in 1897 (39). They were still at Woodcock Heath in 1901, but by 1911 they were living in Kingstone village centre, William Sherratt having succeeded his father Joseph, as tailor in Church View (page 44) (4). Magpie Hall' was demolished and replaced by a more modern house in 1960. Clearly, never a 'Hall' but a single-story thatched cottage, this property is said to have been a shooting lodge for the Shrewsbury Estate (21).

Richard Wood, also an agricultural labourer (and perhaps brother to Edward Wood) was living in a cottage {109} directly opposite that of Edward Wood in 1838; he was still here in 1871 but died in 1875 (24) (4). This cottage is not recorded on the Ordnance Survey map of 1882; it had probably been demolished by this date.
Richard Wood had a son, George , a farm labourer , who in 1851 was living with his wife, Adah in Kingstone. However, in 1861 at Stafford Assizes, George Wood, formerly of Kingstone was charged with bigamy. Richard Stonier, the parish clerk of Kingstone provided evidence that Wood had married Adah Deaville at Kingstone in 1847, but later absconded, leaving her with two children dependent on the parish. He had 'married' Alice Moss at Leek in 1860. Wood was sentenced to 3 months imprisonment with hard labour (2).

The other property {16} at Woodcock Heath was in 1838, owned by Richard Corbett Lawrence of Leese Hill Manor. Charles Campion was then his tenant, and a cordwainer (i.e. maker of boots and shoes). He was recorded in the 1841 census and still at Woodcock Heath, presumably in the same house in 1881 (4). Also in 1881, two cottages (we cannot say which) at Woodcock Heath were occupied by Charles Campion's son, Joseph Campion (later the boot and shoe maker who lived at the Old School in Kingstone, page 46), and Joseph Perkin, a blacksmith, whose wife, Rosetta was a daughter of Charles Campion. Joseph and Rosetta Perkin were still at Woodcock Heath in 1911 (4).


**LEESE HILL MANOR** and **FARM** Leese Hill is an area with its own distinct identity; and with a manor separate from Kingstone. In old wills it is always said to be in Uttoxeter parish. At some point, part of this area, including Leese Hill Manor {5} {15} came to be within Kingstone parish. Leese Hill has been wholly within the parish since 1939. Robert Tixall is said to have purchased 'Loxley Leyes', sometimes called 'Kingston Leyes', about the time of Edward III (14th. century), and by the time of Edward IV (1461-1483) it was called Lees-hill (9). Two particular families are recorded as owning property at Leese Hill before about 1600, namely, the Tixalls and the Normans. Robert Norman of 'Lees hyll' , in his will dated 1538, referred to his house at Leese Hill; he also had a house and land in Kingstone, including a pasture called *blakley syche* (pages 23, 60) (24).
His son, also called Robert Norman, lived at Caverswall (i.e. Caverswall Farm, about a mile away to the north-west at Lower Loxley, in Uttoxeter parish). Robert Norman of Caverswall (who died leaving a will in 1553) was an overseer of his father's will, but 'Robert Tyxall of Lees hyll' was also named as an overseer. [The Norman family had a particular with association with Caverswall. William Norman, who died leaving a will, dated 1693 also lived at Caverswall.] John Tyxall, who died leaving a will in 1550 was also of Leese Hill (24)!

Leese Hill Manor appears to have been in the ownership of the Tixalls following the marriage at Uttoxeter of William Tixall and Elizabeth Norman in 1602. William Tixall of Leese Hill was one of over 200 gentlemen in Staffordshire alone who declined to accept a knighthood on the coronation of Charles I in 1625/6 (36). Also on the list was William Norman of 'Careswell' (Caverswall, Lower Loxley), in addition to Rowland Manlove of Wanfield (page 99) and Henry Goring of Kingstone (page 11). The King's money-making scheme, selling knighthoods (at £60 or £70 a time) was highly unpopular. All the above declined the 'honour' and were later ordered to pay a fine instead (usually £10). William Tixall died in 1632, and with the death of his only surviving son, his four daughters became co-heirs. William Tixall's widow, Elizabeth appears to have continued to live at Leese Hill until her death in 1651. A deed of partition, dividing the Leese Hill property between the four daughters is however dated 1641/2 (37). Rachel Tixall is said to have inherited Knightland (about two miles east of Leese Hill), as her share, while her three sisters each inherited a third share of Leese Hill (10).

Fig. 27 **Leese Hill Manor House**

It is also said that John Goring of Kingstone, who married the youngest daughter, Felice Tixall purchased the share of the eldest sister Sarah (who married John Perry) and came to own Leese Hill (10). This seems to be supported by a document, dated 1646 which refers to a property transaction in which *'lands which were in times past the inheritance of William Tixall of Lees hill, gent.'*, were acquired by John Goring and his wife Phelice (39). John Emsworth, who married another sister, Rebecca 'enjoyed his part' (10). He was a yeoman of Leese Hill and died leaving a will in 1664 (24). It is unclear whether the Goring family ever took full possession of Leese Hill (23). Any interest the Gorings had in the property did not last long. By 1667, Alexander Manlove ,who had married Rachel Tixall, and was the son of Rowland Manlove of nearby Wanfield Hall, was living Leese Hill Manor House {15}, and seems to have then owned the property (39). From this point on, the Manlove family and their descendants were in possession of Leese Hill Manor, in addition to Wanfield Hall. Whether, at an earlier period, the Tixalls or the Normans lived at Leese Hill Manor House or either of the two other properties at Leese Hill is open to speculation. At the time of the Godson survey 'Lea's Hill Hall' {15}, was in the ownership of Mrs. Manlove i.e. Mary Manlove [1662 - 1724], the widow of the second Rowland Manlove.

Leese Hill Manor House {5} is a most distinctive property (Fig. 27). In fact it is a fusion of at least two very different types of building. The taller wing of the property would appear to date from the late seventeenth or early eighteenth century, while the lower range of building has features such as half-timberwork which suggest an earlier date. Detailed inventories, included with the wills of Alexander Manlove and his son Rowland Manlove, both of Leeshill, dated 1688 and 1714 respectively, describe the then room structure of the of the Manor (26)(24). In Alexander Manlove's time there was a hall, evidently the main room of the house which was well furnished with a long (dining) table, chairs, stools, a looking glass and other items; this being also where he kept his books. The hall chamber, also well furnished, appears to have been the main bedroom. Other sleeping accommodation was provided in the parlour chamber and kitchen chamber, and there was also a chamber each for the maids and male servants. The house also had a kitchen, pantry, cellar, washroom, cheese room and a new buttery. The inventory also gives a picture of the farming operation, detailing the livestock, farming equipment and implements, and even the acreage of different cereals under crop (24). These were troubled times, and Alexander Manlove was equiped to defend himself and his property; his inventory reveals that he possessed a musket, a gun, a sword belt and a bandoleer.

In Rowland Manlove's house, the parlour rather than the hall provided the main living space being well-furnished with tables, twelve chairs, also a looking glass, and interestingly a 'payre (pair) of 'verginalls' (virginals) and stand'. Presumably someone could play the instrument and provide the family with entertainment! There was now also a study, rooms called the white chamber, matted chamber, and a brewhouse. Additional sleeping accommodation was available in the 'new garret' (as well as in the old garret). Rowland Manlove, had a similar farming enterprise to his father, both of which provided a high degree of self-sufficiency. Lees Hill Manor was well-furnished in Rowland Manlove' s time; he had tables, chairs, stools, several looking glasses, a clock on the staircase, a large quantity of pewter and brass, and also silver plate. In his will, dated 1714, Rowland Manlove referred to the 'Great Chamber', identifiable in the inventory by its contents as the chamber over the parlour (24). He left to his wife, Mary, a silver tankard and other silver items, as well as furniture in this room which included the best bed and its bedding, eight black japanned chairs, a black stand, a looking glass with a black frame, and chest of drawers, all of which were said to have been hers before marriage. Rowland Manlove bequeathed the bed and furniture in the white chamber to his younger, married daughter, Ellen Vernon, while his elder daughter, Rachel inherited all the other household goods. In her own will, dated 1725, Mary Manlove divided her silver plate between her two daughters (24). Following the death of the then, elderly Ellen Vernon in 1781, Leese Hill descended to her granddaughter, Ellen Hartshorne, who married the Rev. Thomas Lawrence, in 1780 (24). Leese Hill (with Wanfield) totalling 219 acres, was recorded in the 1801 survey as being in the ownership of the Lawrence family, and in 1834, part of the estate of Richard Corbett Lawrence (29), the Lawrence family being descended from the Alexander Manlove of Wanfield Hall, and of Leese Hill. While the Lawrence family lived in the Manor House, the farm was occupied by a tenant.

In 1838 Thomas Ward, (son of John and Mary Ward of Church Farm) farmed 172 acres at Leese Hill, and he was still the tenant in 1861, when the farm comprised 180 acres (24)(4). William Spooner, son of Thomas Spooner (page 86), was tenant at Upper Leese Hill Farm in 1871, followed by William Meakin in 1881, Adam Dawson in 1891 and William Clowes in 1901 (4). Charles Henry Cope was farm bailiff at Leese Hill in 1911 (4). Richard Corbett Lawrence died in 1846, but his widow Elizabeth and son continued to live in the Manor. In 1870 Humphrey Downes - Lawrence was living at Leese Hill Manor (29). He had died by 1876 but his mother, Elizabeth Lawrence remained in residence in 1881, and she died in 1887 (4).

In 1928 Vernon Bathew, the eldest son of William and Lucretia Bathew, was farming at Leese Hill (29). Wanfield Hall no longer belongs to the Bathews but members of the family still live at Leese Hill Manor.

**[The family history of the Manlove family and their descendants is given separately - see page 99-101.]**

**GALLEYTREE COTTAGE /ROSE COTTAGE {132}** Situated on Watery Lane (formerly Park Lane), at the southern edge of Loxley Park, Galleytree Cottage, seems not to have existed in 1838 when four pieces of land totalling 14 acres were recorded as being owned and occupied by Thomas Griffin (24). What appears to have been the same 14 acres of land, owned by Thomas Griffin, was advertised for sale in 1847. There was then a brick and tile barn but no mention of a house (2). The same Thomas Griffin lived for a time at Broomy Leasows (page 74), but by 1841 was farming at Leese Hill (page 65)(4).

In 1838 the land around the present cottage included a slang and three small fields called *Gallows Tree* - was this really a place for hangings? Reference has already been made to the Gresley family who once owned Kingstone, and Sir Geoffrey de Gresley having the right of gallows in Kingstone in the 13[th.] century (page 9) (36). Hanging was the most common way of executing criminals in the medieval period, with the individual being suspended from a tree or from some structure erected for the purpose. A site was usually in an open area on the edge of a town, on a hill or by a road, so that locals and passers-by would have a good view. Such a site could be permanent with corpses being left to rot until fully decomposed, and serving as a means of discouraging others from becoming involved in criminal activities. The position of GalleyTree Cottage alongside the road at the boundary of the parish (next to Loxley Park) seems to fit at least some of these criteria. The narrow winding road which is Watery Lane today may not have always been so quiet. It would once have linked track ways from the north-west through Loxley Park to the Lichfield road at a place called Cuckolds Haven (page 66). At the bottom (east end) of what is now called Watery Lane, Park Lane continued as Cuckolds haven Lane (now known as Holly Lane). The route by-passed the present Loxley Green cross roads, and instead, from the bottom of Watery Lane, the road continued straight across to Holly Lane just south of the present bungalow (the remains of this route being still clearly visible today).

The earliest known reference to this property is in the will, dated 1682, of William Barton, a yeoman of Kingstone, who bequeathed the premises he called 'Gallowtrees' to the children of his cousin John Barton, a tanner of Kingstone (24). However, Ellen Allin of Loxley, in her will, dated 1717 left her lands in Kingston, including 'the Gallowtree house', to her daughter Mary Osbourne, wife of Francis Osbourne of Loxley (24). Henry Chell, an agricultural labourer was living at 'Gally Trees' in 1861; in 1871 he was described as a farmer with 15 acres of land (4). Adam Fradley, a farmer was living with his family at 'Gallow's Tree Cottage' in 1881. Charles Green, a farmer at 'Galley Tree Cottage' in 1891, was still here in 1896, but the property was vacant in 1901 (4). There is some confusion between this property, and the next, with both at times having been called 'Rose Cottage'. In 1898 Kingstone's vicar, the Rev. W.D. Hathaway (also rector of Gratwich) met an unfortunate fate (see Elsie's Story, page 119) whilst walking along the footpath near 'Rose Cottage' at the top of Watery Lane on his way home to Gratwich Rectory. Logically his route would have taken him past <u>this</u> property.


**ROSE COTTAGE /MOUNT PLEASANT {276}** The earliest evidence of a house existing on this site is from the 1801 survey (39). In 1838 this was a cottage with two small crofts of about 5 acres in total, owned by Thomas Harper (a man of independent means living in the centre of Kingstone), with John Cartmail as tenant (24). The 1834 Staffordshire Directory records Thomas Harper, as having been a shopkeeper, but then living at 'Mount Pleasant'. This is confusing as the property more usually associated with the name Mount Pleasant is that found in Potts' Lane (page 60). In 1851 Edward Woolley was living at 'Mount Pleasant', which can be identified from its position in the census record as this cottage, later to be called Rose Cottage. Edward Woolley, who earlier had lived at Blackpits, was described as a tailor, but also a grocer and licensed local 'decenting' (dissenting) preacher (4). He may have preached at the Primitive Methodist chapel. Benjamin Severn, a retired farmer (who was at Broomy Leasows in 1851) lived at Mount Pleasant in 1871, which was also clearly identified as this cottage by the 1882 and 1890 Ordnance Survey maps.

However, by 1901 this property was known as Rose Cottage, a name it retained subsequently. A Monkey Puzzle tree (Chilean Pine), growing in the garden here provided an alternative name - 'Monkey Tree House'. The occupant in 1881 was probably George Smith, a railway signalman (4). Thomas Buckley, a farmer was living in this cottage which at the time of the 1891 census was called Rose Cottage, followed by William Dakin, a farmer who had moved here by 1901. In 1911, when Ernest Gould, a farmer lived here, the house had seven rooms, and the property was a 'dairy farm' (4). In 1928 Mrs. F. L. Brown occupied Rose Cottage Farm (29).


**HOLLYDENE/OLD TOWN {139}** Hollydene, which in the past was called <u>Old Town</u> can be reached by following a track off Uttoxeter Road, at the northern entry into Kingstone.

In 1801 the house was owned by Joseph Hubbard together with about 3 acres of land. The Hubbard family were well established in Kingstone. John Hubbard, recorded on his father's gravestone, that he had inscribed it with his own hand, his father having been Thomas Hubbard (also a builder) who died in 1813 (14). The above Joseph Hubbard was the son of Thomas's brother, also called Joseph, and the two brothers were in turn, sons of Thomas Hubbard, a 'mason' of Kingstone who married Elizabeth Gough (daughter of John Gough (page 84) of Kingstone, in 1721. The building profession was a family occupation, perhaps they built the premises at Old Town?

In 1838 this holding of about 9 acres was owned and occupied by Sarah Hubbard, but Richard Stonier used the land (23). Sarah Hubbard was the widow of Joseph Hubbard, probably the J. Hubbard recorded as a bricklayer in 1818 (page 20)(29). In his will dated 1831, Joseph Hubbard, a builder revealed that the messuage house in which he lived had a dwelling house adjoining, occupied by a tenant (24). His wife Sarah in her own will, dated 1856 also made reference to the two adjoining properties that she owned (24). I have found no references to 'Old Town' before 1841 when the census recorded Sarah Hubbard as living at Old Town. George Wood, an agricultural labourer, also lived at Old Town in 1841, being Sarah Hubbard's tenant in the adjoining house. Sarah Hubbard was still living at Old Town in 1851, the year in which she died (4). All her children appear to have died young except for one daughter, Sarah, whose two young sons inherited the property, held in trust for them by their widowed father. This *'very compact and valuable little farm'*, consisting of the two dwelling houses and 9 acres of land was advertised for sale by auction at the Dog and Partridge in Kingstone in December 1855.

Joseph Sherratt (later, the tailor of Church View, page 44) was then the tenant living in the main house, which had three bedrooms, whilst George Shipley occupied the adjoining house which had one bedroom only. Richard Stonier still rented the land (2). George Shipley, an agricultural labourer who had been Sarah Hubbard's tenant in 1851, was living at Old Town in 1861 and 1871 (4). Joseph 'Sharratt' (Sherratt), the tailor was still at Old Town in 1861, but in 1871 George Evans farmed 10 acres here, living next to George Shipley. William Worsey, a farmer, probably lived at Old Town in 1881 (4). In 1901 Frederic Nash, a bricklayer's labourer was recorded as living at Old Town (probably a single residence by this date) (4).

Joseph Gorse, an estate labourer was the tenant when The 'Old Town Farm' a property with almost 10 acres was offered for sale by auction in 1910 (2).

A map accompanying the catalogue for the 1918 Shrewsbury Estate sale indicated that Mr. Whieldon then owned this property (39). The 1928 Staffordshire Directory lists William Whieldon as a farmer, living at Hollydene, this being the first known use of this name, which does not appear in census records (4) (29). In the same year William Whieldon advertised the sale of Holly Dene, a small dairy farm (then 40 acres) (2). Interestingly, even on an Ordnance Survey map dated as recently as 1955, this place was called Old Town. The name suggests a *dene* i.e. a (wooded) vale or valley where there is holly, a common plant locally (20).


**THE BIRCHES** Anyone travelling towards Kingstone from the north on Uttoxeter Road cannot help but be aware of 'Birches Corner', the sharp bend in the road on entering the village. Old maps (Fig. 25, page 64) show that the road once forked at this point with a track and footpath going westwards in the direction of Leese Hill.

'The Birches', a small farm, was built here, next to the road (and also at the bottom of the track leading to Hollydene), in the late Victorian period. Apparently The Birches was built in 1889 (using timber from the Loxley Estate), in which case the house would have been built, not as commonly believed, by Richard Stonier (who died in 1885), but by his son, John Stonier (later of Broomy Leasows and Kingstone Hall) (21).

The name 'The Birches' was not recorded in the census until 1911; it appears to have been part of the property, recorded in the 1891 census as Stalk Bank Farm, then occupied by John Stonier (4).

The village postman Arthur Fearn was living here in 1901; the letters he delivered were carried on his pony's back. John Shaw, a farmer, was tenant at 'Birches' in 1911, then described as a dairy farm, the house having seven rooms (4). The map accompanying the sale catalogue for the Shrewsbury Estate sale in 1918, indicated that John Stonier owned The Birches (39). In 1926 John Stonier sold Birches Farm which had 10 acres of land and Thomas Bettson (a nephew of John Stonier) bought the property for £1000 (2). His descendants still live there (29).

In 1838 there were several fields called *Birches*, just north-west of this property, but curiously then mostly part of Church Farm (some distance way in the centre of Kingstone village). The field {152} on which The Birches was later built was then called *Stalk balk*, and significantly belonged to Walnuts Farm, where Richard Stonier lived. The field {144} immediately to the north, but belonging to Church Farm, was also called *Stalk balk*, and was also immediately south of Sarah Hubbard's residence at Old Town. [The above-mentioned track separated the two *Stalk balk* fields, the origin of the term *stalk balk* having been discussed earlier, page 23.]

In 1838 Richard Stonier was tenant of all nine acres of Sarah Hubbard's land at Old Town, including a field called *Birches,* west of the *Stalk balk* field belonging to Church Farm (24). It appears the Richard Stonier acquired land from these various sources to create a small farm which was later to be called The Birches.

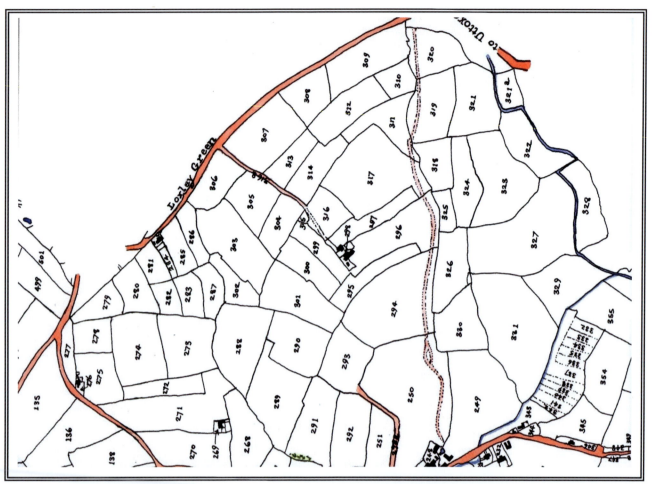

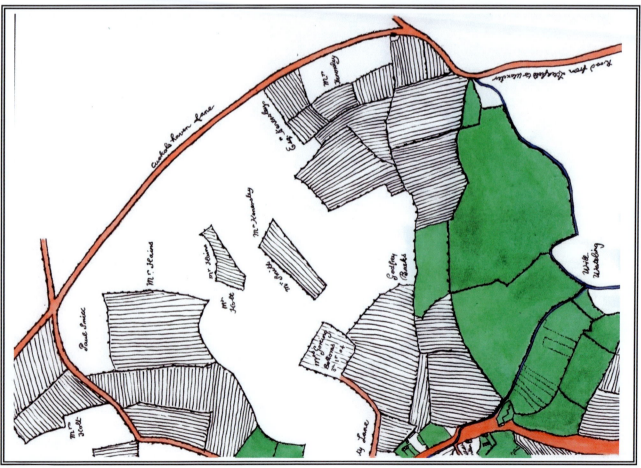

Fig. 28 **Kingstone map** 1717-20 (below) & Fig. 29 **Kingstone map** 1837 (above) **Zone C**

# Park Lane to Cuckold's Haven [Zone C]

The apparent lack of properties in this zone at the time of the Godson map may again be because they did not then exist, or that they were not in John Chetwynd's ownership. Park Lane (Watery Lane) is shown to continue as 'Cuckols haven Lane' (now Holly Lane) which meets the Uttoxeter to Lichfield main road. On the western side of the road, and at the bend in the road just south of this junction was the strip of land which was, interestingly named Cuckold's Haven (not shown on the map)! This is where there was a toll house (built after 1766 when this road between High Bridges (Handsacre) and Bradley Street, Uttoxeter was turnpiked) with fees being collected from road users. James Foster, of Cuckolds Haven and his wife Mary had several children baptised at Kingstone between 1818 and 1827. James Foster was a labourer, and there is no record of him also being a tollgate keeper. However, Ellen Riley, a widow, was living at Cuckold's Haven Gate in 1861 and 1871; she was the keeper of the toll gate and collector of tolls. By 1881, John Foster, a 'late farmer' was living at Cuckold's Haven Gate (4). Evidently by this time tolls were no longer collected as Benjamin Smith, innkeeper of the nearby Red Cow Inn at Willslock had been given £30 in 1878 to release a parcel of land for road widening *where the toll gate house lately stood* (39). Tollgate Cottage had become a farm labourer's cottage attached to Broomy Leasows Farm by 1892 (page 74). In 1901 Thomas Shepherd and his family were living at Cuckhold's Haven. He was an 'agricultural implements painter' which almost certainly means that he worked at Henry Bamford and Sons in Uttoxeter.
A modern house exists today on or near the site of the cottage at Cuckhold's Haven.
How the name 'Cuckold's Haven' may have originated is left to the imagination!

A notable feature at the bottom of this zone is the division of a field into strips called *'In Town Meadows'*.

## HOLLYHAYS {284}

The 1801 survey reveals that William Griffin, probably the brother of Thomas Griffin of Leese Hill (page 65) then owned this house, with about 18 acres of land. In 1834 Charles Sherratt, a button mould turner was living at Hollyhays (29). This was perhaps the same Mr. Sherratt, a maker of wooden buttons (and known as 'the old button flirter') who was living in Abbot's Bromley in about 1860 (34).
In 1838, this property on Holly Lane was a smallholding of about 16 acres, owned by Richard Gaunt with George Durose as tenant (24). George Durose, a labourer (and son of Samuel Durose of The Villa, page 43) was recorded as living here in 1841 (4). 'Holly Hay Farm', a farm of seventeen acres, in the occupation of Joseph Rushton was advertised for sale in 1844 (2). A farm sale was advertised in 1848 on the premises of the late Samuel Rushton (a butcher), at 'Holley Hay'. His widow Harriet remained here until 1856 (2). William Upton, formerly of Church Farm was tenant by 1861, farming 17 acres of land (4). James Woodings and his family were living at Holly Hays in 1871 which at this time

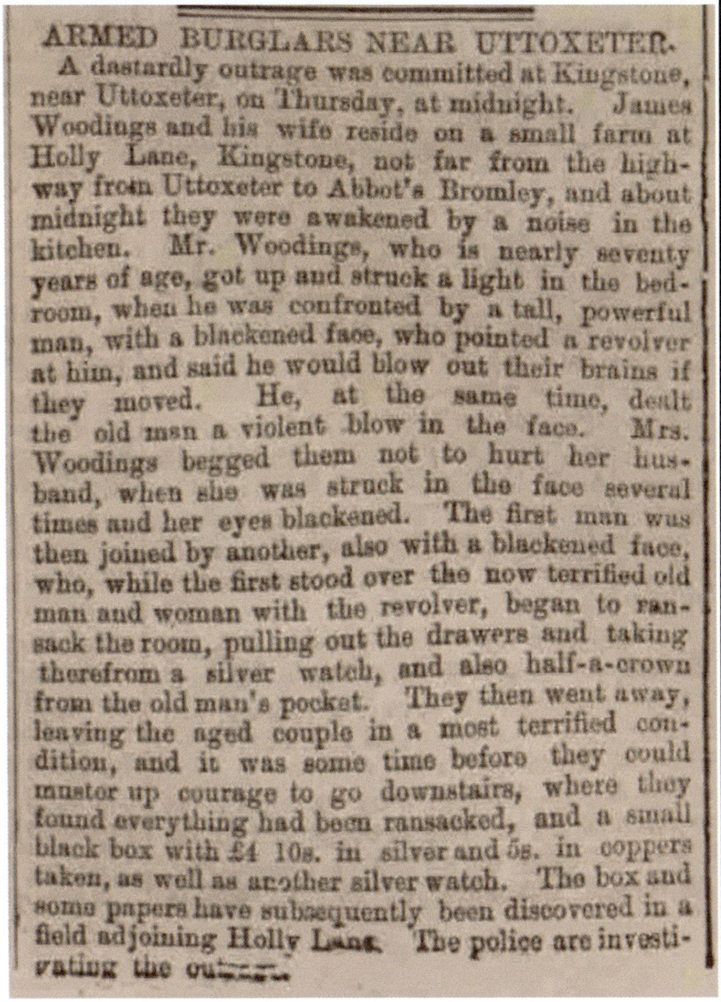

**ARMED BURGLARS NEAR UTTOXETER.**

A dastardly outrage was committed at Kingstone, near Uttoxeter, on Thursday, at midnight. James Woodings and his wife reside on a small farm at Holly Lane, Kingstone, not far from the highway from Uttoxeter to Abbot's Bromley, and about midnight they were awakened by a noise in the kitchen. Mr. Woodings, who is nearly seventy years of age, got up and struck a light in the bedroom, when he was confronted by a tall, powerful man, with a blackened face, who pointed a revolver at him, and said he would blow out their brains if they moved. He, at the same time, dealt the old man a violent blow in the face. Mrs. Woodings begged them not to hurt her husband, when she was struck in the face several times and her eyes blackened. The first man was then joined by another, also with a blackened face, who, while the first stood over the now terrified old man and woman with the revolver, began to ransack the room, pulling out the drawers and taking therefrom a silver watch, and also half-a-crown from the old man's pocket. They then went away, leaving the aged couple in a most terrified condition, and it was some time before they could muster up courage to go downstairs, where they found everything had been ransacked, and a small black box with £4 10s. in silver and 5s. in coppers taken, as well as another silver watch. The box and some papers have subsequently been discovered in a field adjoining Holly Lane. The police are investigating the outrage.

Plate 18 **Assault at Hollyhays** Tamworth Herald - 12 March 1892
Image © THE BRITISH LIBRARY BOARD. ALL RIGHTS RESERVED
http://www.britishnewspaperarchive.co.uk/viewer/bl/0000484/18920312/06

was a small farm with 18 acres of land. James Woodings died in 1900 but his widow, Eliza Woodings continued farming, being still at Holly Hays in 1901 (29)(4). Mr. and Mrs Woodings were the victims of a terrifying assault and armed robbery in 1892, the details of which were recorded in a newspaper report (Plate 18, page 73) (2).
In 1911 Edward John Stephens was farming at Holly Hays. He was later succeeded by his son Frederick Stephens who had taken over the farm by 1928 (and who had married Mabel Whieldon, daughter of William Whieldon who lived nearby at Hollydene, page 71) (4) (29).
The term 'hay' can have many meanings, but in this case probably suggests an area enclosed by a hedge (obviously, of holly) (27).


**BROOMY LEASOWS FARM {298}** (demolished) This farm, which had an access by a track off Holly Lane is not marked on the Godson map. If it then existed, John Chetwynd did not own it, or the land on which it was built. However, Elizabeth Willot, in her will, dated 1746, stated that she was of '*the Broome lesows in the parish of Kingston*' (24).
The 1801 survey indicates that Broomy Leasows was now owned by Earl Talbot and that it was a farm of about 67 acres with William Woolliscroft as tenant. However, Jacob 'Wollescroft', a farmer of 'Broom-Leasow' in the parish of 'Kingston-upon-Toad-Brook', was clearly the previous occupant. In his will dated 1800, Jacob 'Wolliscroft', who was the father of William Woolliscroft bequeathed immediate possession of the farm to his son (24). William Woolliscroft and his wife Ann had several children who were baptised at Kingstone between 1799 and 1808. The family later resided at Poolfields, Lower Loxley.
Thomas and Catherine Griffin (page 65) were farming at Broomy Leasows when two of their children were baptised at Kingstone in the early 1820s.
William Weston and his family, who went to live at Longton were formerly of 'Broomy-leasow'. William Weston's daughter was buried at Kingstone in 1831 when they were living at Broomy Leasows. He was living at Longton, and described as a victualler when he made his will in 1835; he died in 1842 (24).
Benjamin Brooks was listed as a farmer at Broomy Leasows in 1834, and in 1838, he was described as the tenant of this farm of 54 acres, then owned by Thomas Sneyd Kynnersley Esq. of Loxley Hall (29)(24).
Benjamin Severn farmed 70 acres at Broomy Leasows in 1851, and he was still tenant in 1860 when the farm (of 57 acres) was put up for auction by the Kynnersley estate (2).
In 1861 George Sutton was farming 58 acres at Broomy Leasows. '*The Broomy Leasows*' was for sale again in 1869, described by the owner D. B. Fletcher (a hop merchant and man of property of Leeds) *as 'containing about fifty-eight acres, good house, and suitable farm buildings, beautifully situated'* and that the farm '*abounds with game*'. George Sutton had a dispersal sale in 1869 and left the farm.
William Perkin, a cattle dealer was living at Broomy Leasows by 1871, but apparently without any land (4).
In 1881 Thomas Land had only 8 acres of land, evidently because the land (in 1871 and 1881) was then being farmed as part of Kingstone Hall Farm, having been acquired by the Shrewsbury estate (4).
Edward T. Brown (of Heatley, Abbot's Bromley) was at Broomy Leasows by 1885, now farming about 88 acres. This holding included Tollgate Cottage and garden (about ¼ acre) which was said to have late been in the occupation of Joseph Goodwin (39).
John Stonier was tenant of the same 88 acre holding in 1891, and by 1912 he was the tenant of both this farm and Kingstone Hall Farm (4)(29). The farm was sold together with Kingstone Hall in the Shrewsbury Estate sale in 1918 (37). In 1928 Ernest Stonier of Kingstone Hall owned the land but it was farmed by Samuel Gallimore of nearby Wall Heath Farm who had a labourer, Percy Horobin living at the property (29).
After Ernest Stonier died in 1933, Thomas Bettson acquired Kingstone Hall, together with Broomy Leasows. In ruins by the 1980s, all traces of Broomy Leasows farm house and buildings have now gone, the land having been incorporated into that of Kingstone Hall Farm (page 42).

'Broomy' suggests that the land may once have had broom growing upon it (a plant associated with lighter heathland soils, and likely to appear on cleared forest land), while 'lea' is pasture or meadowland. (Similarly derived as in Broomfields, a farm to the south-east of Kingstone, in the direction of Abbot's Bromley, and of course, in the name Bromley, as well as perhaps, Bramshall.)

# KINGSTONE WOOD [Zone D]

Plate 19 **Kingstone Wood** - now a popular place to walk

This was (and still is) another sparsely populated area, with Kingstone Wood occupying much the same area on both maps and the Tad Brook forming the parish boundary to the south-east. A house at Moorfields {16} is the only property recorded in the Godson survey. The track through the Wood going past Moorfields looks like a more established route than in later years. The Dowry Farm {373} although it existed at this date, is not shown. There were many tracks through Kingstone Wood, including those with links to Dowry Farm, other areas of Callowhill, and beyond. The Godson map shows a gate into the Wood at the 'Moss Lane' junction. (Moss Lane had gone by 1838, but the Mosses {223} had been built at the entrance to the Wood by this date) (39).
From Blythe Bridge Bank another gate (Fig. 5 page 30, Fig. 6 page 31) provided a point of entry into Kingstone Wood. This entrance into what was then the 29 acre sector of Kingstone Wood called *Abbott's Wood* still exists today. The Godson survey named the areas of woodland then owned by John Chetwynd.
 [Note that a letter code (*1- 8)* has been added to the Godson map (Fig. 30, page 76) as an aid to identification e.g. *Abbott's Wood (8)*]  Could this name have a much earlier origin reflecting Kingstone's links to the Rocester Abbey? To the east of *Abbott's Wood* was the seven acre wood was called *Brick Leasow Coppy (7)*, alongside the possible brick-making area already referred to (page 23), with the five acre *Little High Wood (6)*, linking to the south with the main central area of Kingstone Wood, the *Great High Wood (4)* which consisted of 72 acres. To the north of Moorfields was *Migery Bank Coppy (5)* (15 acres) and the 18 acre woodland to the south of this dwelling, at the southern limits of the parish was called *Glasshouse Coppy (1)*. There is documentary evidence of an early glassmaking industry during the medieval period, nearby in Bagot's Park. Thomas Sherratt of Callowhill, who died leaving a will in 1634, was a glazier (21). Wood was needed to make charcoal to provide fuel for glassmaking. To the east was *Millpool Coppy (3)* (7 acres), near the Mill Pool Bridge, and going further east was the 12 acre *Srouls Coppy* (**2**) (page 22). Also marked on the Godson map, to the west of *Abbott's Wood* was a woodland area

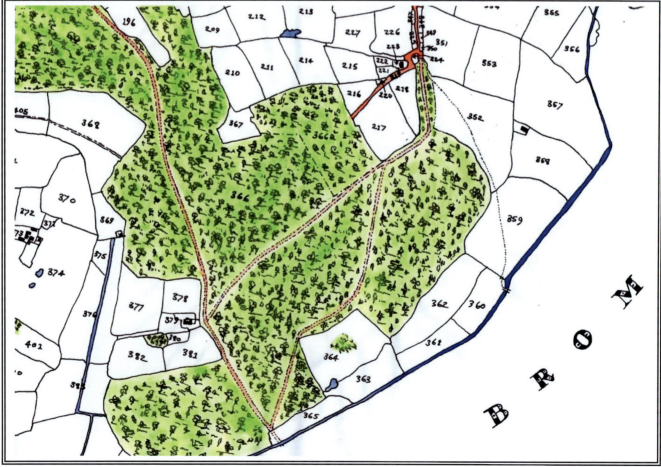

Fig. 30 **Kingstone map** 1717-20 (above) & Fig. 31 **Kingstone map 1837** (below) **Zone D**

called *Mr. Degg's Coppy* (belonging to Simon Degge of Blythe Bridge Hall). By 1838 this woodland had been incorporated into Kingstone Wood as *Degg's Wood.* Similarly, *Katherine Boulton's Coppice* had become part of Kingstone Wood as *Bolton Coppice.* [Katherine Boulton lived at a house {234} next to Moss Farm (Fig. 5, page 30)]. A four-acre field at the south-eastern end of *Abbot's Wood* had become woodland by 1838, called, not surprisingly, *Four Acres.* The 1882 Ordnance survey map gave the name *Alder Carr* for what was formerly called *Migery Bank Coppy.* This map also gave the name *Brown's Rough* to a strip of woodland which consisted of the former *Brick Leasow Coppy,* the *Little High Wood* and extended in a southerly direction into part of the former *Great High Wood. Srouls Coppy,* or *Shoul's Wood* as it was called in 1882, also extended (to Moorfields) spanning the whole width of the lower part of the former *Great High Wood.*

Earl Talbot, and his predecessor, John Chetwynd, like other owners of large estates kept woodlands in their own hands and for their own purposes. They employed gamekeepers and woodsmen to manage the property. For entertainment the Earl and his invited guests could use the woods to shoot game birds and deer. Timber itself was valuable, particularly in the age of wooden ships. A number of newspaper entries advertised timber for sale in Kingstone Wood and other woodland areas which Earl Talbot owned in Kingstone. Generally this was standing timber where lot numbers were painted on individual trees e.g. in a sale of timber: lot 1 - 128 oaks and lot 2 - 72 oaks growing in *Glass-House-Bank,* Kingstone Wood were to be sold at the White Hart, Uttoxeter in April 1812. The timber was said to be *'of great lengths, suitable for ship plank and country purposes'*. The timber was also said to be growing within 5 miles of the Uttoxeter Canal and near to a good turnpike road leading to the Canal. Interestingly the Uttoxeter to Cauldon Canal had only opened in 1811.

In 1817 251 oak trees growing in Abbot's Wood were offered for sale at Sandon. Also for sale, in 1822, at Weston, were 294 oaks growing on *Miry (Migery?) Bank* in Kingstone Wood, and at Rugeley, in 1823, 220 oaks in Kingstone Woods . In each case, John Ward of Kingstone was to show the timber (2)

In 1835, at the Bagot's Arms Inn, Abbot's Bromley there was an auction sale advertised of growing timber including: *'Lot 4 -Three hundred and twenty-one Oak Trees, growing in Kingstone Wood, blazed and numbered with white paint, from 1 to 321 inclusive.'* Viewing was now by application to Thomas Johnson (page 79)(2).

In 1845 a number of competing railway companies were putting forward plans for new routes. One proposal argued that timber from Kingstone Wood, Bagot's Wood and Needwood Forest mostly went to Manchester, and by a tedious canal route. They offered direct, easy, cheap, communication to new markets. It was proposed to use the line of the Uttoxeter to Cauldon Canal as a rail route. This, in fact, is what happened, the Canal being closed in 1847 and the Churnet Valley railway being built along the course . This was part of the North Staffordshire Railway ('The Knotty'), formed in 1845 which had its base at Stoke on Trent. The station at Uttoxeter was opened in 1848. [In addition, the rail link from Uttoxeter to Stafford opened in 1867.] (2).

By 1855 when 119 trees, mostly oak and ash (*the oaks being mostly of very large dimensions*) growing on the farm occupied by Mrs. Williams (of Manor Farm, page 48 ) were offered for sale at the Black Swan, Uttoxeter, the trees were said to be growing near to good roads and about 3 miles from Uttoxeter station on the North Staffordshire Railway (2).

By 1858, timber sales of large trees seemed to be fewer, but at an auction sale at The Vine Inn, Stafford over 80 oaks were for sale in each of *Abbot's Wood* and *Mill Coppice* as well as oak and ash trees growing in *Shrowls Wood* and *Alder Carr Coppice*. Viewing was still by application to Thomas Johnson (2).

At Rugeley, in 1864, three besom makers from Rugeley were charged by Alfred Johnson of Kingstone , woodranger to the Earl of Shrewsbury with having cut a quantity of underwood from a plantation at Kingstone. Johnson's account was corroborated by Charles Limer, who also worked for the Earl. The defendants who were caught in possession of the underwood were each sent to gaol for two months with hard labour (2).

At the time of the Godson survey Kingstone Wood consisted of just under 175 acres. Although further areas of woodland had been added, some parts must have become smaller as it was still the same overall size in 1838. Today, Kingstone Wood, has a distribution pattern broadly similar to that of 1838, with the exception of *Abbot's Wood* which was cleared after the Great War, and a small amount of Kingstone Wood on the Heatley side which has also been felled.

[Elsewhere, in Kingstone, most of the woodland below Woodcock Heath Farm i.e. *Johnny Field Coppice* (called *Johnney Field Coppy* in the Godson survey) was cleared after the Great War, and about half of *Wanfield Wood* (north of Wanfield Hall) was cleared after the Second World War.]

**THE MOSSES** {223} This property is positioned near to the entrance to Kingstone Wood.
In 1801 it was a smallholding with about 10 acres of land, and owned by Francis Deakin (39).
William Durose of Loxley, in his will dated 1820 (but written in 1814), bequeathed the Mosses (then occupied by his son George) to his son George, and jointly with another son, Samuel Durose. His two sons, also jointly inherited three other houses and land in the centre of Kingstone. Another house was left to his youngest son, Thomas Durose (pages 43-44) (24).
By 1838, Earl Talbot was the owner of the Mosses (still a 10 acre holding) and Francis Deakin (probably a nephew of the earlier Francis Deakin), a swine dealer, was his tenant (24).
Samuel Leese, a 70 year old widower and farmer of 11 acres was recorded as living at the Mosses in 1851 (4), but by 1856 Henry Johnson was the tenant (39). Jesse Ainsworth (or Hainsworth), a wheelwright was living at The Mosses in 1861 (4). He had moved to Woodcock Heath by 1871 (page 66), and the new tenant at The Mosses was Elizabeth Finnemore, farming (still) about 10 acres of land.
In 1881 William Ainsworth, the former publican and wheelwright at The Dog and Partridge/Shrewsbury Arms (page 47), and son of Jesse Ainsworth, farmed here on 20 acres. The property was called 'Moss Cottage' in 1891 when William Ainsworth was still living here, described as a farmer and gamekeeper (4).
Charles Beard (step-son of William Ainsworth) was tenant at The Mosses in 1895, and he also farmed about twenty acres of land (39). Charles Beard was still farming at The Mosses in 1901, and similarly in 1911, when he was described as a farmer and gamekeeper (4). In 1911 the house had just four rooms (4).
In the 1918 Shrewsbury Estate sale this smallholding was sold to Charles Beard, the tenant for £550 (39). Charles Beard also 'looked after' Kingstone Wood for the Earl of Shrewsbury and Talbot (page 121).
The Beard family suffered a double tragedy with the loss of two of their sons, John Beard (in 1917) and Thomas Beard (in 1918) who were both WWI casualties. Their names are recorded on a memorial plaque in Kingstone church. [Other young men of Kingstone who lost their lives during the Great War and are recorded on this Roll of Honour include Harvey Brown (page 81), Edward Fradley (page 44), Thomas J. Whitehall (page 66), William H. Harrison and Charles T. Bennett (19).]
By 1928 James Sargeant, a farmer, was living at the Mosses (29). He also used to assist his brother William (Bill) Sargeant, the butcher when he called to visit the homes of people in the area to kill and butcher the family pig. As my father recalled, Jim Sargeant was in the habit of helping himself to some of the fat removed from the pig (every part of the pig was used and therefore valued) earning himself the nickname of 'Old Grab Fat'.


**MOORFIELDS / WOOD FARM** {379} At the time of Godson there was a house here {16}, on the edge of Kingstone Wood, owned by Mr. Holt. The Holts were an old Kingstone family, Thomas Holt of 'Kinston' died leaving a inventory dated 1577/8, and a John Holt was listed in the Hearth Tax record of 1666 (24)(36).
John Holt of Stowe (baptised at Kingstone in 1700) but who died leaving a will in 1729, referred to his father's lands lying in Kingston and Callowhill, where it seems his father Robert Holt lived (24).
The locality seems quite isolated now, but old maps show that, apart from being connected to the centre of Kingstone by tracks through Kingstone Wood, this property was once served by a well-used track and lane from Blythe Bridge bank, which then continued onwards past Moorfields, going via the hamlet of Heatley to the Uttoxeter to Lichfield main road (Figs. 30 & 31, page 76).
A dwelling was recorded on this site in 1801. The then occupant has not been identified, but may have been Michael Crutchley, a gamekeeper. Certainly the Crutchley family lived at the premises in 1813 or earlier. Elizabeth Crutchley, the young wife of Michael Crutchley (son of the above Michael Crutchley) was said to have been of the Dowry when she was buried at Kingstone in July 1813. When, earlier in the same year their daughter Ann was baptised, Michael Crutchley was decribed as a gamekeeper living at 'Kingstone Lodge'. He then married Harriet Beard (daughter of John Beard, the publican) in 1818, and he and his wife were generally said to have been of Kingstone Wood when their children were baptised, but of Moorfields when their son Michael was baptised in 1823. It is clear that they lived at Moorfields, otherwise 'Wood Farm'. Michael Crutchley is first recorded as being Earl Talbot's gamekeeper for Kingstone and Gratwich in 1805 and held this position to at least 1829 (2).
The Crutchley family had moved away (to Stafford) by 1834 when Earl Talbot had a new tenant and

gamekeeper, Thomas Johnson, living at Moorfields (29).
Because of its position next to Kingstone Wood Moorfields provided suitable accommodation for one of Earl Talbot's gamekeepers, or for a worker employed in managing the Wood (24).
In 1838, Moorfields, which adjoined Dowry Farm, was a smallholding of about 13 acres, owned by Earl Talbot, and occupied by Thomas Johnson. Thomas Johnson, a 'wood labourer' was living here in 1841 with his wife Mary and eleven children (4)! He later moved to Moss Farm (page 40).
From 1842, and up to 1871 or later, Thomas Webb lived at Moorfields, described as a farmer with about 24 acres of land (39)(4).
George Johnson (a son of Thomas Johnson who had lived here earlier) was resident from 1877; he had about 13 acres of land, the property then being called 'Wood Cottage' in 1881, and he was described as a woodman (4)(39). He was living at Moorfields in 1891, and was still here in 1896 (4 29).
Thomas Ferneyhough, an agricultural labourer, lived at 'The Wood' with his wife Myra and their sons in 1901, and remained here until 1903 (4).
Charles Noakes was the tenant when Moorfields, which had 14 acres of land, was sold (for £700) by the Shrewsbury Estate, in 1918 (39). In 1920, Moorfields, a smallholding, consisting of a house with three bedrooms, a brick and tile shed for four cows, other outbuildings, about 14 acres, (with a right of road over Dowry Farm), and in the occupation of C. Noakes, was advertised for sale. Mr. Hawthorn purchased the property for £825 (2). In 1928 Thomas Smith farmed at Moorfields (29).
Now gone, this property survived until the relatively recent past.

**DOWRY (DOWERY) FARM** {373} This farm, the most isolated in the parish, has a farmhouse of plain red brick under a roof of blue tile (Fig. 32), which probably dates from early in the nineteenth century.
It seems likely that an earlier farmhouse occupied the same site.
The Dowry Farm is not shown on the Godson map as it was not part of John Chetwynd's Kingstone estate. However, a series of deeds survive which indicate that the 'Dowry Farm' did then exist, but had a different owner (39). These deeds, dating between 1740 and 1772 trace the changing ownership of Dowry Farm.
'Callow hill Farm' (a name by which, confusingly, the Dowry Farm was sometimes known) was stated in the deeds to have been *'the estate and inheritance of Isaac Hawkins Esq.'* (39).
Isaac Hawkins, a gentleman, a barrister, and a man of considerable property lived in Burton upon Trent. After he died, in a will dated 1713, he divided his estate between his three daughters (26). His will made no specific mention of the Dowry Farm, probably because it would have been a relatively insignificant portion

Fig. 32 **Dowry Farm**

of his property, but the deeds suggest that the Dowry Farm passed to his eldest daughter, Rebecca Walthall (of Newport, Shropshire), who had no children, and then to Anne Cheney, the daughter of Rebecca's sister Anne Browne who had married William Browne, the Vicar of Burton upon Trent. [William and Anne Browne also had a son, Isaac Hawkins Browne who became M. P. for Much Wenlock, Shropshire as well as being a barrister, a poet, and a friend of Dr. Samuel Johnson.]

Anne Browne had married Edward Cheney, a wealthy gentleman of Yoxall and she appears to have inherited 'Callow hill farm' in 1760 when the tenant was John Sherratt. Between that date and 1772 Edward Cheney sold the farm to Thomas Dicken, father of another Thomas Dicken, who in turn sold 'Callow hill Farm, otherwise Dowry Farm' to John Chetwynd Talbot of Ingestre (later 1st Earl Talbot, see page 14).

From that date the property remained in the hands of John Chetwynd Talbot's descendants until the sale of the Shrewsbury estate in 1918.

The 1740 deed provides a description of the farm, which then consisted of a dwelling house with barns, stables, cowhouses, outhouses, gardens and orchards and just under 77 acres of land (with all the fields being listed by name). John Cooke was then the occupant and tenant. Whether the farm was known as Dowry Farm in 1740 (or in 1760) is unclear, but the word 'Dowery' was given in fields called the *Long Dowery*, the *Pewlston's* (or *Pewson's*) *Dowery* and *Dowery Coppice*, names which could belong to a distant past. The obvious assumption is that this farm was once part of a marriage settlement, but why should 'dowery' occur in field names? Perhaps the few fields were given as a dowry and the name of the farm is derived from them?

Or could there be a simpler explanation; the word 'dower' can also mean a burrow (of rabbits)!

In 1772, when Thomas Dicken, gent. of 'High-linns' (Highland) Park, Tatenhill, near Burton upon Trent sold the farm, it was also described in detail, with similar field names, and still of about 76 acres. The Dowry Farm was then said to have been in the possession of Richard Croxton, but occupied by John Sherratt his under-tenant. Little is known about Thomas Dicken of Highlins Park, who died in 1772, or of his son Thomas who died in 1786, but the family may have been involved in the developing brewing industry in Burton upon Trent.

The name Hawkins does appear in Kingstone parish registers but no link can be found between them and Isaac Hawkins whose mother was Thomasina Hawkins, and whose grandfather, William Hawkins, was a prosperous yeoman, both being of Muxton, near Lilleshall in Shropshire.

A document dated 1700 seems to have the answer, being a 'final accord' concerning a messuage, garden and orchard, 40 acres of (arable) land, 20 acres of meadow, 100 acres of pasture, 40 acres of woods and 30 acres of scrub in Callowhill and Kingstone (39). The parties involved in this transfer of property were named as Isaac Hawkins and William Hawkins of the one part, and Harry Goreing (Henry Goring), Christopher Sanders, Elizabeth his wife, Samuel Sanders and Susanna Cary, widow (later Suzanna Lambe) of the other part.

In effect it appears that Isaac Hawkins, the barrister, and William Hawkins, his cousin (and also of Burton upon Trent) agreed to acquire the Dowry Farm, together with other property from members of the Goring family (page 12) i.e. Henry Goring (of Wolverhampton), his sister Elizabeth Sanders, her husband Christopher and their children Samuel and Susanna (the Sanders family living in New England).

Elizabeth Sanders (nee Goring), Henry Goring and their brother Lovatt Goring were the children of William Goring who had married Anne Lovatt of Callowhill. Lovatt Goring, as William Goring's heir evidently inherited property at Callowhill (which must have included Dowry Farm). In his will, dated 1697, Lovatt Goring, described as of the Inner Temple and Common Cryer and Sergeant at Arms (i.e. Mace Bearer) of the City of London, made his will in 1695 and bequeathed his Callowhill property to his cousin John Goring and his heirs male, on condition that he paid £20 yearly to his sister Elizabeth for life (26). Failing this, the Callowhill property was to be left to his sister Elizabeth and her heirs. In the event, John Goring (who was already in possession of Callowhill Hall) and his only son John had both died in 1696, before Lovatt Goring who died in 1697, meaning that the inheritance came to Elizabeth Sanders by default. Presumably, Elizabeth Sanders, living in America, decided to dispose of the Callowhill property a few years later, in 1700. As described above, Dowry Farm was later sold by the heirs of Isaac Hawkins to Thomas Dicken, and then sold by Thomas Dicken to Earl Talbot in 1772.

By the time of the 1801 survey Earl Talbot's tenant at the Dowry Farm (now 110 acres) was Jeremiah 'Sharratt' (Sherratt), evidently the son of John Sherratt who was the earlier tenant. Jeremiah Sherratt was still tenant in 1814/15 (39), but was soon to be succeeded by his son, Joseph. Joseph Sherratt married Dorothy Johnson (a daughter of Joseph Johnson of Blithe Bridge Hall Farm) in 1813 at Kingstone, and their two children, Joseph and

Elizabeth were baptised at Kingstone in 1814 and 1816, respectively, their father being described as a farmer of Dowry Farm. Other parish register entries include the burial of Elizabeth Crutchley, aged 20 years, in 1813, and of Sarah Sherratt, aged 29 years, both of Dowry Farm in 1815. They seem to have been daughters of Jeremiah Sherratt, and sisters of Joseph. Michael Crutchley had married Elizabeth Sherratt at Kingstone in 1812. Joseph Sherratt died in 1818, but by this time he had moved away, and was a publican at the 'Bird in Hand' at Hilderstone. His son, Joseph Sherratt, became the tailor who later lived at Church View (pages 44, 121).
John and Jane Elsmore then farmed at the Dowry, their daughters Jane and Elizabeth being baptised at Kingstone in 1820 and 1822 respectively. William Woolliscroft Elsmore, the illegitimate son of Ann Elsmore of the Dowry Farm, was baptised at Kingstone in 1826, Ann Elsmore (who later married Charles Campion, the shoemaker of Woodcock Heath, page 67) having been another daughter of John and Jane Elsmore.
A directory entry in 1834 records Jas. (James) Elsmore as a farmer living at the Dowry (29). James Elsmore, had married Nancy Wilson (a daughter of Thomas Wilson the blacksmith) at Kingstone in 1804.
The Dowry, in 1838, had increased further in size since 1801 and was now described a farm of 127 acres, owned by Earl Talbot with Jane Elsmore as tenant. She was the wife of John Elsmore (a brother of James) although her husband did not die until 1840 (24).
By 1841 Edward Finnemore was tenant and he was later succeeded by his son William (4). William Finnemore farmed at the Dowry for many years. His first wife, Harriet died at the age of only 20, probably in childbirth, and was buried with her two-year-old daughter in Kingstone churchyard - a reflection of the risks of pregnancy and high infant mortality rate at this time (13). William Finnemore had moved away by 1880 when the new tenant at Dowry Farm was George Tams, followed by Thomas Joseph Charles (of the Charles family of Abbot's Bromley) in 1891, and William Titterton in 1901, and until 1904 (4) (39). By 1912 John Brown was the tenant (28).
In the Shrewsbury Estate sale of 1918 this *'exceedingly useful dairy and stock farm'* of 136 acres was sold to the executors of the late John Brown for £3450 (37). John Brown had died in 1917. His son, Harvey Brown was a casualty of WWI, killed in France in 1916 (as recorded on his father's gravestone in Kingstone churchyard). In 1928 Harry Brown, Harvey Brown's younger brother was running the farm (29).

Plate 20 **Kingstone Wood** - more than forestry and pheasants; a wealth of flowering plants, mosses, ferns, fungi and animal life.

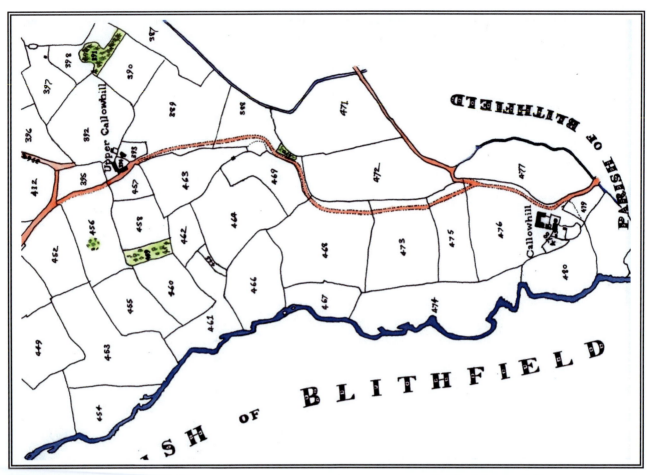
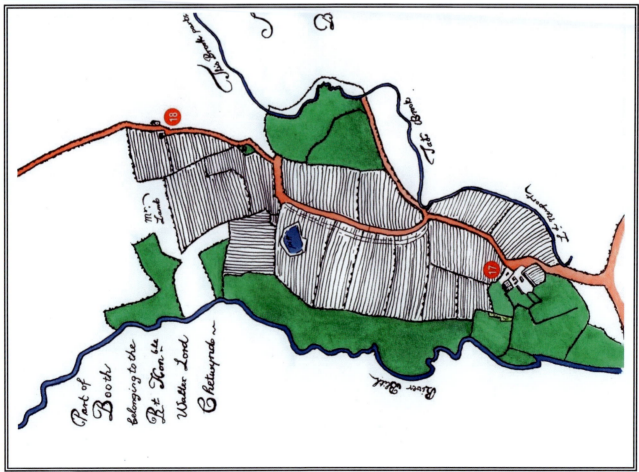

Fig. 33 **Kingstone map** 1717-20 (below) & Fig. 34 **Kingstone map** 1837 (above) **Zone E**

# CALLOWHILL - THE DEEP SOUTH [Zone E]

Leese Hill, Woodcock Heath, Wanfield, and Callowhill are connecting areas of hilly terrain in Kingstone overlooking the valley of the river Blithe which forms the western boundary of the parish. Even in the present era each area is sparsely populated, containing just a few properties (with a single house at Wanfield). Today, Callowhill is represented by just the two farms, (Callowhill Hall and Upper Callowhill Farm), as also shown on the Godson map, although it is evident that in the past Callowhill encompassed a wider area, including what is now Dowry Farm (page 79), and what was Moorfields (page 78). The reference to Blythe Bridge as 'alias Little Callow Hill' in the will of William Whythall (Whitehall) in 1616 is an indication that Blythe Bridge was also then considered part of Callowhill (24). This may account for the higher than expected number of wills (dating from sixteenth and seventeenth century) which were made by residents of 'Callowhill'. Callowhill appears to be very isolated in the southern part of Kingstone parish. Both the Godson map and the 1837 'tithe map' show a lane called Stinkingford Lane (now gone, but still traceable in the 1970s) which crossed the Tad Brook going west towards Heatley, and connecting with Heatley Lane and the Uttoxeter to Lichfield road. Until the later years of the last century Callowhill Hall could be reached from Blythe Bridge by a narrow winding lane (Hollyhurst Lane), but this lane now only goes as far as Upper Callowhill.
Callowhill Hall is however, linked to Blythe Bridge through Booth via Booth Lane.
Additionally, and just to the south, Newton Hurst Lane provided a route to Stafford and Rugeley (via Newton), and also a connection with the Uttoxeter to Lichfield road (via Bagots Bromley).
The word *callow* suggests bare, and land which is bare, open or exposed, and on a hill, perhaps gives a fair description (27). The land may have been considered less productive in the same sense as *wan* in Wanfield.

**CALLOWHILL HALL FARM** {478} {17} Callowhill hall is marked on the Godson map as a large and significant property, the land being mostly arable but with meadow land alongside the River Blythe boundary of the parish. The farmhouse is clearly of considerable age, being a most impressive half-timbered structure, painted in black and white (Fig. 35). Callowhill is an ancient settlement, refered to as 'Kalewehul' in 1355 when also an area of land here was called *le stocking* (36). This may have been the field directly east of Callowhill Hall called *Stocking Field* (page 23) in the Godson survey, and *Stockings* {477} at the time of the 1838 tithe award.

Fig. 35 **Callowhill Hall Farm**

Callowhill (assumed to mean Callowhill Hall, and other property) is said to have belonged to the Lovatt family from the time of Richard II up until the seventeenth century when William Goring of Booth married Anne, eldest daughter and co-heiress of Thomas Lovatt (39). The *'capital messuage and lands at Callow Hill'* were the subject of a marriage settlement in 1646 between Anne, the eldest daughter of Thomas Lovatt and Grace his wife, and William Goring of 'Bould' (Booth), the youngest son of Henry Goring (39). Thomas Lovatt was described as the son and heir apparent of John Lovatt in a document describing the sale of some land at Callowhill in 1619 (36). Robert Lovatt (younger brother of Thomas Lovatt) was named in the Crompton Charity, established by his grandson, Robert Crompton (pages 133-134).

William Lovatt of Callowhill, a likely ancestor of Thomas and Robert Lovatt died leaving a will in 1564/5 (24). The lawyer and eminent antiquarian Sir Symon Degge is generally assumed to have been living in this house in 1655, being described as Symon Degge of Callow Hill (33). This is now viewed as being false and misleading as the term 'Callow Hill' evidently then described a wider area, which included Blythe Bridge. Sir Symon Degge inherited Blythe Bridge Hall, not Callowhill Hall from his Whitehall relatives.

In 1655 Callowhill Hall would have been in the hands of the Goring family, as successors of the Lovatts. John Goring, who died in 1696, was described as being of Callowhill. It was his wish, expressed in his will that Callowhill should not fall into the hands of either the Bagot or the Chetwynd families (page 13) (26). John Goring's heir and only child, his daughter Barbara did however, in 1711, marry Walter Chetwynd! Barbara and Walter Chetwynd, just a few years later, sold the Manor of Kingstone, including Callowhill to another Chetwynd! The purchaser, John Chetwynd who was a relative of Walter Chetwynd, but in another branch of the family (pages 14-16) paid the considerable sum of £12500 for the Manor of Kingstone, including messuages, cottages or tenements with arable land, pasture and meadow. Also included were tolls, stallage, customs and profits from the fairs or markets in Uttoxeter, Birchwood Park, Leigh (consisting of 700 acres) and the capital messuage (Callowhill Hall). The two messuages or farms in Callowhill called Brough's Farm and Motteram's tenement were also part of the purchase. John Gough was named as the tenant at Callowhill. The Godson survey reveals that Callowhill Hall, owned by John Chetwynd, was a farm of 118 acres, the tenant then being Joseph Wakelin (who died in 1733). His wife Mary Wakelin, in her will, dated 1765, left her freehold property (unidentified) in Kingstone to her nephew, Edward Shelley.

John Shelley of Kingston died leaving a will dated 1588/9, suggesting an early family link with the parish, but John Shelley, who died in 1730, and left a will naming his son John as sole executor, was of Callowhill (24). This John Shelley, junior was probably the father of the above Edward Shelley. The property remained in the hands of John Chetwynd's descendants, being owned by Earl Talbot in 1801. Edward Shelley was then the tenant of the farm which had about 138 acres of land (37). In his will dated 1808, Edward Shelley named his wife Ann, son John and daughter, Ann Bakewell (24). Edward Shelley's wife Ann lived to be 95 years old; she was buried with her daughter Ann, at Kingstone (13). In 1838 Anne Shelley, the widow of John Shelley (in turn, the son of the above Edward Shelley) was Earl Talbot's tenant at Callowhill Hall, which was then a farm of 130 acres (24). John Shelley's name is written in Latin as 'Joannis' on his gravestone in Kingstone churchyard (13). His son John went to Cambridge University and became a curate, the Rev. John Shelley M.A. becoming perpetual curate at Bradley, near Stafford. Perhaps the Latin inscription derives from the classical education received by John Shelley, junior. Ann Shelley was still head of the household at Callowhill in 1834 and in 1851 (28)(4).

By 1861, Anne Shelley's eldest son, Edward Shelley had taken over the farm, but he later moved to Colwich. Benjamin Bennett was farming at Callowhill Hall by 1871. Benjamin Bennett had been a visitor of the Shelley family at the time of the 1861 census, and in 1864 he married Mary Hannah Spooner, daughter of Thomas Spooner, junior of Upper Callowhill farm.

Thomas Spooner was tenant at Callowhill Hall Farm in 1876, and was still farming here in 1881 (29)(4). This Thomas Spooner was however, the nephew of Thomas Spooner, junior, being the son of his younger brother, John Spooner who lived at the village of Newton nearby.

By 1891 Luke Mellor (younger brother of Charles Mellor of Blythe Bridge Hall) was farming at Callowhill Hall. After his death in 1898, his widow Maria managed the farm, being assisted by her sons, and she was still at Callowhill in 1911 (4). In 1911 Callowhill Hall was recorded as having 17 rooms, the largest house in the parish. A later occupant, in 1928, was Thomas Charles Brinkler. At the time of the 1911 census he had been working on Charles Mellor's farm at Blythe Bridge Hall (4)(29).

**UPPER CALLOWHILL (LITTLE CALLOWHILL) FARM {394} {18}** This is another isolated farm with what appears at first sight to be a rather uninteresting red brick farmhouse (Fig. 36). Internally, however thick walls of the farmhouse may hide old timbers, with the brick being an outer casing? The farm house is marked on the Godson map but this farm was not then in the ownership of John Chetwynd.

There had however been another house. A valuation of the farm in 1800 made the interesting reference to the *'site of old house near Lower Barn'*, and this seems likely to have been that also shown on the Godson map (Fig. 33, page 82 (39). This map shows what appears to be a house on the small diamond-shaped site, to the south of the current farm house, and alongside Hollyhurst Lane. This lane now ends at Upper Callowhill but used to continue on to Callowhill Hall.

Fig. 36 **Upper Callowhill Farm**

The area of Callowhill in general is intriguing as it has over time attracted those of a higher social standing, amongst them being the families of Lovatt, Goring, Degge, Whitehall, Hawkins, Mott and Cotes.

Of particular relevance here is the family of Cotes, John 'Cootes' (Cotes) of Callowhill being included in a list of gentlemen or landowners 'invited' to accept knighthoods on the occasion of the coronation of King Charles 1st in 1625, but later fined on declining to accept. He was also High Sheriff of Staffordshire in 1629. The 1636 seating plan of Kingstone church (page 129) records John Cotes in one of the 'best seats'.

John Cotes came from a family with ancient lineage who took their name from Cotes, about 4 miles north of Eccleshall, Staffs, his distant cousins, in the main line of the family residing at Woodcote, south of Newport, Shropshire.

Evidence that John Cotes lived at <u>Upper</u> Callowhill stems from an historical trail going back to the early part of the fifteenth century, beginning with Richard Norman 'of the Bold'. Richard Norman (no doubt of the same family later residing at Leese Hill and Caverswall, Lower Loxley) was a man whose property holding was very extensive. He owned land in Draycott in the Moors, Haughton, Stafford, Hixon, Amerton, Chartley, Grindley, Drointon, Newton, Loxley, Heatley, Kingstone and Callowhill, but his main residence appears to have been at 'Bold' (otherwise Booth, just west of Blythe Bridge as already discussed, page 8). At his death his two married daughters Margery Rugeley and Johanna Meverell were co-heiresses, and the above property was divided between them. Margery Norman had married Thomas Rugeley in 1422/3 (39).

The Rugeley (or Ridgeley) family were also a prominent landed family with ancient origins and property in the Staffordshire town of the same name, but had settled at a place called Hawkesyard in the nearby village of Armitage. A later Thomas 'Ridgley' of Hawkesyard, who died leaving a will in 1598, similarly had two daughters, who were his co-heiresses (26). To his daughter Catherine (wife of Francis Aspinall) he left lands and property in Derby, Kings Bromley, Amerton, Hixon, Newton, Kingston and in Callowhill. Francis and Catherine Aspinall's children included a daughter Elizabeth who married John Cotes. It appears the Catherine Aspinall, as a widow, lived with her daughter and son-in-law at Callowhill, and that through his wife's portion John Cotes came into possession of the Callowhill property.

Evidence that the Cotes property was at Upper Callowhill is provided in an indenture (dated between 1654 and 1661) in which John Cotes, the elder of Callowhill, gent, Elizabeth his wife and John Cotes the younger, his son and heir apparent, agreed to sell *'that capital messuage commonly called Callowhill'* (39). The purchaser (or part purchaser) was Phelice Goring of Kingstone, the widow of John Goring (who had died in about 1654). The indenture lists the field names belonging to the property, many of which can be recognised as the same or similar to those later listed for Upper Callowhill Farm in the 1838 'tithe award'. Interestingly this indenture indicated that the property included two farms, i.e. Brough's Farm, and the messuage which was, or had been occupied by Edward Motteram (see the Hearth Tax list, page 18). At this time it appears that the Goring family already owned Callowhill Hall and the Dowry Farm. The acquisition of this neighbouring farm would have been a logical progression and a likely ambition of Phelice Goring on behalf of her family.

The next stage in the ownership of Upper Callowhill is unclear. The indenture, dated 1716 which records the sale of John Goring's Kingstone estate by his daughter Barbara and her husband Walter Chetwynd to John Chetwynd, clearly refers to the two farms, i.e. Brough's Farm, and that occupied by Motteram (39). [The name 'Brough' recalls earlier occupants; a Joan Brough, a widow of Callowhill died leaving a will in 1641.]

Based on this evidence, both Callowhill Hall and Upper Callowhill were included in John Chetwynd's purchase, and yet only Callowhill Hall was recorded as being the property of John Chetwynd in the Godson survey, just a few years later. Perhaps John Chetwynd sold Upper Callowhill again before the Godson survey was carried out. All that is known is that towards the end of the eighteenth century the property was in the hands of William Mott. William Mott was the owner in 1800 when a valuation of his Callowhill estate was given as £130 a year (39). At this time Earl Talbot, through his agent was negotiating the purchase of Blythe Bridge Hall Farm and was considering other options, including the possibility of acquiring this farm from Mr. Mott (39).

Edward Shelley was then William Mott's tenant, in addition to being Earl Talbot's tenant at Callowhill Hall.

The 1801 survey reveals that the farm, still owned by Mr. Mott consisted of about 106 acres. William Mott held the prestigious post of deputy registrar of the diocese of Lichfield, and lived in the Cathedral Close, but he also owned an estate at the village of Wall, south of Lichfield. John Mott succeeded his father, William as deputy registrar and also lived in the Cathedral Close. John Mott also owned Upper Callowhill Farm. *'A messuage with 104 acres at Callow Hill, parish of Kingston'* had been part of John Mott's marriage settlement in 1814 (24).

John Elsmore, who died in 1817, had farmed here with his family. He was described as a farmer of Callowhill in his will, dated 1818, but he also the owned a house, malt house and land on Blythe Bridge Bank (pages 95-96) (24). John Elsmore was succeeded at this farm at Callowhill by his son Robert Elsmore. Robert Elsmore and his wife Sarah had a number of children who were baptised at Kingstone, but the family had moved away to Hill Ridware by 1830. Robert Elsmore's brother, John Elsmore farmed at the neighbouring Dowry Farm at a similar period (page 79-81).

In 1838, the farm owned by John Mott, was described as comprising 102 acres with Thomas Spooner, senior as tenant (24). Thomas Spooner, senior died in 1858 and his son, Thomas Spooner, junior, who had been a shopkeeper, and a farmer of a few acres in the centre of Kingstone (page 43-44), had succeeded his father as tenant by 1861. Thomas Spooner was still at Callowhill in 1871, but died in 1879 and by 1881 Eli Herbert Deakin had taken over at the farm (4).

In 1888, (presumably following the death of John Mott's son, William Mott in 1887) the farm left the ownership of the Mott family. Ralph Heath had been tenant at the time. The farm was sold to Benjamin Charles Bloor of Cage Hill Farm, Chartley for £3000 (39).

Joseph Leadbetter, an agricultural labourer had taken 'Callow hill Farm', by 1891, and he was still living at 'Lower Callow Hill' in 1901, then as a farm bailiff (4). In 1911, Joseph Shaw, an agricultural labourer, lived with his family at this farm, the house then being described as having ten rooms (4).

Charles Bloor, son of James Bloor of Gratwich (in turn a son of Benjamin Charles Bloor), was farming here in 1928 (29).

# BLYTHE BRIDGE TO WANFIELD [Zone F]

Blythe Bridge, or 'The Blythe', to give it its modern name, remains a tiny settlement at the crossing over the River Blithe (a name suggesting a gently-flowing river) at the western limits of Kingstone parish. The Godson map shows the existence at the time of two important properties i.e. 'Windfield' (Wanfield) Hall and Blythe Bridge Hall, with the mill and smithy at Blythe Bridge also shown. This map also reveals that another large area of common land then existed at top of Blythe Bridge Bank, and alongside the road going past Wanfield Hall towards to Leese Hill (39).

This common land had been encroached by 1838 with several house or cottages built upon it (24). In 1914 the ford at Blythe Bridge was replaced by a road bridge; the only other means of crossing the river before that date having been by a wooden foot bridge (2).

This zone still has very little housing today, mostly of houses built by the rural district council in the 1950s.

## BLYTHE BRIDGE HALL FARM {445} {19}

The present farmhouse was built in the mid - 1920s, following the demolition of the old house, an event witnessed by my father.

It seems that the Hall, an ancient structure of brick, half-timberwork and stone was in a dilapidated state (Figs. 39 - 41). Its loss is regrettable, partly because Sir Symon Degge had owned the property, and also died there aged 90 in 1702/3 (9)(33). In an account written in 1870 by a visitor to Kingstone, Blythe Bridge Hall was reported as having been a good example of timbered architecture (page 117)(2). Richard Tooth may have lived and farmed at the Hall in the middle of the seventeenth century, and as a tenant of Symon Degge (page 18-19).

Ellen Beard, a widow, in her will dated 1724 is recorded as being of Blythe Bridge Hall (24). She had married Thomas Beard of Ipstones in 1689. Their relationship with other members of the Beard family of Kingstone has not been established.

In the late eighteenth century Thomas Wilson and his wife Margaret lived at Blythe Bridge Hall. Thomas Wilson married Margaret Woolley at Bramshall in 1735, although they both appear to have been from Marston Montgomery in Derbyshire. Their gravestone in Kingstone churchyard has the thoughtful epitaph:

*'Praises on Tombs are Trifles vainly spent, A Man's good Name is his own Monument.'* (13).

Thomas Wilson would have been a tenant as this property was owned by the descendants of Sir Symon Degge, cousins of his great

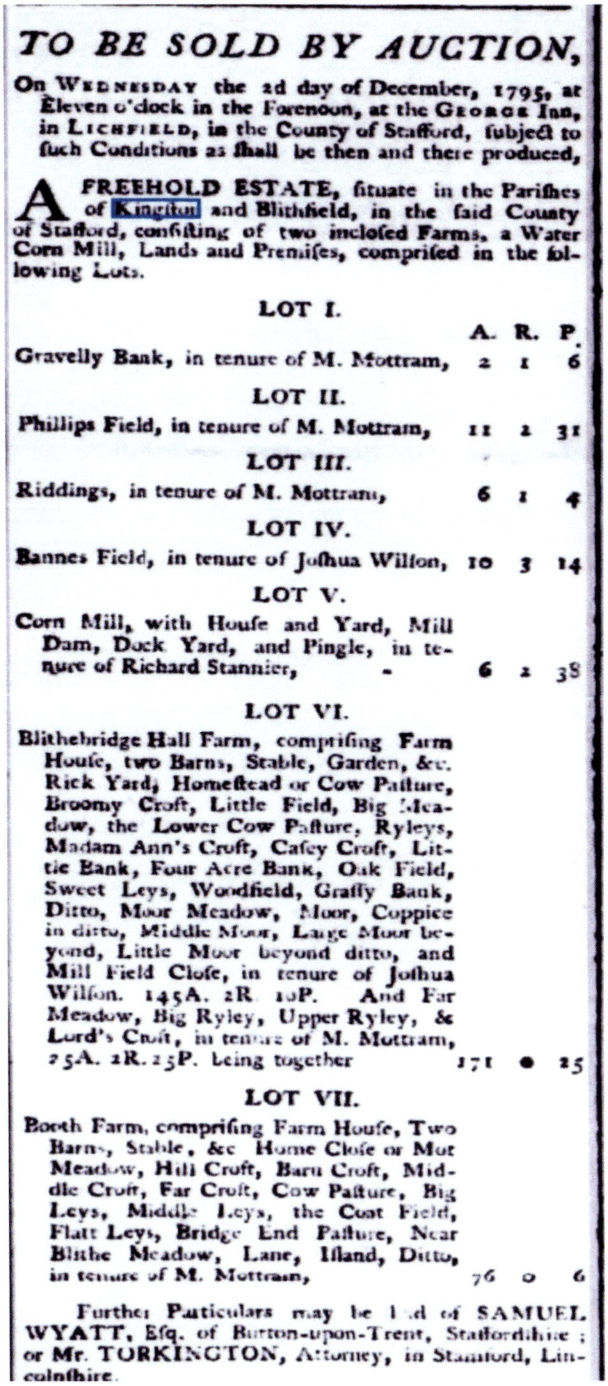

Plate 21 **Sale of Blythe Bridge estate**
Staffordshire Advertiser Saturday 28 November 1795
Image © THE BRITISH LIBRARY BOARD. ALL RIGHTS RESERVED
http://www.britishnewspaperarchive.co.uk/viewer
bl/0000215/17951128/016/0001

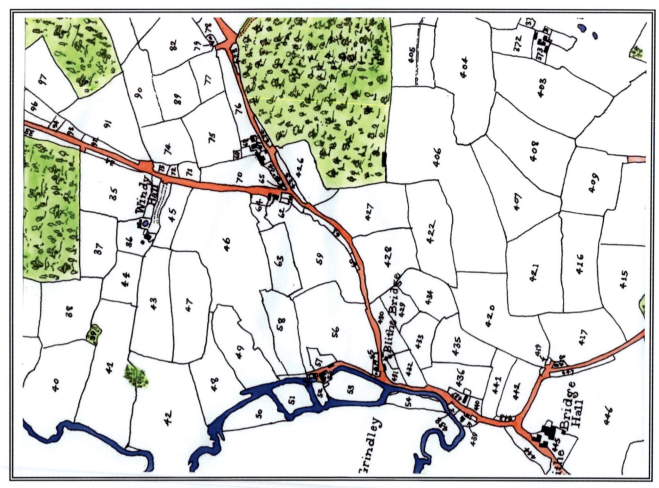

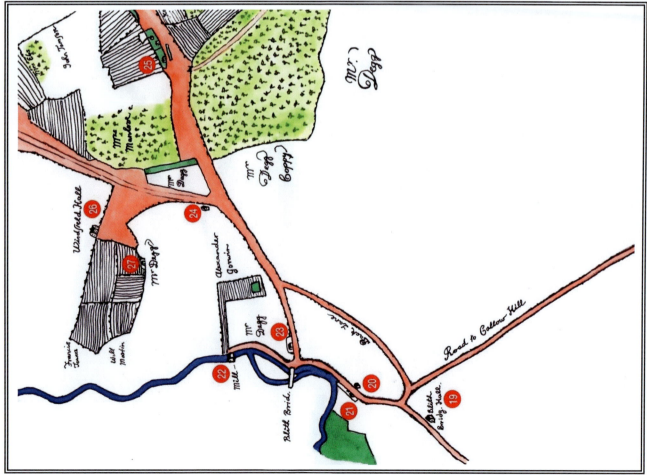

Fig. 37 <u>Kingstone map</u> 1717-20 (below) & Fig. 38 <u>Kingstone map</u> 1837 (above) **Zone F**

grandson, also called Simon Degge who died in about 1765. On the death of the last of these cousins (four sisters without children), in 1795, the Blythe Bridge estate was put up for sale, the tenant then being Joshua Wilson, one of the sons of Thomas and Margaret Wilson (Plate 21, page 87). Blythe Bridge Hall Farm was described (with field names given, including *Casey Croft*) as comprising 171 acres. Also included in the sale were Blythe Bridge Mill, and a farm at Booth (about a ½ mile to the south) with a farm house and 76 acres of land. During 1795 -1796, in letters to Thomas Mills, agent for the Talbots, Colonel Talbot expressed regret that they had failed to purchase Blythe Bridge Farm (39), but in 1800 the Earl purchased the property from the then owner, Mr. Locker. It appears that the farm was valued at £4160 in 1795 and £4190 was then bid on Earl Talbot's behalf. By 1800, in a note to the Earl it was written *that 'times have very materially advanced since the sale of the Blythe Bridge estate in 1795'*. The agreed purchase price in 1800 appears to have been £7500 plus the valuation of timber and 'compost' (manure?). By the time of the 1801 survey the farm was in the ownership of Earl Talbot, and William Johnson was his tenant. In 1838 the property was described as a farm of 160 acres, and Joseph Johnson, William Johnson's son was Earl Talbot's tenant (23). Joseph Johnson had retired by 1871 and his son, also called Joseph Johnson was the tenant of the farm, by now of 180 acres, and he was still farming here in 1876 (4)(29).

Charles Mellor had taken over at Blythe Bridge Hall by 1881 (4). He died in 1895 and his widow, Cicely then ran the farm, being still here in 1901(4). By 1912 Charles Mellor (son of Charles and Cicely) farmed at the Hall (29).

Fig. 39 **Blythe Bridge Hall Farm** ( demolished 1925/6)

Fig. 40 **Blythe Bridge Hall Farm** ( demolished 1925/6)

Fig. 41 **Blythe Bridge Hall Farm** ( demolished 1925/6)

The property was certainly large and rambling, described in the 1911 census as having 14 rooms - one of the largest houses in the parish (4). I was able to complete the above drawings (Figs. 39-41) using photographs loaned to me in the 1980s by Mr. Mellor, whose family owned and still lived at the Hall.

In 1838 (as earlier, in 1801) a house {418} with about ¾ acre of land existed at a sharp bend on Hollyhurst lane, just east of Blythe Bridge Hall, the tenant being Thomas Wood, a sawyer (and grandfather of Thomas Wood, later the sexton at Kingstone Church) (24). Thomas Wood, a widower, was living with his family at Blythe Bridge, and probably still occupied this property in 1841, but by 1851 they had moved into the Poor House (page 58) in Kingstone. This house or cottage (which had also existed at the time of the 1801 survey) appears to have been demolished by 1882 as it is not marked on the Ordnance Survey map of that date.

**THE BLYTHE INN** {437} {20} The early eighteenth century Godson map shows a house on this site (39). The 1801 survey also showed a house here in Blythe Bridge, and described a property with about 15 acres of land which was said to be in the ownership of George Atkins. William Atkins, a gentleman of Newton, in Blithfield parish died in 1804, at the advanced age of 94, and in his will he bequeathed his messuage in Kingston parish, called 'Blithebridge Farm' to his son, George Atkins (24). This property was evidently passed down to William Atkins, great-grandson of the above William Atkins. In 1838 this was a small holding of 15 acres, owned by William Atkins, but occupied by James Wright, a cordwainer (shoe maker) who was still living here in 1851 (24)(4). William Atkins, a farmer, was born at Newton in 1810, but lived for most of his life at Rocester, dying there in 1881.
William Woolliscroft (with his wife Jane and son Alfred) was living here by 1861, described as a publican and farmer with 15 acres of land. In 1871 and 1881, William's widow, Jane Woolliscroft was the beer house keeper (4). In the 1891 census this property was called 'The Blythe Inn' for the first time, run by 'Arthur' Woolliscroft, clearly an error as Alfred Woolliscroft (son of William and Jane) was recorded as beer retailer in 1896 (28).
In 1901 Richard William Brandrick was publican at the Blythe Inn. He had married Alice Woolliscroft who had been living with her grandmother, Jane in 1881, and as housekeeper to her uncle in 1891. Herbert Alfred Plant, who managed the Black Horse in Rugeley (in 1901), had taken over as the publican (and farmer) by 1911 (4).

Throughout this period this property had also been a small farm. Herbert Plant remained at the Blythe Inn until he retired in 1938 (2). The Blythe Inn, in Booth lane, survives today as a popular country public house. The land in 1838 included a piece of ground known as *Kissey Croft* or *Cosy Croft* which is referred to as a source of income for the Whitehall Charity, the oldest of the Kingstone church charities (pages 133-134) (24).

Opposite the Blythe Inn, on a small strip of land near the River Blithe, the Godson map appears to show another house or cottage {21} which was also marked on the 1801 survey map. A house on this site {439}, with almost an acre of land was also present in 1838, then owned by Earl Talbot, with Mary Harper as tenant (24). Joseph Sherratt, the tailor (who later lived at Church View), then unmarried, was lodging here with Mary Harper at Blythe Bridge in 1841 (4). [He married Ellen Deakin, daughter of Francis Deakin, pig dealer of The Mosses, at Kingstone in 1843.]

In 1891, Henry Johnson, a platelayer lived with his wife and daughter at 'Blythe Bridge Cottage', but in 1899, at Uttoxeter, he was charged with deserting his four children who had been received into 'the union' (workhouse) at the cost of £12 for their maintenance. Johnson's wife was said to be in the asylum. Johnson was sent to gaol for one month with hard labour (2).

A house called 'The Cottage' still exists on this site today.

**BLYTHE BRIDGE MILL** {52} {22} This water mill on the River Blithe is another interesting ancient property of the 17th. century, or earlier. The mill house is constructed using half-timberwork, the timbers painted black, and with the brick infill painted white (Fig. 42).

Henry Crompton (page 10) appears to have held the lease of this mill in 1593 when Thomas Gresley sold the Manor of Kingstone, with Edward Cartwright (page 129) being Sir Walter Aston's tenant in 1625 (39). Richard Stonier, described as a miller at the time of his first marriage, at Kingstone in 1755, was presumably then resident here, being the miller at Blythe Bridge Mill at his death in 1809 (15). In 1795, Blythe Bridge Mill was up for sale, along with Blythe Bridge Hall as part of the former estate of the Degge family. It was described as a corn mill with house and yard, mill dam, dock yard and pingle, in the tenure of Richard 'Stannier' (Stonier), with about 6½ acres of land (page 73) (2). In the 1801 survey, Blythe Bridge Mill, with about 8 acres of land appears to be in the ownership of Richard 'Stanier'. Richard Stonier's name is however scored out and replaced with that of William Clarke, a much later owner or tenant. Richard Stonier's will, dated 1810 indicates that he then owned Blythe Bridge Mill, although it was mortgaged (24).

William Stonier, a son of Richard, succeeded his father as miller; he was recorded as corn miller here in

Fig. 42 **Blythe Bridge Mill**

1818 (page 20) (29). However, he became bankrupt at some point, the London Gazette, for April 30th 1822 recording his discharge from Stafford Gaol. William Stonier (the father of Richard Stonier, Kingstone's schoolmaster) later lived on Blythe bridge Bank (page 96), being then described as a shopkeeper in 1834 (29). The present mill building, constructed in red brick, and in a gothic style, (Fig. 42, page 91 to the left of the mill house) bears the date 1823. This date, together with the coat of arms of Earl Ferrers appears on the front of the building, indicating that Earl Ferrers then owned the mill, which he had also rebuilt following William Stonier's bankruptcy. A newspaper advertisement dated 1823 confirms this stating that there was a newly erected mill at Blythe Bridge which was available immediately for letting (2).

In 1838 the mill was owned by Duchess Sforza and there were 10 acres of land (24). The somewhat exotic name of the owner is intriguing. In fact her full name was Caroline, Duchess Sforza Cesarini [1818-1897].
Born in Brewood, Staffordshire, Caroline Shirley, was the only child of Viscount Tamworth, heir to Robert Shirley 7th. Earl Ferrers. Her father died when she was five, and when Earl Ferrers, her grandfather later died, in 1827, he left her a considerable amount of property. Earl Ferrers' primary seat was at Staunton Harold, and his estates were mostly in Leicestershire, but his secondary seat was in Staffordshire, at Chartley (hall and castle) .
In his will the 7th. Earl Ferrers referred to estates in Staffordshire, which *'I have purchased at various times'* - including those in Hixon, Weston on Trent, Grindley, Fradswell and also Kingstone (26). The Kingstone property bought by Robert Shirley, 7th. Earl Ferrers evidently included Blythe Bridge Mill, which was then amongst the property left to Caroline Shirley by her grandfather. Although Caroline Shirley was wealthy in her own right she married, in 1837, a wealthy Italian aristocrat, Duke Lorenzo Sforza Cesarini. They seemed to have lived most of their lives in Italy (35). Later documents, dated to 1865 refer to a purchase of lands in Staffordshire, including at Kingstone (with the specific mention of freehold estate at Blithe Bridge, Kingstone) from the trustees of the Duke & Duchess of Sforza Cesarini (22).

In 1838 William Clarke, (the son of a prosperous baker and confectioner of Uttoxeter) was the miller, being the tenant of Duchess Sforza. He was still at the mill in 1851 (24) (4).

George Webb (son of Richard Webb, miller of Haywood Mill, Great Haywood) was the miller here in 1861 (4). In 1840 he had married Elizabeth Stonier, daughter of the former miller, William Stonier, but now had a second wife, Ann. Blythe Bridge Mill, with ten acres of land, let to Mr. Webb was advertised for sale in 1864 (2). Later occupants included Joseph Fisher in 1870 (who went on to became miller at Burndhurst Mill, further up the River Blithe at Lower Loxley), Thomas Goodall (apprentice miller to George Webb in 1861), who was miller in 1876, and John Moss in 1881 (4) (29). Samuel Jackson, a miller's son from Dilhorne had become the miller at Blythe Bridge in 1891 and was still living and working here in 1912 (4)(28).

Ernest Fisher (son of Joseph Fisher) was tenant at the mill between 1919 and 1925, but by 1928 William Raynes was listed as the miller at Blythe Bridge (29).

**BLYTHE BRIDGE SMITHY** A house on this site was indicated in the Godson survey, with George Smith as John Chetwynd's tenant. It is not known if he was a blacksmith, and all he had was a small garden {23}.
[There is evidence from the wills of Arthur 'Cowappe' (Cope), dated 1598 (21), Humphrey Gaunt (page 19), dated 1667, and John Martin, dated 1700, indicating that all of these men were all blacksmiths in Kingstone parish, but where they lived and worked is unknown.]
The house which stands today (Fig. 43, page 93) is where several generations of the Wilson family worked as blacksmiths. The first Wilson blacksmith appears to have been Thomas Wilson [1705 - 1776]. Confusingly, there were two Thomas Wilsons, each with a wife called Margaret whose children were baptised at Kingstone during the 1730s and 1740s. Thomas Wilson, the blacksmith originated from Alton, Staffs. and had married Margaret Wakefield at Uttoxeter in 1726. The other Wilson family farmed at Blythe Bridge Hall (page 87).
In the 1801 survey Thomas Wilson [1744 - 1832], (son of the above Thomas Wilson) was the blacksmith, and tenant of the property (with about three acres of land), then owned by Earl Talbot.
The 1818 Staffordshire Directory records Thomas Wilson as a blacksmith in Kingstone parish, and also a Thomas Wilson (thought to be his son) who was a blacksmith, farrier and farmer in Gratwich, (page 20) (29). Thomas Wilson, senior, blacksmith of Blythe Bridge died in 1832 at the age of 87, and in his will he left his tenant right of the house, blacksmith's shop and smithy, working tools etc. to his son, Thomas (24).

In 1838 the house and smithy {55} and almost 2 acres of land were owned by Earl Talbot, with Thomas Wilson as tenant (24). In 1851 the same Thomas Wilson [1778 - 1852] was the blacksmith at Blythe Bridge (4). This Thomas Wilson's eldest son, Thomas, was also a blacksmith, but he moved to Gratwich, being recorded as resident in 1841 and still there in 1881 (4). [His wife Harriet was the daughter of John Green, the butcher who lived (page 94) in the house opposite the Blythe Bridge smithy.]

Thomas Wilson, blacksmith at Blythe Bridge was succeeded by his second son Edward, recorded as blacksmith here in 1861 and 1871. By 1881 Edward Wilson had moved to Mount Pleasant in Potts' Lane, Kingstone where he had a small farm, his son William then being the blacksmith at the smithy in Blythe Bridge, but also a farmer with 19 acres of land. In 1901, William Wilson's wife, Salome was at the smithy, with a servant, William Hall as blacksmith, while her husband William Wilson was farming at Lower Booth, which is where they were both living in 1911, Charles Wilson having taken over at Blythe Bridge smithy (4). Interestingly, Charles Wilson was not the son of William Wilson, but the son of his cousin, Thomas Wilson. This Thomas Wilson was blacksmith at Gratwich, while his brother, John Wilson lived and worked at the Loxley Green smithy (now Forge Cottage) in Holly Lane, near Holly Hays Farm. These two brothers were sons of the Thomas Wilson (elder brother of Edward Wilson) who had been the blacksmith for many years at Gratwich.

Charles Wilson was still the occupant at Blythe Bridge when the Shrewsbury Estate sold the house (of 4 bedrooms) and blacksmith's shop (for £170) in 1918 (39). There was also a shed with tying for 4 cows, a piggery and a hooping yard. The present range of buildings (Fig. 43) still bears traces of the former smithy. In its final phase the area below the brick arch was open to the street and was able accommodate up to three horses for shoeing, the forge being next door.

In 1928 William (Bill) Roberts was the blacksmith. He was also the last blacksmith at this smithy, working here until the 1930s (29). [Note: There was no smithy in Kingstone itself, the nearest smithy

Fig. 43 **Blythe Bridge smithy**

other than that at Blythe Bridge being at Loxley Green.]

My father recalled that in later years Bill Roberts became a travelling smith. His 'bullnose' Morris car pulled a trailer with an anvil in the back, and with ready-made shoes to fit the horses.

In the mid- twentieth century there was a shop and post office here, having been transferred from the Old School building (page 46) in the centre of Kingstone. Mrs. Mould and her sister Harriet Fradley, daughters of Sarah Fradley who had earlier kept the post office and shop in Kingstone, were here during the 1950s.

**BLYTHE BRIDGE BUTCHER'S SHOP/ WHEELWRIGHT'S HOUSE {431}** A house existed on this site (opposite the smithy) in 1801. Formerly owned by William Martin it was conveyed to Edward Shelley of Callowhill Hall. He wrote his will in 1804 leaving his Blythe Bridge estate to his wife Ann for life, then divided between his son John Shelley, and daughter Anne Bakewell. The property, with butcher's shop, other buildings and about 4 acres of land was conveyed (following some legal wrangling) to John Shelley in 1827, the tenant then being John Green (39). The butcher, John Green was also the tenant in 1838 when the owners were the executors of John Fox (24), John Shelley (page 84) having died in 1830.
John Fox, a currier of Uttoxeter, aged nearly sixty, and a wealthy bachelor, made his will in January 1835, with various relatives and friends being beneficiaries, including his 'friend', the much-younger Ann Bakewell who he married about a month later. Interestingly, Ann Bakewell was the daughter of above Ann Bakewell (page 105). John Fox died in May 1835, of apoplexy, and his widow, Ann gave birth to a son in October 1835! Redfern records that the subsequent protracted litigation was followed with great interest in Uttoxeter (33)! This small 4 acre farm (still in the occupation of John Green) was advertised for sale by auction in 1860 as part of the property of W. J. Fox Esq. (William John Fox, gent. of Uttoxeter, the son of John Fox)(2).
By 1870 Charles Green, also a butcher had succeeded his father John Green, and was still here in 1881 (29)(4). Thomas Edward Brandrick had set up a wheelwright's business here by 1896, being still present in 1928 (29). Thomas Brandrick's business was of course conveniently placed. Wheels he made could be fitted with iron hoops just across the road at the blacksmith's hooping yard. Thomas Brandrick, (the brother of Richard Brandrick, publican at the Blythe Inn ,page 90) also worked as a coffin maker and undertaker. In 1919, this small holding, in the occupation of Mr. Brandrick was offered for sale. It was still a property of just 4 acres (2). After the Great War, as my father recalled, the felling of trees for pit props took place in parts of Kingstone Wood and a light railway brought wood down the valley to the woodyard here by the wheelwright's house. Kingstone Wood had formerly extended right up to the roadside on Blythe Bridge Bank between Kingstone and Blythe Bridge. Trees were also then felled in woods at Woodcock Heath.

**BLYTHE BRIDGE BANK** In the eighteenth century there were large areas of common land associated with the road between Kingstone and Blythe Bridge. Some of the properties in this area were therefore built later, on encroached strips of land, the common having been enclosed by 1801 (39).
At the junction with the road leading to Wanfield Hall and Leese Hill there was only one house {24} at the time of the Godson map (39). When Earl Talbot was negotiating the purchase of Blythe Bridge Hall Farm in 1800 he was also considering the possible option of purchasing the neighbouring small, 23 acre estate belonging to Peter Heathcote of Walsall. This estate, which lay on both sides of road leading up the bank from Blythe Bridge was valued and assessed. Thomas Wilson (of Blythe Bridge) was said to be a good tenant, and there was *'an indifferent house and a tolerable good barn'*. The Earl's agent otherwise referred to a *'not so very desirable house, is almost worn out'*. Another account in 1803 mentioned a stable and cowhouse. It was revealed that in 1800 the whole property had been valued at £800 plus £100 for timber, and that £1000 had been asked for. Evidently Earl Talbot decided not to buy Mr. Heathcote's estate (39).
Thomas Wilson, senior, the blacksmith at Blythe Bridge, in his will dated 1833, left the lease and tenant right of the farm he held from Mr. Heathcote 'at *Gravelly Bank*' to his son Richard (24). Richard Wilson died in 1838, and in the same year, this house {64}, with about 23 acres of farmland, owned by Peter Heathcote (24), had Edward Wilson as the tenant. Edward Wilson was Richard's brother, and being a blacksmith he is likely to have assisted their other brother, Thomas Wilson, who had taken over from his father at the smithy at Blythe Bridge. Thomas Wilson, junior probably lived at the property at an earlier period. He and his wife, Sarah were described as living on Blythe Bridge Bank when their children Mary, and William, were baptised at Kingstone in 1815 and 1822 respectively. William Wilson, another relative, aged about 60, was living here in 1841.
This farm, a 24 acre estate, then with Edward Wilson as a tenant, and consisting of a cottage, barn, stables, cow-shed, orchard and gardens was advertised for sale at the White Hart, Uttoxeter in 1847 (2).
It was described, effusively, as being - *'situated on the banks and is surrounded by the romantic scenery of the River Blyth, and adjoins Blyth Bridge Mill …. is bounded by the lands and woods of Earl Talbot, Earl Ferrers …. It abounds with game, its surface is extremely diversified, commanding views over the surrounding country,*

*and is very eligible for the erection of a good residence, or as an investment'.*
Whether or not Mr. Heathcote was then the vendor was not revealed.
William Bridgwood, a retired farmer may have been living in this property in 1861 (4).
The house is not recorded on the Ordnance Survey map of 1882; it must have been demolished by that date. The site does offer a fine view today, but there is no trace of this house or buildings.

Three other houses had been built on a roadside strip of encroachment on the opposite roadside corner by 1838. Five houses exist there today, on much the same footprint. However, in 1801 there was only one cottage{67}, together with a building later identified as a malt-house (39). John Elsmore, junior was recorded as being a maltster, living on Blythe Bridge Bank in 1834, and in 1838, still described as a maltster, he occupied this house with a malt-house and garden, totalling ½ acre {67} (24)(29). The property was owned by John Elsmore i.e. himself, or otherwise his father of Dowry Farm (pages 79-80).
The 1801 survey records James Bakewell (page 104) as owning houses and land, including a croft of about 1½ acres with three houses and malt-house. The fact that in 1801 the property {67} stood by itself suggests that James Bakewell's malt-house was elsewhere, probably in the centre of Kingstone - on the site where The Villa and some other cottages then existed (page 43) (39).
John Elsmore, a farmer of Upper Callowhill (page 71), who was grandfather of the above John Elsmore, in his two wills, dated 1811 and 1816 revealed that he then owned the house, malt-house and land at Blythe Bridge Bank, and that it was occupied (in 1811) by John Lymer, (who was also his son-in-law having married his daughter, Ellen Elsmore) (24). John Lymer, a maltster, presumably ran the malting business at this time. John and Ellen Lymer were bequeathed the Blithe Bridge Bank premises in 1811, but John Elsmore changed his mind, leaving it, in his 1816 will, to his sons John, Thomas and Robert. John Elsmore made provision for his wife Ann through a rent charge on the property, but also bequeathed her *'the dwelling that is made out of the barn at Blithe Bridge Bank'.*
William Titley, a maltster and miller, appears to have occupied the Elsmore property in 1861.
He had been living, working, and assisting the miller at Blythe Bridge Mill in 1841 and 1851, and it is likely that he was still working there, as well managing a malting business at Blythe Bridge Bank. William Titley had moved to Uttoxeter by 1871, by which time John Elsmore, then described as a farmer with six acres of land, had returned (4).
John Elsmore still occupied the property in 1881, then called *'Gravelly Bank'* (the name of the field behind the house), and was succeeded by his son, also John Elsmore, a farmer and labourer who lived here until at least 1901, and probably until his death in 1908. This must certainly have been the property on Blythe Bridge Bank advertised for sale in 1909 which consisted of a house with outbuildings, including a *'large well-built malt-house'*, together with a two acre close of land.
E. J. Elsmore (Ernest Elsmore), son of the deceased John Elsmore was recorded as the occupier (2). The same property, although reduced to ¾ acre was advertised for sale again, in 1912 when it was occupied by Richard Willan at £9 a year (2).
The former Elsmore house or cottage {67} survives as '<u>The Malthouse</u>', although it is much enlarged. The long, single-storey house next door, known as '<u>Holly Trees</u>' was (until 1975) a building (or two linked buildings) which formed part of 'Malt House Farm'. Before being converted into a residence (in the 1960s), and separated from the house (which became The Malthouse), the building was used as a butchery. In reality, <u>this</u> building was the true malt-house where malt was produced for making beer. Most people used to drink beer, and in large quantity, it being safer than just water, and many villages had a malt-house in the 18th, and into the 19th century. Such buildings were typically long, low, narrow buildings no more that two storeys high, and with a large floor area over which the grain was spread while it germinated. Barley and malt could to be stored at opposite ends of the building.

In 1838 Earl Talbot owned two small cottages {66} and {68}, one on each side of John Elsmore's property, each with about 3 acres of encroached land. John Lymer was the tenant in one of these cottages {68}, in 1838. He and his wife Ellen, both elderly, were still living in their house in 1841, but by 1851 John Lymer was dead and his wife, Ellen ('a former maltster's wife') was householder. Their son, Charles

Lymer was here in 1861, and in 1871, when he was described as a farmer of three acres of land. David Bentley, a flour miller was also living at Blythe Bridge Bank in 1861 in a house next to Charles Lymer (on the Kingstone side). Where there had been one house {68} in 1838, there was now a pair of semi-detached cottages. John Pountain, an agricultural labourer and Eli Fradley, a foreman platelayer were living in the pair of cottages in 1901. Mary Webster had replaced John Pountain as tenant in 1903, and Joseph Leadbetter lived in one of these cottages between 1905 and 1907.

The two cottages were sold by the Shrewsbury Estate in 1918, but as one joint lot, with about 3½ acres (39). Eli Fradley and Thomas Beard were the tenants, and Thomas Beard bought the two four-roomed cottages and land for £350. Thomas Beard (son of Charles Beard of Mosses Farm), a general estate labourer, was here by 1911. Eli Fradley, who had lived in Kingstone all his life was listed as a foreman railway platelayer in the 1901 census (4). He is recorded as having worked on the railway for 54 years; he also (in the 1860s) cut the first sod of the Uttoxeter to Stafford railway, at the Lower Loxley tunnel (page 21)(2). By 1911 Eli Fradley had retired and was farming on a small scale at Blythe Bridge Bank (4). The two cottages still existed in the 1970s, but they have since been replaced by two detached houses.

Anne Bentley was the Earl's tenant in the other cottage {66}, nearest the junction with the road to Leese Hill. In 1844, probably the same Anne Bentley was sentenced to six months in prison for stealing a silver watch from Thomas Johnson of Kingstone (2). Henry Wood, an agricultural labourer was householder at Anne Bentley's cottage in 1841 and 1851, and Thomas Titley, an aged farm labourer was there in 1861(4). By 1871, Dorothy Wood and Jane Capewell (sisters of the above Henry) were living in this cottage. In 1881, Thomas Wood (a son of Jane Capewell), who was an agricultural labourer lived here alone, and he was still here in 1891, his home then being called Yew Tree Cottage (also its present name)(4). He seems to have continued to live here as tenant up until 1918 when this 'cottage holding', with two acres of land was sold (for £230) at the Shrewsbury Estate sale (38). Thomas Wood was Kingstone's bell-ringer, sexton etc. (page 106), and it seems likely that this was when he then moved in to the centre of Kingstone at 'The Barracks'.

Further along Blythe Bridge Bank, towards Kingstone, and opposite the footpath leading into the woodland called *Abbot's Wood*, John Chetwynd owned a house {25}, occupied by William 'Armes' (Orme), which at the time of Godson, existed on a narrow strip of land by the roadside. John Chetwynd also then owned another house, with Thomas Bentley as his tenant, on a similar roadside plot on the side nearest Kingstone.

At the time of the 1801 survey there appeared to be just one house at this point.

In 1838 a house {79} on or near this site with about one acre, owned by Earl Talbot, was occupied by William Stonier (24). In 1841 John Phillips, an agricultural labourer was the householder, living here with his wife Ellen and father-in-law, William Stonier (the former miller at Blythe Bridge Mill, still described as a miller) (24)(4). William Stonier, described as a grocer was again head of the family in 1851, but he died in 1854 and by 1861, John Phillips, a grocer and labourer was again 'head', and still here in 1871 (4). Thomas Phillips, John's son, a general labourer was living here with his family by 1883 (39). This house was occupied by Albert Fradley when it was sold at the Shrewsbury Estate sale (for £115) in 1918 (39). Today is called 'Woodside'.

**WANFIELD HALL (WINDY HALL or WINFIELD HALL) {36} {26}** This old house is a large and impressive 'gentleman's residence' (Fig. 44, page 97), once the family seat of Rowland Manlove.

In his History of Uttoxeter, Francis Redfern makes reference to Wanfield Hall, in Kingstone (33):

*'Wanfields belonged to the Manloves, and was bought by Rowland Manlove by the wealth he obtained in the naval service under Sir Walter Leveson; it having previously belonged to Sir Walter Chetwynd. It was enjoyed by his son Alexander in 1660. Dr. Wilks, who made extensive collections towards a History of Staffordshire, in 1725, married Rachel Manlove, of Leese Hill. Wanfield subsequently came to the family of Lawrance, and till 1871, the time of his death, was owned by Humphrey Lawrance, Esq., whose only issue is a daughter married to William Bathew, of Blunt's Hall, and who has taken the name of Lawrance.'*

Redfern does not tell us how Wanfield Hall was ultimately inherited by the Bathews. In fact this was to a large extent by descent through the female line. Members of the Bathew family, still live in Kingstone at Leese Hill, an ancient manor in itself, in Kingstone parish (page 67-69). Up to the middle of the 20th. century the family also owned Wanfield Hall.

The Manlove family link with Kingstone began with Rowland Manlove [? - 1653] who apparently came from Wem in Shropshire, but as indicated above, is said to haved served in the Navy under Walter Leveson.

Sir Walter Leveson was a Shropshire and Staffordshire landowner. He had a lucrative business in North Sea trade but become involved in piracy for which he was imprisoned and heavily fined. In his later life he was accused of sorcery and attempted poisoning, and he may have been deranged. He died in prison leaving his son Richard with large debts (30). It would appear that Redfern was mis-informed, and that Rowland Manlove is more likely to have served under Walter's son, Sir <u>Richard</u> Leveson [1570 - 1605].

Richard Leveson was a volunteer aboard the Ark Royal at the time of the Spanish Armada in 1588.

The Lord High Admiral, 'Howard of Effingham' was his father-in-law, and this can only have helped his further advancement. Richard Leveson went on to have a distinguished and career in the Navy, although whatever fortune he may have obtained through the capture of Spanish and Portuguese ships seems to been insufficient to meet his father's debts. Richard Leveson was appointed Vice-Admiral of England in 1604, but died in the following year aged just 35 (30).

[The wealth of the Leveson family was built on wool, Richard Leveson's grandfather having been Sir James Leveson of Wolverhampton, a Merchant of the Staple.

Fig. 44 **Wanfield Hall**

James Leveson purchased estates at Trentham and Perton, Staffordshire and Lilleshall, Shropshire. The heirs and successors of the Levesons were the Leveson-Gore family, Dukes of Sutherland who retained the Trentham and Lilleshall estates into the 20th. century.]

Assuming that Rowland Manlove obtained wealth by serving in the Navy under Sir Richard Leveson, why should he have used it to purchase property in Kingstone? Had he perhaps heard that Sir Walter Chetwynd wished to realise some of his assets? It was then 'a small world', and Sir Walter Chetwynd's neighbour was Sir Walter Aston of Tixall, who then owned Kingstone. Sir Walter Aston was related, not only to the Gresleys at Drakelow, but also to the Leveson family (page 10).

Evidence survives in a document dated 12th. August 1614, of a sale agreement between Sir Walter Chetwynd and Rowland 'Menlove' (Manlove), gent. of Perton for lands in Kingston and Loxley (36). The present Wanfield Hall presumably dates from around 1614. However, Rowland's Manlove's purchase included an existing messuage, suggesting that a house already occupied the site (36). At the time of the purchase of Wanfield, Rowland Manlove was living at Perton (just west of Wolverhampton), the village which Sir Richard Leveson had owned. Rowland Manlove died in 1653 and his son Alexander inherited the Wanfield property. Alexander Manlove also acquired Leese Hill Manor and when he died in 1688, his son Rowland inherited both properties. Rowland Manlove died in 1714 followed by his wife Mary in 1724. Shortly afterwards the family seemed to have had a tenant. Walter Leigh of Kingstone, in his will dated 1730, was recorded as being of 'Windfield Hall' (24). Wanfield subsequently came to the family of Lawrence (descendants in the female line of the Manloves from Rowland and Mary Manlove's younger daughter, Ellen), and was recorded as belonging to the Lawrence family in the 1801 survey. In 1834 Wanfield Hall was described as the seat of Richard Corbett Lawrence Esq.. His estate also included Leese Hill (29), but the family retained Wanfield Hall, in which they had tenants.

In 1838 'Windy Hall' was a property with about 14 acres, and the tenant was William Fletcher (although William Fletcher, a gentleman of Uttoxeter, had actually died in 1837) (24). In 1851 Josiah Jessop, a landed gentleman (of a family of cabinet makers in Uttoxeter) was living at Wanfield Hall (4)(29).

Joseph Woolliscroft Goodwin, a retired merchant (from a family of potters in Longton) was tenant in 1871 (4). The Bathew family came to Wanfield in 1874 when Lucretia Lawrence married William Bathew. William Bathew was a farmer and cattle dealer on quite a large scale, he would drive as many as 100 cattle by road to the May and November fairs at Uttoxeter. Following Lucretia Bathew's death, William Bathew, continued to live (with his family) at Wanfield Hall, being still here in 1912 (29). William Bathew died in 1921 and in the same year the Wanfield and Leese Hill estate, by direction of trustees, was put up for sale. Wanfield Hall was described as a choice and compact dairy farm and sporting property of about 92 acres, and with a picturesque and substantially built residence. It was sold to Mr. Prince for £5800. (Leese Hill Manor House and the Manor Farm, Leese Hill were also sold as part of the estate (page 64) (2). In 1928 Mr. and Mrs. Samuel Weston Prince, farmers, were living at Wanfield Hall (Mrs. Violet Prince was one of twin daughters of William and Lucretia Bathew).

**[The family history of the Manlove family and their descendants is given separately - see page 99-101.]**

The Godson map shows that there was a large area of common land near to, and to the south of, Wanfield Hall, and what appears to be a house {27} on nearby land owned by John Chetwynd, with William Martin as tenant. William Martin farmed about 18 acres of land here and closer to Blythe Bridge (39). It is clear from his will, dated 1731 that William Martin, a yeoman of Blythe Bridge had land of his own which he bequeathed to his eldest son, and he probably did not live in this property (24).

Mary Jenkinson of Kingstone, the widow of John Jenkinson, a yeoman of Kingstone stated in her will, dated 1728 that she was of was of 'Wanfield Green' (24). Mary Jenkinson may have occupied a house here.

*Wan* in Wanfield suggests an area of gloomy or unattractive / sickly pale appearance, or that the land was poor and unproductive (20). Possibly the location was also found to be an exposed and windy site, hence 'Windfield'?

Fig. 45 <u>**Manlove Coat of Arms**</u>

*Azure, a chevron ermine between three anchors, or.*

Rowland Manlove's naval experience seems to be represented by (golden) anchors set against the background of an azure (blue) 'sea'.

The Coat of Arms of Alexander Manlove 1664 (39). This Coat of Arms was later claimed by The Rev. Thomas Manlove who died in 1802. He was descended from Edward Manlove, second son of Rowland Manlove of Wanfield, and was said to have been the last representative of this family.

# Chapter 5: Some Kingstone Families

This chapter is devoted to some particular inhabitants of Kingstone. The Goring family has already been discussed, but there are some other families and individuals of interest.

## 1. The Manlove family and their descendants

The earliest evidence of a link between the Manlove name, and Kingstone, is of Rowland Manlove and his purchase of Wanfield in 1614, as already described (pages 96-98).
The name Manlove (or Menlove) has a particular association with Wem, Shropshire where it is said that Rowland Manlove originated, the Manloves in Wem being a yeomen family. No detail seems to be known of his service in the Navy. He was living at Perton at the time when his purchase of Wanfield was agreed. Rowland Manlove's second son, Edward and other older children (up to 1620) were baptised at nearby Tettenhall. It therefore seems likely that the family did not move to Kingstone until after that date.
Rowland Manlove I was one of a number of the local gentry (also Henry Goring of Kingstone) summoned to attend the coronation of Charles I in 1625, and to also accept (and pay for! ) a knighthood. He was fined £10 for non-attendance (36). In his will, dated 1656 Rowland Manlove left his Coat of Arms to his son, Alexander (26).
Rowland Manlove's son, Alexander Manlove [c.1614 - 1688], at some point also acquired Leese Hill. His wife Rachel was one of the daughters of William Tixall of Leese Hill (page 68).
Rowland Manlove [c.1644 - 1714] inherited Leese Hill from his father Alexander Manlove. He had two daughters Rachel and Ellen. These were the last of the Manloves of Kingstone.
In his will Rowland Manlove II left to his daughter Rachel *'my Coate of Arms, and bigger Silver Seale that hath my grandfather's Coate of Arms on it'*. To his daughter Ellen he left *'my lesser Silver Seale that hath my grandfather's Coate of Arms on it and also my Great Gold Ring'* (24).
Rachel Manlove [1696 - 1756] married Dr. Richard Wilkes [1690 - 1760] of Willenhall, a physician and antiquarian, but the marriage produced no children.
The younger daughter, Ellen Manlove [1697 - 1781] married John Vernon [1682 - 1756] of Abbots Bromley. John Vernon was an ironmaster, and although he lived in Abbots Bromley his family appear to have roots in Cheshire where they had a role in the early development of iron working there. His brother, William Vernon managed the Warmingham Forge (west of Sandbach) and was related to all three of the ironmaster families of Cotton and Kendall and Hall, who played a leading role in the development of the iron industry in Britain (24). John Vernon may have also been involved in iron working locally. There is evidence that Forge Farm, at Abbots Bromley is the site of a former foundry - one of a group of sites where iron working took place, which together with others on Cannock Chase were set up probably in the late 16th. century by the Paget family. [The Paget family then owned Abbots Bromley, but lived at Beaudesert, their mansion on the edge of Cannock Chase.]
John Vernon, and his son Edward, a physician, are both commemorated in a memorial in Abbots Bromley church . [Edward Vernon [1723 - 1780] also lived in Birmingham. Edward's will is interesting in that he mentions 'Mathew Bolton' as a trustee. This is almost certainly Mathew Boulton who formed a famous partnership with James Watt in the manufacture of steam engines in Birmingham.] (26).
John and Ellen Vernon's daughter, Mary Vernon [1720 - 1780] married Reverend Thomas Hartshorne [1726 - 1779], Rector of the Shropshire village of Badger, at Wolverhampton in 1754.
Ellen Vernon's will, dated 1781, is particularly interesting. Written on a large piece of vellum it details her considerable property, including that in Kingstone, and a 12th. share of the Manor of Uttoxeter (24). Her husband John Vernon, in his will had left her (for her lifetime) the property that she owned on her marriage to him, which was then to be inherited by their eldest son Edward (24). However, she lived to a great age, and outlived not just her husband, but also her son and daughter. She bequeathed most of her property (which presumably included Wanfield Hall and Leese Hill) to Ellen Hartshorne [1754 - 1822], the only child of her daughter Mary.
Ellen Hartshorne married Reverend Thomas Lawrence [ ? - 1812] at Wolverhampton in 1780 and they produced several children, all baptised at Albrighton between 1782 and 1791. Their eldest son was called Manlove Vernon Lawrence; he died without an heir and was succeeded by his brother Richard Corbett Lawrence [1791 - 1845].

[The naming of family members with the incorporation of ancestral surnames seems to have become something of a tradition; a practice which continued into more recent times within the Bathew family. The surname Corbett occurs within the family tree of the Hartshorne family].

Humphrey Downs-Lawrence of Leese Hill, the son and only child of Richard Corbett Lawrence, in turn had just one surviving child, a daughter, Lucretia who was to be the last of the Lawrences.

Lucretia Lawrence married William Bathew [1845 - 1921], (the eldest son of William Bathew of Blount's Hall, south-west of Uttoxeter) at Kingstone Church in 1874. According to Redfern, Blount's Hall had been bequeathed to the father of William Bathew, senior [1815 - 1872] i.e. to John Bathew [c. 1783 - 1856]. The Bathew family had moved to Blount's Hall from the Tutbury area (33).

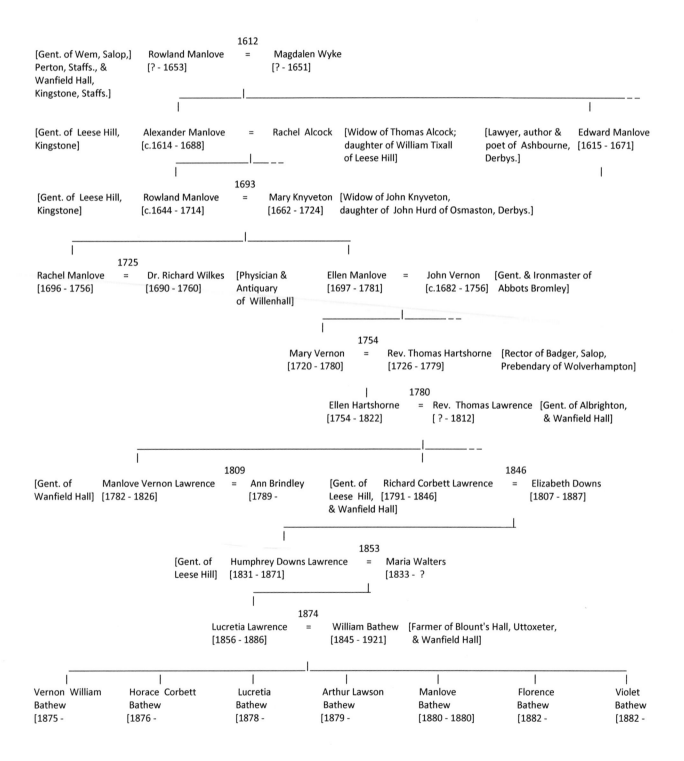

The wedding of Lucretia Lawrence and William Bathew at Kingstone church is said to have been the most spectacular wedding ever held in Kingstone church. Red carpet was laid for the bride on the church path and wines specially imported from France to ensure the right bouquet!
William and Lucretia Bathew had a number of children, but Lucretia sadly died at the age of only 29 in 1886. Interestingly, their children included a son, Manlove Bathew, who unfortunately died as an infant.

An issue of the Kingstone Local Newsletter, in 2008 included a copy of a letter from the Heraldry Society, concerning a pair of funeral hatchments (large paintings on canvas of the coat of arms of deceased gentry) studied by the Society, which the writer suggested once hung in Kingstone old church. The hatchments (said by the writer to be in the collection of a theatrical properties company) commemorated Ellen Lawrence, formerly Ellen Hartshorne, and her son Manlove Vernon Lawrence (as above) who both died in the 1820s. The hatchment illustrated in the painting of the interior of Kingstone old church (Plate 35, page 130), hanging on the wall of the chancel (with the other hatchment probably hanging opposite) is likely to one of these.

## 2. Sir Symon Degge and the Whitehall family

In Kingstone churchyard, just to the west of the two Sherratt family chest tombs (page 35), hidden and protected under the turf, are three memorial stones that were once within a chapel on the north side of the old church. These memorial tablets, presumably placed where they are now when the old church was demolished in 1860, record the burial of someone who was as near to a celebrity as Kingstone has produced - Sir Symon Degge (buried here with some of his family).
The historian Francis Redfern, writing in his history of Uttoxeter, copied the inscriptions on the tablets, which he thought had been later obliterated (33). Some years ago, however, when the tablets were visible, I was able to read the inscriptions clearly, and attest to Redfern's accuracy.
Although the engraver used Roman numerals in a somewhat curious way, it was possible to read Symon Degge's date of birth, recorded as 5th. January 1612, and that of his death as 10th. February 1702.
[Note: At this period the year began on 25th. March. This means that, in modern terms Symon Degge's date of birth was 5th. January 1613, and that of his death was 10th. February 1703!]
Symon Degge's birth date (the same date as on the tablet) and baptismal date are recorded in the Uttoxeter parish register. He was the second son of Thomas and Dorothy Degge. The Degge family had ancient links with Stramshall (then in Uttoxeter parish), and the nearby place, Deggs Leasow probably indicates their long association with the locality.
Symon Degge is generally considered to have lived to the age of 92, rather than 90 as his memorial suggests. Unfortunately the Kingstone burial register for this period has been lost and cannot be used to confirm the true year of his death as 1702, rather than 1704. Symon Degge's own son (or grandson?) had recorded (erroneously) that his father had died in his 92nd. year, which means, of course, he would have been 91!
Redfern gave some detail of the life of Symon Degge, who trained as a lawyer and became an eminent barrister and judge. Charles II appointed him as Judge for West Wales. He was knighted in 1669/70, was Recorder of Derby for 39 years, and High Sheriff of Derby in 1675. He also wrote on legal matters, being the author of '*The Parson's Counsellor*', the clergyman's guide, a leading text for many years.
Sir Symon Degge is mainly celebrated as an antiquary. He added extensively to the works of earlier writers on the history of Staffordshire. This included, for example, a description of the Abbots Bromley Horn Dance which he himself had often observed in the years before the Civil War.
Symon Degge lived in Derby for much of his later life. He owned a number of properties and apparently lived for some time at Fenny Bentley, just north of Ashbourne. He probably moved from Uttoxeter (or Stramshall), at an early age to live in Kingstone parish with relatives by the name of Whitehall. It is likely that he would have met, and married his first wife in Kingstone, where he was certainly living by the 1630s.
Symon Degge was a Royalist during the Civil War when he was said to have been 'of Callowhill'. This has led to an assumption that Symon Degge lived at Callowhill Hall, the ancient half-timbered house which still stands in the

southern part of Kingstone parish, which for centuries the home of the Lovatt family, and which then passed to the Goring family (page 84). The reference to Blythe Bridge as *'alias Little Callowhill'* in the will of William Whitehall, dated 1616 indicates that the area called Callowhill then included Blythe Bridge.

Symon Degge was the heir of Symon Whitehall, who died in 1630 (in turn, the son of William Whitehall) and inherited the Whitehall property at Blythe Bridge (24). Symon Whitehall of Blythe Bridge was responsible for one of the Kingstone charities (page 133-134).

Symon Degge is said to have died at Blythe Bridge Hall (i.e. Blythe Bridge in Kingstone, not the Blythe Bridge near Stoke-on-Trent).

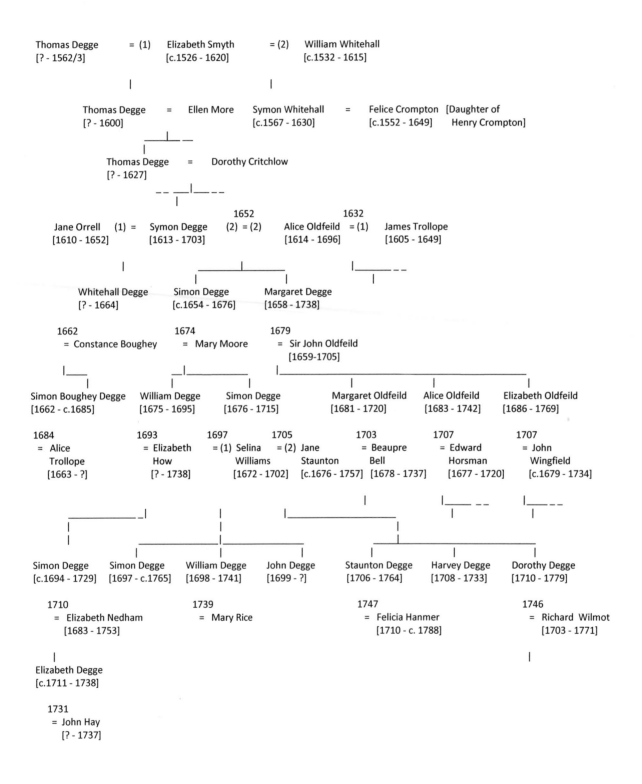

Symon Degge married twice, and had a daughter and two surviving sons. His great-grandson, called Simon Degge, and the fourth in a succession of Simons, died a bachelor in about 1765. He was the last male Degge descendant of Sir Symon. He had inherited the Blythe Bridge Hall estate (which also included Blythe Bridge Mill where Richard Stonier was tenant). Simon Degge's property passed to some cousins (four sisters) and his estate at Blythe Bridge was advertised his estate for in 1795 when the last of these sisters died (page 87). John Degge, son of his Sir Symon Degge's brother, Isaac Degge, left for America, probably in the 1670s, and settled in Virginia. He was the ancestor of numerous descendants living in America.

For a more detailed account, see - 'Sir Symon Degge his Family and Their World' (14).


Memorial tablets of the Degge and Whitehall families

[The three tablets relating to the antiquarian Sir Symon Degge and his family now lie in the churchyard. The inscriptions on the tablets were copied by Redfern (33). It has been assumed that they were mural tablets, but a description of the interior of the old church indicates that they were in the floor of the chapel (page 117).

1. 'Here lyeth the body of Sir Symon Degge, Knt., who was judge of West Wales, to Civri the 2nd XIV years, and of the same King, Counsel in the War of Wales 12 years, and then upon his petition (his) discharge he was in the commission of peace for the counties of Derby and Stafford, and Recorder of Derby above thirty-five years. Was born Jany. vth, MDCIXII. Dyed February X, MDCICII.'

2. 'Here lies the body of Dame Alice Degge, daughter of Anthony Oldfield, of Spalding, Lincolnshire, Esq., and second wife of Sir Symon Degge. Was born and christened June xxvth, MDCIXIV. Died March xxxth, MDCIXCVI.'

3. 'Against this place, in the body of the church, was buried the bodies of William Whitehall, gent., who died 12 March, 1615, aged 83, and Elizth., his wife, formerly the wife of Thos. Degg, of Stramshall, gent., great grand-mother of Sir Symon Degg, ys built this chapel. She died 10 June, 1620, aged 94, and Symon Whitehall, their son, gent., who died 17 May, 1630, aged 63; and Letice, his wife, who died Octbr 20, 1649, aged 97; and Dame, first wife of the said Sir Symon Degg, who died 2 July, 1642, aged 42 years.'

Comment: The inscriptions giving the year dates on tablets 1. and 2. do not make sense as they stand. The stonemason seems to have had some difficulty with Roman numerals.
If we remove the 'I' from the middle of each date then most dates do make sense e.g. for Dame Alice Degge her date of death becomes MDCXCVI (1696) instead of MDCIXCVI.
(From Bishops' Transcripts (24) we know that she was buried at Kingstone 2nd. April 1696.)
Similarly Sir Symon Degge's date of birth becomes MDCXII (1612), and his year of death, MDCCII (1702). Sir Symon Degge wrote his will on 16th. January 1702/3, and the will was proved on 21st. April 1703, dates which are consistent with the date of death recorded on his memorial as February 10th. 1702/3 (26).

## 3. The Bakewell family

Hidden away, behind the present church, and attached to its outside wall are two stone memorial tablets. They are of an earlier date than the church, and were formerly attached to the inside wall of the old church (page 117). The tablet in memory of Sarah, first wife of James Bakewell [1765 - 1826] of Kingstone reveals that she died 11th March 1801 *'of a decline in the prime of life, leaving a young family to lament her loss with pangs of woe. The pensive husband viewed her slow but certain fate, whilst infant tears in artless grief bewailed a parent's loss'*. Records show that at the time of her death, Sarah Bakewell was only forty, and had five children, between 2 and 11 years of age. We don't know why she died at a relatively young age, but death associated with pregnancy and childbirth was frequent during this period.

> Sacred to
> The Memory of Sarah [ wife of
> James Bakewell ] late of Kingstone
> and daughter of the late
> Wm. Smith of WildPark, Derby-
> shire. She died of a decline
> in the prime of life on Wednesday
> the II th of March
> MDCCCI leaving a young
> family to lament her loss
> with pangs of woe. The pensive
> husband viewed her slow but
> certain fate whilst infant
> tears in artless grief bewailed
> a parents loss .

> Sacred to
> The memory of
> Elizabeth, second wife of
> James Bakewell late
> of Kingstone and daughter
> of the late Wm. Towers
> Minors Esqr. of Knipersley
> in a few months after her
> marriage and in the prime
> of life. She was taken by
> an apoplexy on Wednesday
> the XXVII of Oct'er MDCCCII.
> Her sudden death was
> very much and deeply
> regretted by her family
> and friends.

Fig. 46 **Bakewell Family memorials**

The second memorial tablet tells us that the apparently grief-stricken husband married for a second time, just one year later. On 30th March 1802, at Kingstone, James Bakewell married Elizabeth Fenton, a widow. She died suddenly, just a few months later, *'taken by an apoplexy'* (an internal haemorrhage, probably a cerebral haemorrhage or stroke). She was only 34 years old.
It might be assumed that this was the end of the story, but James Bakewell married for a third time!
He married Elizabeth Webb at Leicester on 21st January 1804, and had a further six children! James Bakewell died at Prestwich, Lancashire in 1826, having outlived his third wife by two years.
Francis Redfern, in his 'History of Uttoxeter' (33) refers to the family of Bakewell and mentions a Thomas Bakewell who was said to have been a soap boiler in Kingstone, but gave up the business and left the village when his premises burnt down. He also mentions a Thomas Bakewell, said to have been a geologist.
We tend to assume that a village such as Kingstone has a purely agricultural history, and don't imagine that industries such as soap or glue manufacture would have existed here. These occupations are, of course, related to agriculture, and would have involved the boiling up of animal bones, and processing of other animal waste products. No doubt some rather unpleasant smells would permeate the air, and if indeed such industries did once operate in Kingstone, villagers would have had reason to been relieved when they disappeared!
The first member of the Bakewell family to live in Kingstone appears to have been John Bakewell [1687 - 1764] of Normanton-le-Heath, Leicestershire. He married Mary Griffin of Leese Hill, and must have moved to Kingstone

by the late 1730s, the last five of their eleven children being baptised in the village. His gravestone still survives in the churchyard (13). His son Thomas Bakewell [1731 - 1816] could have been the soap boiler, although there seems to be no evidence for it. Thomas Bakewell's eldest son, also called Thomas, was certainly not a soap boiler.

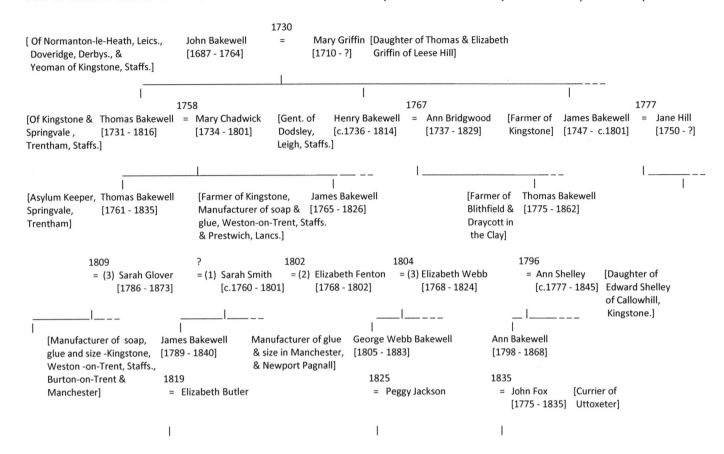

Thomas Bakewell [1761 - 1835] (who also married three times) became a highly respected keeper (for 27 years) of an asylum he established at a place called Springvale, near Trentham and published a family guide in 1805 on the management of the insane. Redfern's source of information was incorrect; it was Thomas Bakewell's younger brother, James Bakewell [1765 -1826] who became a manufacturer of soap (and also glue).
'James Bakewell' ( either the future soap boiler or his uncle) was recorded in the 1801 survey as owning houses and land in various parts of Kingstone (page 43), including a malt-house, but probably not the malt-house owned by John Elsmore (page 95). Whether any soap boiling operation ever took place in Kingstone is unknown. James Bakewell was in partnership with his son James Bakewell, the younger [1789 - 1840], as manfacturers of soap and glue. In 1814 their premises were burnt down, but this was in Weston-on-Trent, not in Kingstone, and resulted in their bankruptcy. In 1815 the Bakewell soap boilers were forced to sell their Weston-on-Trent premises, and also 16 acres of land which lay between *Johnny Field Coppice* and the road to Blythe Bridge (2). James Bakewell, junior continued in business on his own account as a glue manufacturer and bone calciner in Burton on Trent, but was bankrupt again in 1828. After that he and his family left the area, and he set up business in Manchester where he became bankrupt for a third time, in 1837. His wife having died, and close to the end of his eventful life, the bankrupt James Bakewell married again in 1838, having taken a trip to Gretna Green! As for Thomas Bakewell, the geologist, this was another error. The noted geologist was not Thomas, but Robert Bakewell [1768 - 1843]. This Robert Bakewell was however, sometimes confused with Robert Bakewell [1725 - 1795], famous for his pioneering work in the selective breeding of cattle, horses and sheep. Robert Bakewell, the geologist was apparently once asked 'was he related to the Mr. Bakewell who invented sheep' ? He replied, with some forbearance to the aristocratic lady who posed the ludicrous question, that he was not! Interestingly, the two Robert Bakewells were related, and also related to John Bakewell, the first of the Kingstone family branch. Another Thomas Bakewell [1775 - 1862], the son of Henry Bakewell (above) married Ann Shelley of Callowhill. Their daughter Ann became the wife of the wealthy, and much older John Fox, who died soon after (page 94)!

# 4. Thomas Wood

Thomas Wood [1850 - 1938] is remembered with some affection. The fact that his photograph remains on display in Kingstone Church, many years after his death is testimony to the regard that the people of Kingstone had for him.

The photograph, with the caption below, shows him standing outside the porch of Kingstone Church in 1927. Apart from giving recognition to what he achieved in his life, another reason for mentioning him in this book is that his story would have been typical of many people who had a fairly meagre existence in Kingstone during this period. So many, who like him spent all their lives in Kingstone would have had to work hard for long hours, without enjoying much in the way of a monetary return, or a comfortable home of their own. Tommy Wood did not have the best start in life; his mother was a servant and unmarried, and he was the third of her illegitimate children. [Her situation was by no means uncommon in Kingstone in the first half of the nineteenth century, with many young women from all levels of society producing children which the vicar, in the parish register, labelled as 'bastards'.] Thomas Wood's mother, Jane Wood did marry, in 1858, but by the time of the 1861 census, he was not living with her and her husband. At the age of only ten Tommy was a farm labourer living in the household of Henry Cotterell (son of Clement Cotterell of Kingstone Hall) at High Trees Farm, Bagot's Bromley. Ten years later he was a live-in servant at John Bettson's farm at Woodcock Heath.

Tommy Wood never went to school; sixpence a week for tuition was unaffordable, and he was never able to read and write, relying on his wife in later life to do any necessary writing (2).

By 1881 he was a farm labourer living by himself in a small cottage on Blythe Bridge Bank (called Yew Tree Cottage in 1891) (page 95), and working for William Bathew at Wanfield Hall nearby. He married Annie Locker, daughter of Joseph Locker, a labourer, at Kingstone in 1883. He and his wife were still living on Blythe Bridge Bank (in the cottage which had a few fields attached to it) until at least 1911, but later moved to a house in the 'Barracks' in central Kingstone. They had no children.

Apart from working as a farm labourer and in his several church - related roles, Tommy Wood worked for the rural district council as a road labourer. He was a lengthsman, employed to maintain the local roads around Kingstone. My father remembered him working in the gravel pit behind Kingstone Hall, loading gravel into a wheelbarrow, and dumping it over a large area a yard high so that it could be measured for road mending. The gravel was then loaded by hand into a horse - drawn cart to be taken to where it was needed for road repairs.

In June 1937, Tommy Wood's devoted service, of more than sixty years was recognised by the parishioners of Kingstone. A subscription list was opened *with the object of providing weekly necessaries to Mr. and Mrs. Wood in their declining years'*. Tommy Wood was then aged 88, and it was said that for 40 years he never had a doctor. His wife, Ann was aged 76. Tommy Wood died in August 1938, followed by his wife, Ann, just eleven days later (2).

**THOMAS WOOD**
Still in office at the age of 77 October 1927
He tidied the Churchyard and acted as Sexton, Bell Ringer, Organ Blower and Grave Digger at St. John's Church, Kingstone, for the last 55 years.

Plate 22 **Tommy Wood**

# CHAPTER 6: SOCIAL GATHERINGS

In centuries past the church was much more a part of everyday life. People inevitably met for 'hatches, matches and dispatches' (baptisms, marriages and burials), and most forms of social activity was likely to revolve around the church.

Most villagers would have spent their time working to maintain the basic necessities of life, rather than attending social events or indulging in leisure activities. Ensuring that their families had enough to eat, and somewhere to live, would have been their priorities, hoping also not to succumb to disease or suffer an early death.

There were, however, holiday periods at Christmas, Easter and May Day when there was time for relaxing and there could be feasting with recreational activities such as games, dancing or other entertainment.

Kingstone has never been a prosperous place; for most people their livelihood depending directly or indirectly on the land, working mostly as servants and agricultural labourers. Those who were craftsmen, tradesmen and farmers had more freedom, but would still have been mostly tenants of an absentee landlord, even as recently as a hundred years ago. There was little opportunity or need to leave the village, and people would have found simple pleasures where they could. Kingstone, like other communities did what it could to care for the poor and needy. The following provides evidence that Earl Talbot, as the principal landlord made some contribution.

The Staffordshire Advertiser in early January 1838 reported that *'We state with pleasure that Earl Talbot with his accustomed bounty has bestowed upon the Kingstone and Gratwich clothing club; enabling each poor family to supply themselves with sheets, blankets, flannel, calico and other articles needed by them at this inclement season'*.

Years later, the same newspaper reported that at Christmas 1893 *'the usual presents of clothing and beef were distributed to the poor of the parish'* of Ingestre, Kingstone and Gratwich, amongst others, by Lord and Lady Shrewsbury (2).

It mattered little to the villagers of Kingstone whether the nation was governed by Whigs or Tories, or who was King or Queen, but if celebrations were organised to mark an event such as a royal birth they were no doubt happy to take part. Following the birth of Queen Victoria's son and heir (the future Edward VII) in November 1841, Kingstone joined in the national celebrations, as reported below (Staffordshire Advertiser 19 Feb. 1842) (2).

*'There were spirited doings at Kingstone and Gratwich, to commemorate the birth and christening of the young Prince. The Gratwich people were exceedingly liberal on the occasion, and their Kingstone neighbours were not a whit behind-hand with them. On the 25th. (January) mutton was given to all the poor families, and a comfortable dinner was provided for the other inhabitants at the upper house, the Dog and Partridge Inn. On the 27th. (January) there was a great tea-drinking at the lower house, where 94 merry faces sat down to tea, &c. After tea, ale and wine were handed round, so that every one present might drink the health of the infant Prince, and other members of the royal family. Dancing was kept up till a late hour at both houses. On the 3rd. of February, the school children were regaled with currant bread and a glass or two of ale each to drink the "Young Prince of Wales." The boys and girls were afterwards taken into an adjoining croft, and twenty of the stoutest lads had a scramble for an odd loaf. They were drawn up into two companies, and that party which could carry the bread out of the field were to have it. The scramble afforded great amusement: for it was plainly to be seen that the loaf never would have been got away if it had not broken to pieces, such was the determined spirit of the competitors for the prize.'*

Note: The 'upper house', is identified as the *Dog and Partridge* (now the *Shrewsbury Arms* or '*Shrew*'. The 'lower house' is assumed to have been the *Barley Mow*, down the hill in the centre of the village (where the present school is now situated).

## 'Let's all go down the pub!'

**The Dog and Partridge** (which today is the **Shrewsbury Arms**) has long been a gathering place for social functions. According to the a visiting tourist (page 118) a maypole once stood on what was then a green in front of the Dog and Partridge Inn. Each year, on the 1st. day of May, the return of Spring was celebrated here. Wild flowers were gathered and the villagers danced around the maypole on the green.

'Welcome Home' - return from the Boer War - June 1901

This above photograph (Plate 23) was a copy belonging to Elsie Gallimore, and previous to that was owned by her mother, Mary Ellen Bettson. Several members of the Bettson family appear on the photograph as well as other Kingstone people, and some visitors from Uttoxeter. The following account of the proceedings was given to me by my grandmother Elsie Gallimore.

The photograph was taken in Mr. Derry's field opposite the Shrewsbury Arms, Kingstone and celebrates the return of three young men of the Kingstone area from the Boer War. They were troopers Ernest Brown of Grindley and Vernon Bathew of Wanfield Hall, and Corporal William Clowes of Leese Hill Farm. The others in khaki are the young men from Uttoxeter who also went, including troopers Hill, Hall, Horace Stretch (son of William Stretch, the brewer of Uttoxeter), and James Bagshaw (son of W.S. Bagshaw). All were presented with an illuminated address and walking sticks by Mr. Bunting, the Uttoxeter Urban Council chairman (2).
The top row includes Mr. Fisher of Burndhurst Mill, Mr. Durose, a farmer of Caverswall, Mr. Charles Bunting, the brewer of Uttoxeter, Mr. W.S. Bagshaw, the founder of Bagshaws of Uttoxeter, Mr. William Steele (Police Constable of Kingstone), Mr. Payne Hall of Uttoxeter, Mr. George Bathew, Mr. Samuel Prince, of Gratwich and later of Wanfield Hall, Mr. Alfred Johnson and Mr. Thomas Johnson, brothers of Moss Farm, Kingstone and Police Constable Fisher, then stationed at Kingstone.
In the centre row were the farmers of the village who subscribed to the **'Welcome Home'** for the returning men. Also present was the Leighton Ironworks Band under Bandmaster Tildesley. Just who is who within the photograph is in most cases difficult to say with certainty, but some individuals are identified as follows:
[1] Police Constable Steele ?; [2] Mr. Durose of Caverswall ; [3] Joseph Fisher, Burnhurst Mill ; [4] and [6] the Johnson brothers of Moss Farm, Kingstone ; [8] Mr. W.S. Bagshaw of Uttoxeter ; [18] John Bull, Leese Hill ?;[27] Mr. Tildesley, bandmaster ; [30] Bernard Bettson ?; [31] Ernest Stonier ; [32] John Holland, Kingstone Hall Farm ; [33] John Bettson, Woodcock Heath Farm ; [35] John Stonier; [37] Mr. Johnson, Moss Farm, Kingstone ; [39] Richard Taylor, schoolmaster; [41] William Bathew, Blount's Hall Farm; [52] Ernest Brown ; [53] William Clowes ; [54] Vernon Bathew ; [57] Thomas Bettson ? (Yeomanry).

Note: In January 1900, before they departed for South Africa, the three volunteers from Kingstone had been entertained at a farewell dinner at the Shrewsbury Arms. At the dinner Mr Jackson presented each of them with a silver-mounted pipe, pouch, spirit-flask and 1 lb. of tobacco (2).

The Barn Ground (the field next to the Shrewsbury Arms) provided space for village events including e.g. celebrations to mark Queen Victoria's Diamond Jubilee in 1897.

In 1901 a 'Welcome Home' was provided for soldiers returning from the Boer War. All involved gathered together in the field opposite the pub. for a photograph, recording the occasion for posterity (Plate 23).

Before the days of national insurance and the welfare state Friendly Societies were formed to provide community support. The Kingstone Friendly Society was apparently founded by Richard Stonier in 1854 (2). During the early years of the twentieth century the chief officials for the management of the Society were John Stonier, Samuel Jackson (of Blythe Bridge Mill), William Bathew and Richard Taylor (the schoolmaster).

The Society or 'Club' held their meetings in the large club room at the pub. and each year in first week in June the Friendly Society held a Club Day. All the members, preceded by a brass band (usually the Rocester Brass Band or Bamford's band of Uttoxeter) marched to the church for a short service with a sermon, and then back again to the Shrewsbury Arms for 'a real old-fashioned hot dinner of several kinds of roasts with appropriate vegetables and sauces, then plum pudding, trifles and jellies to follow, with, of course, beer! In the adjoining field were shooting galleries, swing boats, all kinds of stalls and amusements and four or five donkeys for the children to ride. The event concluded with dancing on the field accompanied by the brass band. All the village enjoyed the day and most had their old friends to visit them.'

Around the time of the Great War many Friendly Societies were disbanded following the introduction of Lloyd George's National Health Insurance Act in 1911. The Kingstone Friendly Society still existed in 1936, but by this time, on an occasion when members met in the Institute for an evening supper, together with some entertainment and a dancing competition, the Society was struggling to survive (2).

[The above formed part of my grandmother's recollections (page 119-123) but my father, John Gallimore also had a long memory and recalled, amongst other matters and events, the Kingstone Show.]

The Shrewsbury Arms (courtesy of Edward Lovatt) was also the location for the annual 'Kingstone Show', otherwise the Kingstone, Gratwich and District Agricultural and Horticultural Show which took place in the Barn Ground. At the third annual show in August 1924 there were numerous classes for a whole variety of vegetables, fruit, flowers and dairy produce. There was a marquee in which refreshments were served, and also 'a bit of a fair' with sideshows, skittles, bowling and sports events, including a cycle race. There were 'turn-outs' i.e. drays and carts (e.g. milk and butcher's carts) all presented in a clean and smart condition to be judged. There was a heavy horse race, and the horses had to walk, trot and gallop around the field. There were also races for hackney and hunting horses. A tent provided plentiful supplies of beer! The event concluded with a dance in the Institute in the evening. The Show continued to grow, and by 1930 silver cups and prizes totalling £100 were on offer. By the time of the tenth annual show, in 1931, the Kingstone Show had become the principal show in the Uttoxeter area. The Show was however defunct by the late 1930s (2).

## Kingstone gets an 'Institute'

After World War 1, whilst the Shrewsbury Arms remained an important social centre, the village was provided with a new gathering place. A new use was found for many former wooden army huts, and so it was at Kingstone where one of these huts became Kingstone Village Institute.

The Village Institute, during the period of about fifty years that it existed in Kingstone had many uses which included dances, many whist drives, parties, public entertainments, and meetings of various organisations such as the youth club, and especially the Women's Institute. Dances were popular events during wartime years of the 1940s. A dance programme card (Plate 24, page 111) dating from 1946 gives a flavour of the sort of dances which were then often used to provide entertainment in the Village Institute.

Entertainment provided in the Institute included, in January 1953, a performance of the pantomime 'Cinderella'. The pantomime, presented by the residents of Kingstone of Gratwich, was written and produced by the vicar, the Rev. Donald Watson, who himself played the part of one of the ugly sisters. The cast list also included the vicar's son together with Mrs. Watson as the cow, Dorothy Gallimore as Cinderella, her brother Ernest Gallimore as Buttons and Kathleen Capewell as Prince Charming (2).

The Women's Institute (WI) movement was founded in 1915 to revitalise rural communities and encourage

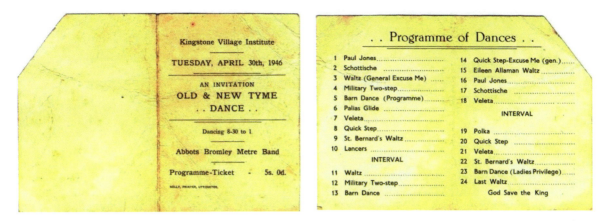

Plate 24 **Dance Programme** for a dance in Kingstone Village Institute in April 1946

women to produce food during the First World War. Kingstone WI (an early foundation, in 1918, and still going!) has therefore certainly been the most significant organisation to use the Institute, and meetings of the WI were often reported in newspapers. The history of Kingstone WI is a worthy topic in itself, but beyond the scope of this book. One of the many occasions when the WI met in the Institute was in 1952 (Plate 25, page 112) when members and guests celebrated Kingstone WI's 34th. birthday(2).
There was an air of nostalgia on the 1st. October 1971 when the old Institute building was sold by auction (for £165), soon to be replaced by the present Village Hall.

## Kingstone celebrates the Coronation

Most gatherings in Kingstone Institute have been undocumented or not reported in detail. The following account of the 1953 Coronation preparations is an exception. A series of meetings took place in 1952 and 1953 to plan for the celebration to mark the occasion of the Coronation of Queen Elizabeth II, on 2nd. June 1953.
This is relatively recent history, but the discovery of a minute book (kept by my mother, Olive Gallimore) recording the careful planning for the event makes for interesting reading, and is therefore included here.
The following extracts are taken from Kingstone with Gratwich: Coronation Minutes:
A Coronation meeting was held in the Institute on December 2nd. 1952. A committee was formed, with Norman Capewell (of Gratwich) elected as Chairman, Arthur Derry as Treasurer and Olive Gallimore as Secretary.
It was decided to hold a dance in the Institute on February 3rd. 1953 to raise funds.
Regarding Coronation Day itself, Mr. Capewell was to arrange for the provision of television sets in Kingstone School so that the Coronation Service and procession may be viewed (with most, including me, then watching television for the first time). This would be preceded by a church service in Kingstone Church. A meal for all and sports for all were to be arranged. A house to house collection was to be made with subscribers to the fund outside the parish being able to join in the festivities. Norman Capewell was to find out if music could be provided in the afternoon, and a band for the evening to give a grand finale. At the next meeting collectors were appointed to visit different areas of the parish, and also record the number of people in each house who might attend.
The dance in aid of Coronation funds took place as planned on February 3rd., with music provided by Madame Bruce and her band. A ladies committee provided refreshments, and there was a draw for a bottle of sherry; the whole event yielding a profit of £13-1s-2d.
At the following Coronation meeting on April 2nd. a suggestion was made to consider the erection of a street lamp outside the Institute as a Coronation memento. Catering provision was discussed and the printing of tickets. A church service was to be held at 7.30 pm the previous evening, followed by a celebration of Holy Communion on the day itself, thus leaving time after for the Westminster Abbey service. The timing of the meals was discussed, and also arrangements for the sports, Mr. S. Derry offering his field for the childrens' sports.
At the next meeting on April 27th. the matter of the street light was again discussed with the objective of having it in place in about six months time, or at any rate before the dark nights began. Mrs. Mould (who ran the local

Plate 25 **Kingstone WI** birthday party celebration, held in the Institute on Friday 26 June 1952.

Those identified on the above photograph include: 3 ........Wilks; 4. Lily Turner; 5. Rene Hanson (Morris); 6. Rose Hine; 7. Kathleen Capewell; 13. Mabel Stephens?; 16. Betty Arthur; 17. Margaret Collier; 19. Kathy Jackson; 22. Beatrice Capewell; 23. Doreen Capewell (Gee); 24. Mary Plant; 25. Olive Gallimore [Secretary]; 26. Elsie Cotton [Vice-President]; Frances Warrington; 28. MaureenTurner; 29. Beatrice Warrington; 30. Margaret Cotton (Povey)?; 31. Frances Warrington [President]; 32. Cicely Causer; 35. Anne Watson [Vice-President]; 36. Margaret Lowe; 37. Elizabeth Bettson; 38. Doris Adams (Darby); 39. Millie Hampson; 40. Norah Pughe; 41. Dorothy Derry; 42. Janet Watson; 45. Jane Austin Hine; 47. Marjorie Bebbington; 48. Beatrice West.

Note: This photograph includes WI members from neighbouring WI groups who were invited to the party.

shop, then at Blythe Bridge) had offered to do the catering but it was decided that a ladies and gents committee be formed for the purpose instead. [The names of those involved were listed separately]. The meeting felt that *'more satisfaction would be gained by our own labours provided that as many ladies as possible would help us during the day'*. Miss Guntripp offered to assist with the sports, assisted by Mr. N. Capewell, Mr. Lowe and Mrs. Chilton. A general Coronation meeting took place in the Institute on May 11th. It was announced that the total

number of people to be catered for in the parish on the day was 339 adults and 182 children. It was decided to have 80lb. of ham and 50lb. of beef and 6 tongues, all ready cooked. £30 was to be allocated to the ladies for the rest of the refreshments, two 18 gallon barrels of beer, 8 bottles each of port and sherry, and 6 bottles of sherry for making trifles. Also £5 was to be spent on minerals and squashes. [Further detail about the catering was recorded separately from the minutes which included, amongst other items, the provision of forty 2 lb. loaves, 4 lb. tea, 60 jellies, 80 dozen cakes, 40 lbs tomatoes, 12 cucumbers, 60 lettuces and nearly 40 dishes of trifle!] The times of the meals were to be 2.30 pm, 3.30 pm and 7.00 pm for adults, and 4.30 pm for children. The childrens' sports were to be held from 2.30 pm to 4.30 pm, with £15 allocated for prizes.
*A small number of the younger ladies were to be asked to take care of the children*' while watching television in the school', and forms from the Institute were to be provided for children in the school to sit on. '*A few kind gentlemen*' were to see that the forms were replaced in the Institute in time for the first meal.
Other entertainment on the day was to be bowling, adult sports and a dance in the evening.
The last Coronation meeting took place on 28th. May and made final arrangements for the dance at the end of the day. It was also decided that the adult sports would include a comic football match.

## A Day at the Fete

An event which formed a significant part of Kingstone's relatively recent history was the annual church fete, set up to raise funds for Kingstone and Gratwich churches.
My own memories of the church Fete in Kingstone go back to the 1950s and 1960s, but its origin is clearly earlier. A fete was organised to take place in August 1941 (and this may be the earliest date) to raise money for church expenses and the Vicarage Restoration Fund. There were stalls, side-shows and competitions on the Chapel Field, teas were served, and a dance held in the Institute in the evening, the event raising £154 (2).
An old notebook records the (following) detailed preparations for the Fete, the first entry being over 75 years ago, in 1943. A meeting was held on May 12th. 1943 when villagers from Kingstone and Gratwich gathered in the Institute to discuss arrangements. The Vicar, Rev. Neaum presided. Mr. R. C. Whittaker proposed that the Fete should take place on Whit Monday June 14th., this was seconded by Mr. T. Causer.
[Whit Monday became the traditional Fete day until it ceased to be a bank holiday in 1971]. The Countess of Shrewsbury was to be asked to open the Fete. Messrs. G. Deaville and N. Capewell were appointed Treasurers, and Mr. R.C. Whittaker, Vice-Chairman. Mr. T.B. Bettson offered a pig, and Mr. Deaville a bottle of whisky as prizes for bowling. Mr. A.J. Bettson offered a calf as a prize for a draw. [What would most people do with a live pig or calf today?!] Miss Guntripp was to be asked to take charge of children's sports, and Miss. C. Rees offered to make arrangements for a baby show. Messrs. R.C. Whittaker, S. Jackson, J. Doughty and L. Plant were appointed doorkeepers for the dance, with Mr. E. Brinkler as M.C. The Women's Institute offered to serve teas and have a stall. The Young Peoples' Club (Youth Club) also offered to have a stall. Mrs. Poole undertook to make a bouquet and this was to be presented to the opener by Freda Whittaker.
A meeting to finalise arrangements took place in the (former) Chapel on June 2nd. Bowling for a pig was to be priced at 6d.(2½ p), and the same price for the kagle (for which Mr. S. Jackson had also offered a pig). The Vicar offered to give a bottle of whisky as a prize for shooting. Saving stamps were to be given as prizes for the baby show, judged by Dr. Parry Evans. Mrs. and Miss. Deaville offered to have a stall for plant roots and Gratwich villagers were to have a miscellaneous stall. There was also to be an auction sale in the evening, with Mr. C. J. Blore as auctioneer. On June 21st. a follow-up meeting was held. Gross takings were £220-19s-9d. Various expenses included 15s to Mrs. West and 17s-6d to Mrs. Derry for washing up and cleaning, 10s rent to each of the Institute and the School, and £1 for ammunition, leaving a profit of approximately £208. £15 was to be given to the Bishops Fund for churches, and £17-4s-5d to pay for the dilapidations of the (Gratwich) Rectory. Kingstone Church was to receive £95 and Gratwich Church £45. Thanks were given to Mr. S. Derry for the use of his field – the Chapel Meadows. [The Fete was held on Mr. Derry's field, for many years; the access being via a track between Nene House and the former Chapel, both, in recent years, being owned by the Cotterill family].
The 1944 Fete had some extra features, including a bran tub (Miss. D. Whittaker & K. Jackson), pony rides (Miss. N. Whittaker), a treasure hunt (Amy Capewell), and hoop-la, with lemonade and ice cream also

available. The R.A.F. Band were engaged to play. There was also a tug-of-war for teams of eight Home Guards, this being of course, war-time.

In 1945 there was also a fortune teller. The old notebook (authorship unknown) details arrangements and records outcomes for the Fete up to 1948, and also contains balance sheets up to 1952. During this time the arrangements were generally similar but the Fete grew, more stalls and sideshows were being added. By 1952 expenditure had risen sharply to over £140 (which included tents for the first time, advertising costs, and £48 for pigs and a calf – no longer donated, it seems), leaving a net profit of about £270. By 1956 there was a coconuts shy, as well as other sideshows, and sports. You could have a go at the more traditional bowling, or on this occasion, watch hay bale tossing.

Other records of the Fete show that by 1955 there was a crowning of 'the Queen of the Carnival', later better

Plate 26 **Some ladies try their luck** at the fete - early 1950s

Plate 27 **The 'Queen' and her retinue** - c. 1957

Included in this photograph: *Back row, left to right:* Jean Smith, Val Turner, Sonia Gallimore, ................[Fete opener], Audrey Lowe, June Dyche, Anne Derry, Noreen Cole
*Front row, left to right:* Connie Jackson, David Somerville, Margaret Hine [Queen], Lynda Probyn.

known as the Sunday School Queen. The 'Queen' always had a sizable retinue, which added to the spectacle (as in Plate 27, page 114 & Plate 30, page 116). A procession of decorated vehicles (trailers from local farms) departed from Church Lane, outside the lych gate to slowly progress to Chapel Field.
In the 1960s the artistic flair of Mrs. Upton, wife of the then vicar contributed greatly to this display.

Plate 28 **The opening of Kingstone Fete** (held on the Chapel Field) - c.1958

*Left to right* (on the 'stage'): Nola Whittaker, Rev. Donald Watson (former vicar of Kingstone and rector of Gratwich), Jane Watson, Mary Deacon, Rev. Charles Upton, Olive Gallimore, Roland Bebbington. Mrs Winifred Upton is seated on the grass.

The children's fancy dress parade was a popular event. I particularly remember one year in the about 1960 when my sisters and I converted an old pram into a 'horse-drawn gypsy caravan'. My eldest sister Sonia was (played the part of!) the back end of the 'horse' and I was the head-end. My sister Joan pushed the 'caravan' (pram) at the back, and my other sisters, Lindsay and Jill were in the 'caravan'. Lindsay held the 'reins' (baling string) although rather too tightly at times, but I think we won first prize!

Plate 29 **Fancy dress parade** - c. 1960

Other notebooks and papers, some kept by my mother provide records of the Fete, up 40 years later in 1983. There was still bowling (but not for a pig!), pony rides, hoop-la and the Gratwich stall, but now also a tombola, plant stall, a bouncing castle with hot dogs available, and an evening disco now rather than a dance. You could get a special bus to and from Kingstone from Uttoxeter. Expenditure was now in excess of £500 (the marquee alone costing £120 to hire) leaving about £720 net profit. The fete was always hard work for the organisers (as I often witnessed), but worthwhile in this small community.

Plate 30 **Queen Noreen is crowned** as Sunday School Queen in 1959

Included in this photograph are: 1. Margaret Probyn; 2. Joan Gallimore; 3. Geoffrey Doughty; 4. Lynda Probyn; 5. Clifford Cotterill; 6. Connie Jackson; 7. Christine Derry; 8. Christopher Lowe; 9. Gladys Bettson; 10. David Somerville; 11. Robert Somerville; 12. Charles Hayford; 13. Noreen Cole; 14. James Gallimore 15. Michael Hayford; 16. Robert Derry; 17. Philip Derry; 18. Lindsay Gallimore; 19. Judith Derry; 20. Janet James; 21. Kathleen Gallimore; 22. Geoffrey Sargeant; 23. Alan Derry.

# CHAPTER 7: RAMBLING AND RECOLLECTION

This chapter gives two views of Kingstone. The first - 'A RAMBLE ROUND KINGSTONE' is a tourist's view i.e. that of G. F., an unidentified visitor to Kingstone who reported on his 'ramble' in 1870. His account is given below, as it was reported in a newspaper article (2).
The second view is quite different, being that of a native. ELSIE'S STORY records the experiences of someone born in Kingstone in the 1880s, and who lived all her life in, or close to, the village.

## 1. A Ramble Round Kingstone

'There are about twenty-four Kingstones in England, but it is our Staffordshire village of that name to which my present ramble refers, generally called by the natives 'Kin-son'. It is the most southerly parish in Totmonslow Hundred, situated on the 'Toad Brook,' or commonly abbreviated 'Tad brook'. We have recently heard a good deal of the want of bridge accommodation near one of our market towns. We have here two bridges over the same stream, at right angles to, and within thirty yards of, each other. Perhaps our grandfathers considered it more economic to build a second bridge than to make a very short diversion of either the road or the water course. There is a curious legend associated with the 'Tad brook,' but it would expand this 'ramble' too much to relate it here. This village has not the advantage of convenient railway communication, the nearest stations being Grindley or Uttoxeter, two-and-a-half and three-and-a-half miles distant. But to the tourist, with his eyes and ears open, noting all that may be enjoyed by the way, and not afraid of modestly questioning the simple country people that come in his way, it may become a very agreeable walk from either station. The general isolation from society of the inhabitants, and the habit of spending much of their time alone, make them naturally taciturn; yet they can, if they wish, while away the hour by many a sporting or poaching adventure in the preserves of Lord Talbot or Lord Bagot, by which their village is so conveniently surrounded. Kingstone Old Hall is an interesting specimen of the half-timbered, many-gabled style of the sixteenth century. It was occupied by a family of the name Wood for several generations. Another very old house, occupied by Mrs. Williams, is perhaps older than the 'Hall,' but not so interesting. Blythe Bridge Hall, once the residence of Sir Simon Degg, the antiquary, is a mile from Kingstone, and was also a good example of timbered architecture. It has, however, been so altered and modernised a few years ago that the old antiquary would scarcely recognise his home again. The river Blyth crosses this hamlet, but the name is a misnomer; cattle and carriages have still to ford the river.
There is no resident clergyman in Kingstone, but an excellent substitute will be found in Richard Stanyer (Stonier) for reference in any local matters; I believe he has been parish clerk between forty and fifty years.
The old church was taken down in 1861, and rebuilt a little more to the east. The patron is the Earl of Shrewsbury, who owns most of the village and the lands adjoining. I am not aware whether there is any drawing of this old church amongst the manuscripts so handsomely presented to the county by Mrs. Salt; but I took the opportunity of having careful drawings of both north and south elevations, taken before its destruction ; as the late Judge Temple observes, 'Let us remember that our day will ere long be the olden time, and let us try to preserve for those who follow us what, alas, we have many times lost, for want of a little thought and a little pleasurable exertion'.
Our forefathers had a very objectionable custom of burying ordinary persons under the floors of their churches, and a goodly number found a sepulchre within the late old church, but only one historic personage amongst them -- Sir Simon Degg, the lawyer and antiquary. He was buried in the northern chancel. The inscription, much worn by the tread of the congregations, reads as follows:
-- 'Here lieth the body of Sir Simon Degg, Knt., who was Judge of West Wales 10 civri the 2nd fourteen years, and of 4 the same King's Council. In the marches of Wales 12 years, and then upon his petition discharged He was in the Commission of the Peace for the counties of Derby and Stafford, and Recorder of Derby above 35 years. Was born Jany. 5, 1611 ; died Feby. 10, 1701.'
His second wife also rests beside him, with this inscription :- 'Here lieth the body of Dame Alice Degg, daughter of Anthony Oldfield, of Spalding, in Lincolnshire, Esqr., and 2nd wife of Sir Simon Degg. Was born and christened June 26, 1613 ; died March 30, 1696.'
There was a tablet near the communion, with an inscription in Latin, recording the death of Dorothea Hurd in 1735, aged twenty-two years ; another tablet, on the western wall, to the memory of Sarah, wife of James Bakewell who died in 1801 ; also to Elizabeth, the second wife of the above, a few months after her marriage, in 1802.
The latest interment that I can find within the church is the Rev. Thomas Lawrence, and Ellen, his wife, who both died in 1823.

There is an old oak register chest, with an inscription deeply cut into the front, which, being in crabbed capitals, without stop or break, puzzled me for a time to make out, the plain English of which is 'Hugh Needham gave this chest who died September 1601'.
    R.B --- T.B --- 1608.

Our forefathers had a beautiful and poetic idea of celebrating the return of genial spring by floral festivals, such as dancing round the Maypole, appropriately decorated with flowers on the 1st. of May. These Maypoles used to be very general throughout 'Merrie England,' but in this age of progress are fast passing away, to make room for the more prosy poles of the electric wires. One of these Maypoles still stands on the green here before the Dog and Partridge Inn, and many a joyous young spirit has lightly skipped around it. Another kindred custom is also practised in the districts round here. On the last day of April baskets of wild flowers were collected (principally marsh marigolds and ladysmocks) to strew on the doorsteps before going to bed, to usher in on the following morning 'Beautiful May.'

The tourist who has a taste for forest scenery must not fail, when here, to pay a visit to Bagot's woods and Park, about one-and-a-half miles distant. A foot-road near the 'Hall' will take him either by 'Cuckold's Haven' or Broomyfields. In this park will be found some of the most ancient and majestic oaks in the county. Tradition points out several as being a fair size in the reign of King John. A brother tourist took this route in the last century, and wandered several miles out of his way (if a naturalist ever can be out of his way), but eventually got safe to the Goat's Head Inn at Abbots Bromley. He had certainly a very Irish Way of expressing his gratitude for the hospitality of the 'Goat.'

Here is his ***'Grace after meat'*** --

> *'At a village remote*
> *At the sign of the 'Goat,'*
> *A publican who was a sinner*
> *Charged fourpence one day*
> *To a traveller this way,*
> *For only a bread-and-cheese dinner,'*

*With this I must wish the reader good-bye.*

              G. F.

---

**Staffordshire Sentinel and Commercial & General Advertiser - Saturday 14 May 1870**
Image © THE BRITISH LIBRARY BOARD. ALL RIGHTS RESERVED
http://www.britishnewspaperarchive.co.uk/viewer/bl/0000345/18700514/042/0006

---

Comment:

1. The Tad Brook runs from the north-west into the centre of Kingstone village to meet the Uttoxeter Road opposite Kingstone School. A bridge existed at this point, and in fact still exists on the western side. The Tad (now piped in ) used to run down the east side of Uttoxeter Road (and alongside the School fence) to the second bridge which was over the Church Lane junction (as illustrated- Plate 1, page 1).
2. The 'curious tale' about the Tad is (frustratingly) unknown to me. I have only heard about the alleged source of the Tad, said to be from seven springs at Woodcock Heath.
3. Grindley Station was on the Uttoxeter to Stafford branch line.
4. The Wood family of Kingstone Hall has already been mentioned (page 42).
5. The other very old house occupied by Mrs. Williams is identified as Manor Farm (page 48).
6. Kingstone's vicar was also rector of neighbouring Gratwich, and lived at Gratwich Rectory. The parish clerk 'Richard 'Stanyer' was Richard Stonier who was also schoolmaster in Kingstone.
7. There are some views of the old church, some of which are included in this book. The writer makes reference to what is now the William Salt Library at Stafford.
8. The memorial tablets of Symon Degge and his family were assumed to have been mural tablets, but the evidence here

is that they were placed in the <u>floor</u> of the chapel which Symon Degge had built on the north side of the church. Note that the inscriptions were recorded incorrectly (see page 103 for the correct versions).

9. Dorothea Hurd was a relative of the Manlove family, being a niece of Mary Manlove (died 1724). She was also a niece of Dorothy Bassett, wife of the Rev. Richard Bassett, Kingstone's long-serving curate. Richard Bassett had married Dorothy Hurd (sister of Mary Manlove) in 1725. Statements of witnesses to the will of Dorothy Hurd, dated 1736 record that she died at the house of her uncle and aunt, and it was her 'usual habitation' (24). The statements also record that the house was in Kingston. Where the Rev. Bassett and his wife lived in Kingstone is unknown. During periods when the curate at Kingstone was not also rector of Gratwich (where there was accommodation at the rectory), we can assume that the curate lived in Kingstone.

10. The memorial tablets of the Bakewell family still exist and are now fixed to the <u>outside</u> wall of the vestry of the present church (Fig. 46, page 104).

11. Funeral hatchments of Thomas Lawrence and his wife Ellen were also thought to have been hanging in the chancel of the old church (Plate 35, page 130)

12. The church chest, dated 1608 is of course that now in the present church (page 39)

13. The Dog and Partridge Inn still exists as The Shrewsbury Arms (page 47).

14. Footpaths near Kingstone Hall lead to Cuckolds Haven (on Uttoxeter to Lichfield Road (Fig. 29, page 72) and to 'Broomyfields' - this is Broomfields Farm.

15. The Goat's Head Inn still exists in Abbot's Bromley.


## 2. Elsie's Story

My grandmother, Elsie Gallimore [1888 - 1985] (born Elsie Bettson, the elder daughter of John and Mary Ellen Bettson) spent all of her 96 years living in Kingstone parish, or close by. In the following account she recalls her earliest years living at Church Farm in Kingstone, then (after 1901) at Woodcock Heath Farm, and into the 1920s at Wall Heath Farm where she lived after her marriage to Samuel Gallimore in 1913.

In later life Elsie often talked about earlier years in Kingstone and fortunately (in the 1970s) also recorded her memories in writing. It was clear that she wanted those who came later to know what life was like in past times. These were personal recollections, but are included in this book because they provide a unique perspective. They are recorded as far as possible using Elsie's own words.


'My earliest recollection was when I was five years old and had just started at the village Church of England school. I felt very hot and not well so my mother sent me to bed and called in Dr. B. Heywood Herbert, grandfather of Dr. Arthur Herbert (of Uttoxeter). It was in April, some days were very sunny and some very cold, as it often is this month. I had pleurisy and inflammation of the lungs, which made me very poorly and weak for a very long time. When I gradually improved my mother gave me port wine and a biscuit at lunch time and I got stronger.

The Vicar Rev. W. D. Hathaway and his wife often called to see me and I remember they brought beautiful flowers with maidenhair fern, which I thought was lovely.

Unfortunately, one very cold frosty night in November 1898, the Rev. Hathaway was walking back to Gratwich Rectory by the footpath near Rose Cottage at the top of Watery Lane when he collapsed. Mr. John Fradley found him frozen and dead in the morning, his dog by his side. He was interred in Kingstone churchyard, just outside the porch. He was a very kindly man, and often came into the school to talk to the children. There was no motor transport or buses, so he arrived at church on Sundays in a four-wheeled 'black basket' carriage drawn by a black pony which he put in the stable at Church Farm. If he did not bring his pony he walked.

Our resident schoolmaster was Mr. Richard Taylor who lived in the School House near the Chapel with his wife and two sons, Richard and Basil. [Basil Taylor died from pneumonia in 1911, aged just 23 - he is commemorated on a brass plate in Kingstone Church.] Mr. Taylor called his home Nene House after the River Nene near Wisbech where he originally came from, in 1886 (and taught until his death in 1924). He was paid by Government grant, helped by yearly subscriptions from all parents in the village who could afford to give. Nobody seemed to have much money. Sovereigns and half-sovereigns were used but very few cheques. I do not remember the use of cheques until I was about twelve years old.

The School had been given by the Earl of Shrewsbury, and was opened by Lady Shrewsbury in November 1877. There were about 80 children attending school when I was there (Plate 11, page 52). There was no large class room then, the room with wash basin was the infants room, and a porch for a cloak room was where the new cloakroom is now, which was built after I left in 1902. Mr. J. Stonier was one of the School managers, and with other well-known gentlemen made the children's school life happy, with their visits, tea parties, prizes and outings. Mr. Taylor was a very persevering, upright and just man but he made school enjoyable and useful, and did not believe in wasting time. He kept his garden so nice with both flowers and vegetables. His wife (Amelia) taught the infants; she also took the sewing lessons which I enjoyed most of all. She was an expert seamstress herself and made the boys' suits until they grew big. The boys kept a collection of various animals in their shed which is still at the house occupied by Mrs. D. Cotterill; guinea pigs, hamsters, rabbits and white mice, even a snake in a glass case which they kept very clean and fed them well. When Mr. and Mrs. Taylor went to Stafford on Saturdays they took the ten o'clock train from Grindley station and returned by the afternoon train.

In my early days the winters were much more severe than now and as the horses and trap were the only transport (no cars or buses), if there were icy roads the horse had to have his shoes 'sharped' at the blacksmith before we drove to market.

There were blacksmiths shops in the vicinity, one at Blythe bridge, occupied by the Wilson family, and one at Loxley Green occupied by the Martin family. There was also a blacksmith's shop at Gratwich occupied by Mr. Wilson. Mr. Lyons, at the Red Cow (Willslock) was the wheelwright. He was also a general workman, which included making coffins for the local people who passed on.

During my early years living at Church Farm my mother made cheese and butter from our own milk, and we reared calves and fed pigs with the whey and buttermilk. The cheese and butter was made every day when there was a flush of milk as our cows were calving, so there was most milk in summer. Cheese was 6d per lb. in the Spring. The butter was sold to the villagers for 1/- per lb. (in summer, and 1/2 per lb. in winter), and any left over was taken to Uttoxeter market. We also supplied the villagers with their milk who came with jugs and cans at 1½d per pint. We also kept fowls; the chickens were all hatched under hens. As I got older it was a job I liked to do, looking after and feeding them and looking for the eggs. We reared several litters of pigs and a few sheep.

We also had several cade lambs which were given to me by Uncle Tom Bettson. When at Kingstone I reared several orphan lambs. One of these, when he got bigger would roam the village, even going to the children in the school yard. He also got into the schoolmaster's garden and ate some plums. I had a blue ribbon round his neck with a bell on. However he had to go to market when fat in the autumn. He was sold for 30/-, which went to my pocket money. I think I had quite a full and busy life.

We fattened a good pig each year which we killed for our own use in the home around Christmas time.

When the weather was cold then my mother made pork pies, black puddings and sausage. The lard was put in large earthenware bowls and used for mince pies and all kinds of pastry. Neighbouring farmers bought young pigs from each other. The litters were weaned when about eight to ten weeks old for about £1 each, and got on well for they were allowed to run outside, and fed on Sharps bran mixed with whey from cheese-making and buttermilk and skimmed milk when cream was taken off for butter-making. The schoolmaster had all his butter, eggs and milk from us until we left to live at Woodcock Heath Farm when I was thirteen years old.

When I was nine years old my father bought a new piano from Allin's of Stafford which came from Stafford in a horse-drawn vehicle. I started having music lessons with the schoolmaster (Mr. Taylor), and went for lessons on Tuesday evenings at 6 pm. He was very keen on teaching us to sing at school. We had hymns and prayers every morning, and also read a small piece each from the Bible which after the reading was fully explained to us.

I enjoyed my school life, as we lived so near the school and could go home for our midday meal. Many children walked a long way to school; the Emerys from Loxley Park Cottage, the Wilsons from Booth Farm, the Tittertons from Caverswall, Sally and Harry Durose, also from Caverswall (near Burndhurst Mill) and the Mellor family from Callow Hill Hall.

When we went to Uttoxeter it was by horse and trap (which everybody did) and stabled our horses at different inns. We used the Black Swan which had a large number of stalls for horses. It is in Balance Street. All the family stabled there for about forty years until motors arrived. In those days public houses kept open from eight in the morning until ten o'clock at night.

My mother brewed our own beer for the harvest; two large casks in April to last through the summer.

The workers were allowed a large bottle to take to into the field in harvest time. It was very good, made of pure malt, hops and plenty of sugar, and was very refreshing. We brewed all our own until I was twenty one.

My mother also made cowslip and elderberry wine. If a cow got a chill we gave her either a quart of warm ale with ground ginger in, or a bottle of elderberry wine and kept her warm in a shed. If the lambs got cold we brought them by the kitchen fire and gave them warm brandy and water, and a good rubbing, and wrapped them in something woollen. I had several lambs who had lost their mothers and reared them on the bottle. We kept them until big enough to go to the butcher in the winter.

We also had a few rabbits but I didn't much care for them. There were plenty of wild ones running in the fields near the Ashcroft Wood (on which there are two new houses built by Mr. Bernard Beard and Mr. Ron. Beard). At the little Ashcroft Farm opposite lived Mr. and Mrs. Frank Sherratt and their family. She was a very tall person; a dressmaker who made quite a lot of our dresses. My mother made as many as she had time for.

We had a resident policeman (Mr. Steele) whose children all went to school with us. We also went to their Christmas tree party. He lived in the end house in Church View. The sign 'Policeman's House' was over the door. The middle house was occupied by Mr. Joseph Sherratt, the tailor who sat in the front of the big window making cord breeches with boxcloth leggings for the farmers and labourers of the district costing 19/- to 25/- per pair. When he died (in 1896) his son William followed his father's trade, but he was troubled with ill health (pernicious anaemia) and sometimes could not work; so the farmers had to wait a bit for him to finish the making of their clothes. His wife took up midwifery and went into homes to live-in whilst nursing. In fact she nursed me over five of my family. Her daughter Annie was my best friend at school and sat next to me for a long time. I also had two girl friends at Kingstone Hall. They were Florence and Sallie Holland who were the same age as my sister and myself. We went down to Kingstone Hall quite a lot to play hide and seek in the cowsheds and blow bubbles with old-fashioned clay pipes which we bought from the Shrewsbury Arms for 2d each. The Hall then belonged to the Earl of Shrewsbury, as well as the Shrewsbury Arms, most of the farms, cottages, the school (built in about 1874). [All the Kingstone Estate was sold soon after the Loxley Estate on November 25th 1918.]

There was a Friendly Society instead of a Health Scheme, and they held their meetings in the large club room at the pub. Then about the first week in June the Friendly Society held a Club Day when all the members went to a church service and back at the Shrewsbury Arms for hot luncheon. There was a band to play them through the village to the church, and played for dancing in the field in the evening. All the village enjoyed the day. How nice if we could have such a day now. After the First World War was over (I don't remember the exact date) Lloyd George introduced stamps for the work people at 10d per week. So after that many Friendly Societies were disbanded.

[For a more detailed account of the events of Kingstone Friendly Society Show, as described by my grandmother, and of the annual Kingstone Show -See Chapter 6, page 110].

On going up the hill (out of the village towards Uttoxeter) where a bungalow now stands (below the Walnuts Farm), there was a house with old lattice-paned windows which was used as a school in my father's time, but then used as a shoemaker's workshop. It was occupied by an old boot and shoe maker named Mr. Joseph Campion who made hand sewn boots at about 19/- to 25/- a pair. He also repaired (soled and heeled). All the farm workers wore strong boots as all had to do a lot of walking with horses following the plough and chain harrow. He liked his beer and sometimes spent the whole day drinking at the Shrewsbury Arms. In that case, your shoe mending had to wait. [Charles Bunting's of Uttoxeter supplied the beer (in barrels) to the Shrewsbury Arms, beer was then 2d to 3d per pint.]

The Post Office was later there for many years, kept by Mrs. Edward Fradley, and after her death by her daughter, Harriet. Before that, in about 1900, the Post Office, kept by Mrs. Fradley, was at the other end of the row of cottages where the policeman lived (in Church View).

The present shop was the well-attended Methodist Chapel until about 1900, and was looked after by Mr. Alfred Johnson of the Moss Farm, who died at a rather early age.

There was a very pretty thatched cottage below the Moss Farm on the left hand side occupied by Mr. and Mrs. Tom. Ferneyhough. Their only son lived with them who had the misfortune to have had an accident in his early days which meant the removal had one leg off above the knee, but he was a very useful man. He got about with a crutch and was the handyman for the village, doing painting, papering and house repairs. He could see to pumps which were relied upon for water supply. However he did not live to a very great age. His father was a good gardener. His mother, a very small woman came each week to Church Farm for her butter and cheese. Their garden was a pretty picture of flowers with edgings of red daisies, white nancys and other cottage flowers. The damson trees still stand in the hedge where his house stood.

Mr. Charles Beard lived at the Mosses Farm near Kingstone Wood, and he had a family of lads who were all starting work. He looked after the woods for the Earl of Shrewsbury and did the splitting of rails and posts for farmers. Harvest time was busy. All hay was pitched by men with forks and unloaded with forks on to the ricks or barns. The corn was cut by mower with reaper attachment and tied with straw bands by hand. It was then stacked in barns or stacks until the threshing machine arrived, the threshing going 'round the farms' in winter. At the Church Cottage there was a small sweet shop kept by Mrs Jemima Fradley; she was also the church cleaner. The church key was kept there too.

Bread was delivered to the village in horse and covered van by Mr. Tom Fradley of Bramshall (son of John and Jemima Fradley of Church Cottage, page 43), three days a week, Monday, Thursday and Saturday. He supplied lovely large homemade loaves at 4½ d per four pound loaf. Pakeman's of Uttoxeter and other carts came round with groceries. Coal was 6d per cwt if you sent your own cart to the Wharf at Uttoxeter. Meat was supplied by Mr. W. Sargeant who came to Mount Pleasant. The house and cowshed were thatched before Mr. Sargeant came. Our M.P. was Col. R. F. Ratcliff of Newton Park, Burton on Trent. During the Boer War The Col. got the Burton Daily Mail sent to the village so that the villagers could follow the progress of the war with the Boers in South Africa.

When I was thirteen years of age we moved up to Woodcock Heath, and my uncle Richard (Bettson) took over at Church Farm.

I left school at Christmas 1902 when I was fourteen and began helping on the farm and in the house. I enjoyed working outside most of all, hatching chickens, feeding calves and pigs. My mother was still cheese-making and butter-making every Tuesday. When we fattened calves for the Easter market they were given as much hot milk as they could take that night and morning and given plenty of clean straw. Some of the farmers sold milk to London, taking it to Grindley Station each night, but we could not send ours as our water supply was very hard to pump up from the deep well in the garden. [The milk which went to London had to go from Grindley station by the 7.00 o'clock train in the evening. The empties were returned by a train about 2.30 pm. the next day and were picked up each evening when the day's milk was put on the train. About 100 seventeen gallon churns went every evening to Finsbury Park or Kings Cross, whichever station was nearest the buyer.]

Apart from the cows we also kept fifty breeding ewes as the forty acres of land at Wanfield was away from home. The young stock and ewes were kept there except at lambing time, then they were brought home. The lambing was usually of about three weeks duration, and we sat up at night so that no lamb was neglected at birth. When lambing finished the lambs were tailed and castrated and moved back to Wanfield, and given some corn in their troughs until there was plenty of grass.

There were no motors or tractors and all farm work was done by horses. We kept four heavy horses for the work and a cob to drive and take the milk float to the station.

About this time Rugeley Horse Fair was held in the street around Whitsuntide, and my father bought us a donkey so we could ride. Ted Brown from Heatley said he would ride it home for us to Woodcock Heath. I believe it cost £2 - 5 - 0. Miss Violet Bathew (later Mrs. Sam. Prince) lent us an old side-saddle on which my sister Hetty and myself and the boys (my brothers) learned to ride. I remember saddling him to go to music lessons. I put him in the stable at Church Farm but my ride down was very slow. I could have got there quicker had I walked, for I didn't get a trot out of him. We had only had the donkey for a few months when he ate some yew from the trees adjoining the garden, and of course he died. We all cried and he was buried in a deep grave beside the wood near the old pit.

We used to grow wheat, oats, barley, mangolds and turnips which helped the winter feed for all the stock. Sheep and pigs would feed on the turnips with some meal added. Most of the corn we used was delivered by Mr. Jackson's mill cart. He ground the Indian meal from the Indian corn at the Blythe Bridge mill. Farmers and all small-holders fattened a pig for their own use in the winter. Bran was then 5/- per sack and Sharps about 7/6 per sack.

Life went on steadily during my teenage years, all my brothers growing up. The County Council sent a dairy van equipped with all butter making utensils which travelled through the Staffordshire villages. My sister and I attended the classes which were held in a field at Church Farm. The classes were held every afternoon two to five pm. They took eight pupils. The classes were very interesting and we learned quite a lot. The cream was provided by the County Council, and the butter weighed and made into 1lb blocks by Scotch hands. Of course we made butter at home to supply our customers. When farmers began to sell milk some still made butter, and also kept fowls for eggs. After supplying our regular customers we stood in the market at Uttoxeter to sell butter and eggs. We also sold eggs in the market at 1/- per score, perhaps as high as 1/6 per score in winter, when they were scarce.

When I was seventeen to eighteen we began to think of learning to dance. Miss. Violet and Miss. Florence Bathew of Wanfield Hall came to our granary in the evening to learn to dance. As the school had been taken over from Church of England to Council School we could no longer use the School, so we cleaned out our granary, (green-washed and decorated it), scrubbed the floor, put dance polish on it and made it quite tidy.

[The granary at Woodcock Heath Farm - Fig. 26, page 66.]

Mr. Harrison (who lived at the Manor House, Kingstone) could play the violin so we engaged him at 3/- per night on a Thursday evening to play (from seven to eleven) and we had weekly dances.

At Christmas we got up a Fancy dress Dance and got a better band.  Refreshments were got by my mother and ourselves in the house.  We decorated the room with gay material and evergreens.  Miss. Jenny Mart of Loxley Green Farm was dressed to represent a pillar box in red, Miss. V. Bathew as Daughter of the Regiment, myself a gypsy and my sister Hetty as Harvest viz. a cream frock trimmed with oats, poppies and cornflowers. When I was nineteen I went to my first whist and dance afterwards, it was arranged by Mr. Taylor in aid of School children's prizes.  I was learning to play and after that I went to quite a few, especially at Abbot's Bromley.  We had a nice dance organised by Dick Stonier and the Wilks family.

When I was about 18, after Rev. J. R. Palmer, our new vicar arrived (in 1905), his sister Adelaide Palmer gave me organ lessons.  I took over the post as organist ( in Kingstone Church) until I was married.  Old Thomas Wood blew the organ which was hand years blown at the time I played, and also rang the three bells on Sunday (as well as being sexton and grave digger).

Plate 31 **Elsie Gallimore** -
in her garden at Sunset Cottage
(formerly a farm cottage belonging
to Wall Heath Farm, Willslock).

I was married on April 3rd. 1913 at Kingstone Church at Easter.  I was taken to church by hired carriage from Carter's Mews, Uttoxeter, cost £2 – 5 – 0.  That was the first bill I put on our file as we started married life at Wall Heath. [Elsie said that her wedding was then the last by a horse and carriage; for later weddings at Kingstone cars were used.]

In 1914 we had the Great War which lasted until 1918. We had German prisoners to work on the farm and had some exciting experiences. Food stuff for the cattle became very dear, and we had ration cards, and 'evacuees'. Farming suffered a slump up to 1925 when there was a slump in everything.

The milk situation was in a bad way, the milk buyers only paying about 6d per gall.  In September 1925 there really was a strike of milk producers at Uttoxeter (September 1925 was the time for renewing milk contracts). We kept ours at home and I was faced with the task of making 100 gallons daily into cheese. I made nineteen (Derby type - each 30 lb.) cheeses in ten days which we sold to Mr. Deaville of Carter Street, our grocer at 1/- per lb.  Amy Cope came from Broomy Leasow to help me.  Things began to improve and a better price was obtained, and the dairies began to come round to collect the milk.

All my children were born at home at Wall Heath Farm (about one mile north-east of Kingstone village centre). [Elsie also said that her son Sidney, had died of pneumonia, following whooping cough, in 1929.]

During an epidemic of whooping cough (or diptheria?) in the early months of 1929, three children had died in Kingstone. 'A very cold winter - it froze from Christmas to the end of March.'] That was in 1928 (to 1929). They were bad years for farming; money was scarce.'

Plate 32 **Kingstone Old church** - from a series of watercolour paintings by Miss. Theodosia Hinckes and Mrs. Rebecca Moore, dated 1857-1861.

This view shows the chancel at the east end, and the Degge chapel built on to the north-facing side of the church.
Reproduced with the permission of Lichfield Cathedral.

# CHAPTER 8: CHURCH AND CHARITY

This chapter addresses various matters relating to the present and previous churches at Kingstone, supplementing information already given in Chapter 4, and includes details of Kingstone Charities.

## 1. A note on Kingstone parish registers

From 1538 all churches were ordered to keep registers of births, marriages and deaths, and also from 1597 to send each year transcripts of the register to the Bishop. Commonly with old documents, losses occur but Kingstone seems to have been particularly unfortunate, or some earlier custodians somewhat lax. A relatively recent source of the late nineteenth century (11) suggested that registers existed dating from 1571, and this suggestion was repeated in a Post Office directory dated 1912(29). A note in the front of the Kingstone register of baptisms for 1813-1873 records the response to an enquiry made in 1832. This note stated that there were three registers containing entries prior to 1813. These included, firstly, a register of baptisms, burials and marriages between 1571 and 1678 (legible to 1598, and partially legible to 1678). The second register recorded baptisms and burials between 1679 and 1812, and marriages from 1679 to 1752, with some separate leaves for marriages between 1755 and 1802. The third register recorded marriages between 1803 and 1812. The actual situation is rather different with no registers surviving of a date earlier than 1755, and only marriage registers existing from 1755. From 1813 onwards all registers survive. The parish registers (apart of course from those in current use) are preserved at the County Records Office at Stafford.
On a happier note Bishop's Transcripts of an earlier date do survive (24). They date from 1679, although with a number of gaps [1682-1685; 1701-1705; 1791-1794].
So what has happened to Kingstone's parish registers? Could some documents dating from 1571 still exist? Could they be in private hands? We can only hope that they have survived somewhere and that they will someday reappear.

The following list is of surnames of individuals recorded in the earliest surviving Bishop's Transcripts from 1679 - 1708: Hawthorn ; Martin ; Harvy ; Ensworth ; Coapstake ; Adderly ; Elsmore ; Harris ; Barks ; Carrington ; Thurffield ; Holding ; Hawkins ; Sherratt ; Manlove ; Jenkinson ; Barton ; Orme ; Holt ; Holland ; Brinly ; Wilson ; Jackson ; Hitchcox ; Houle ; Norman ; Briggs ; Greatrix ; Fisher ; Emery ; French ; Tallary ; Bolson ; Oakley ; Mottram ; Wilkinson ; Stokes ; Cooke ; Sherriffe ; Crutchley ; Belcher ; Kinsorsley ; Croxon ; Walker; Degg ; Goring ; Tompson ; Prince ; Mills ; Madeley ; Embry ; Cox ; Bentals ; Marrat ; Palmer ; Toft ; Lathbury ; Mayson ; Harding ; Nixon ; Woodhouse ; Green ; Beard ; Starky ; Bentily ; Watkins ; Hudson ; Potts ; Dawson ; Pegg ; Ensor ; Crawley ; Ward.

## 2. Kingstone incumbents

Kingstone old church, an ancient foundation, dates from about 1175 (16)(36), or perhaps from before the year 1166 (page 9).
No list of incumbents for Kingstone church appears to exist before the 1530s, except for Richard de Blifeld (Blithfield), and a priest called Radolphus (Ralph).
A dispute over the advowson of Kingstone followed the death of the priest, Radolphus in or about 1199. William de Greseleia (Gresley) wished to present a replacement, but his right to do so was challenged by John de Blifeld (Blithfield), then Lord of Blithfield, who claimed it for his 'mother - church' of Blithfield. This is thought to have meant that Richard de Blifeld (Blithfield), Rector of Blithfield from about 1185, (and probably a brother of John), held both Blithfield and Kingstone. John de Blithfield asserted that that his father, William de Blithfield had presented Richard de Blithfield to Kingstone to be held together with Blithfield, and that Richard still held both positions. He also claimed that his father had presented Ralph, but that Ralph had only been a 'locum tenens', not the parson.
On the other hand William be Gresley argued that his grandfather, also called William de Gresley (who

| Date | Incumbent | Post | Patron |
|---|---|---|---|
|  | Richard de Blifeld |  |  |
| -1199[d] | Radolphus |  | William de Greseleia 1199 |
|  |  |  | Abbot of Rocester (by c.1240) |
| 1533 - 1558[d] | John Abell*[w1558] | curate |  |
| 1561 - | Ralph Lompe | curate |  |
| 1561 - | John Russell | curate |  |
| 1565 | Thomas Bickley | rector |  |
| 1573 - 1581[d] | John Russell[w1581] | rector |  |
| 1579 - | John Mansfield | curate |  |
| 1580 - | Christopher Preece | curate |  |
| 1580 - | Robert Daye | vicar |  |
| 1584 - | Edward Cheshire | curate |  |
| 1593 - | Thomas Eckles | curate |  |
| 1596 - | Thomas Bolton | curate |  |
| 1604 - 1609[d] | William Lynney*[w1609] | curate |  |
| 1609 - | Robert Gee | curate |  |
| 1616 - | George Dale | curate |  |
| 1630 - 1674[d] | Lawrence Dawson | curate |  |
| 1636 - 1640 | Ralph Rodes | curate |  |
| 1651 - 1652 | no curate |  |  |
| 1652 - | John Beeby | curate |  |
| 1659 - | Thomas Hele | pastor |  |
| 1666 - | Thomas Orton | curate |  |
| 1693 - | William Lynes | curate |  |
| 1698 - | Jonathan Wilkinson | curate |  |
| 1717 - | Richard Bassett | curate |  |
| 1755- | Edward Shaw | curate |  |
| 1782 - 1820[d] | John Hilditch* | curate | Earl Talbot |
| 1821 - | Evan Lewes | curate | " |
| 1822 - | John Hanbury | curate | " |
| 1824 - | Thomas Powell Browne | curate | " |
| 1854 - | John Hempsted | curate | " |
| 1861 - | Samuel Gilson | curate | Earl of Shrewsbury & Talbot |
| 1864- | Henry Matthews | curate |  |
| 1867 - | Samuel Gilson | vicar |  |
| 1873 - | Charles Osborne Gordon | vicar | " |
| 1883 -1898[d] | Edward Drury Hathaway* | vicar | " |
| 1900 - | Arthur Thomas Brereton | vicar | " |
| 1905 - | John Richard Palmer | vicar | " |
| 1941 - | Joseph Bowman | vicar | " |
| 1943 - | David Neaum | vicar | " |
| 1946 - | Harold Hollingworth | vicar | " |
| 1951 - | Donald Wace Watson | vicar | " |
| 1955 - | Norman Myatt | vicar | " |
| 1958 - | Charles Treyhern Upton | vicar | Bishop of Lichfield - from 1961[T] |
| 1971 - | Peter Gledhill | Priest in charge | " |
| 1982 - | Stuart Munns |  | " |
| 1986 - | Mark Vidal Hall |  | " |
| 2002 - | Dominic Stone |  | " |
| 2011 - | Joseph Cant |  | " |

Table 3 **Incumbents of Kingstone Church**

**Key:** <sup>d</sup> indicates date of death; but not necessarily when still in post at Kingstone
\* indicates burial at Kingstone    <sup>w</sup> (with date) indicates that the incumbent left a will

<sup>T</sup>The transfer of the advowson in 1961 was said to *'make better provision for the cure of souls'*.

died in 1166), had presented Ralph, and that the advowson was in <u>his</u> gift (34).
The case appeared to have been settled in favour of William de Gresley, but around 1240, when William Gresley gave certain lands in Kingstone to Rocester Abbey, together with the advowson of Kingstone church, it becomes clear that the earlier dispute had not been resolved. The right of William Gresley to gift the advowson was then challenged by James de Blithfield, then Lord of Blithfield (and grandson of John de Blithfield) (36). This dispute over the advowson was linked to the ownership of Kingstone itself. When the Gresley family acquired Kingstone is unknown; perhaps the Blithfield family were previous owners or had claims over some of the land (page 9).
The situation with Gratwich is simpler with an almost complete list of incumbents (usually rectors) going back to the church's foundation in about 1230, and with the Chetwynd family of Ingestre (and their successors, the Earls Talbot, and Earls of Shrewsbury and Talbot) listed as patrons listed as far back to about 1300.
More recent rectors of Gratwich have also been vicars of Kingstone, with their residence at a rectory at Gratwich. Exactly when the two posts were combined is unclear, but the acquisition of the manor of Kingstone by the Chetwynd family, in 1716, to add to their manor of Gratwich would seem to a logical starting point. However Thomas Orton, preacher at Gratwich from 1663 was also curate at both Gratwich and Kingstone from 1666. Also William Lynes was rector at Gratwich as well as the curate at Kingstone from 1693. In 1692 there was a dispute which split the parish with some members of the congregation being dissatisfied with Thomas Orton. A physical encounter is also reported to have taken place in the church between Thomas Orton and Mr. Goring (probably John Goring). The outcome was that Thomas Orton was relieved of his post at Kingstone (although he was at Gratwich until 1701) (20). During this time Jonathan Wilkinson was the curate at Kingstone, and Kingstone seems to have had a separate incumbent for a number of years after that.
From Thomas Powell Browne onwards, into modern times, the incumbent has been the same at both churches.

Plate 33  **St. John the Baptist Kingstone**

Plate 34  **St. Mary the Virgin Gratwich**

The above images are taken from the front cover of the Kingstone-with-Gratwich parish magazine for May 1913.
[Note: There was no church clock at Kingstone in 1913, and no lych gate until 1929.]

## 3. Nonarum Inquisitiones

The *Nonarum Inquisitiones* relates to a grant by Parliament to Edward III in 1342 to assist him in his wars in France, of one-ninth of the corn, wool and lambs produced in the kingdom. The value of these items was assessed for the year 1341, parish by parish (including for Kingstone) by groups of parishioners under oath.
In this early record the local jurors were asked to provide a valuation (as follows) using as a guide a tax on clerical incomes imposed by the Pope in 1291. However, as the 1291 tax took into account other contributions to clerical income, the jurors in 1342, in almost every case judged that the assessment for their church based on the 1291 valuation was too high.

**Church of Kyngeston**   Taxes, X marks (in 1291)
Richard de Gretewych, Hugh Gamel, William Clericus, John Osbarn, Richard de Paynlowe,
John Meriel, parish jurors, present that the ninth is worth this year 6 marks and no more,
and so they cannot reach the true value of the said Church because the rector holds:
1 messuage, 10 acres, value ½ mark; tenth of hay, value 20s; oblations, profits, and small tithes 26s 8d.

## 4. Inventory of Kingstone Church goods 1552

In the reign of King Edward VI (soon after the introduction of the Second Prayer Book) the King's Commissioners were appointed to travel around the country making inventories of every parish church and its contents and take away for the King's use (i.e. to make money to swell the Government coffers) everything not considered necessary for the reformed church services. Everything was removed except one chalice and paten, the church bells, one cassock and a linen cloth for the communion table. (Private persons had already plundered many churches so that the inventories may not be complete).

*'A just trew and parfett survey and inventorie of all goodes, plate, juelles, vestments, belles and other ornaments, of all churches, chapelles, brotherheddes, gilds, fraternities, and compenies, within the hundred of Totmordislowe in the Counti of Stafford, taken the first day of October, in the sixth year of the reigne of our Sovereign Lord King Edward the Sixthe, by Walter Vicounte Hereford, Edward Lyttleton esquier, and Thomas Fitharbert, Knighte, by Virtue of the Kinges Majesties Commission to them directed in that behalfe, as hereafter particularli appereth '*

'KINSTON

   Fyrst, a challes of silver with a patent, parcell gilte.
   Itm, iiij old vestements, ij ameses, ij albes, iiij alterclothes.
   Itm, a surples, a rochet, ij towelles, iij belles, a sanctus bell.
   Itm, a hande bell, a sacring bell, a crosse of brasse.
   Itm, ij cruetts of tinne, a sensor of brasse, a cope of seye.
   M.D. delyvered by ----------------------- to John Les and William Alsbye, Churchwardens
   there, on(e) chales of silver with a patent parcell gilte, ij lynen Clothes for the Holli Comunyon
   Table, iij bells and a sanctus bell in the stepull, and on Surples for the Curat to ministre with,
   safeli to be kept ------------------------ the viij th of May.

   Indorsed Kinston. '

   [ M.D. = memorandum of what should have been there ] (16).
   Comment - Note that a 'sacring bell' was a little bell tinkled at the altar at the elevation of the Host, while a sanctus bell hung in the steeple and gave warning to parishioners at home at the Sanctus, that the Consecration and central act of worship was approaching.

It is interesting to see that (the old) church had ' iij belles' i.e. three bells, as now. Two of these bells would presumably have been those still in existence today (cast in the early 16th. century). The third bell must have been replaced later, in the reign of King Edward's half-sister Queen Elizabeth I. Kingstone's (now recast) third bell dates from 1595.

## 5. Kingstone Old Church Seating Plan

This is a fascinating document (Fig. 47) dating from more than 380 years ago (36).
The general layout is interesting in suggesting that the present church was in part modelled upon it.

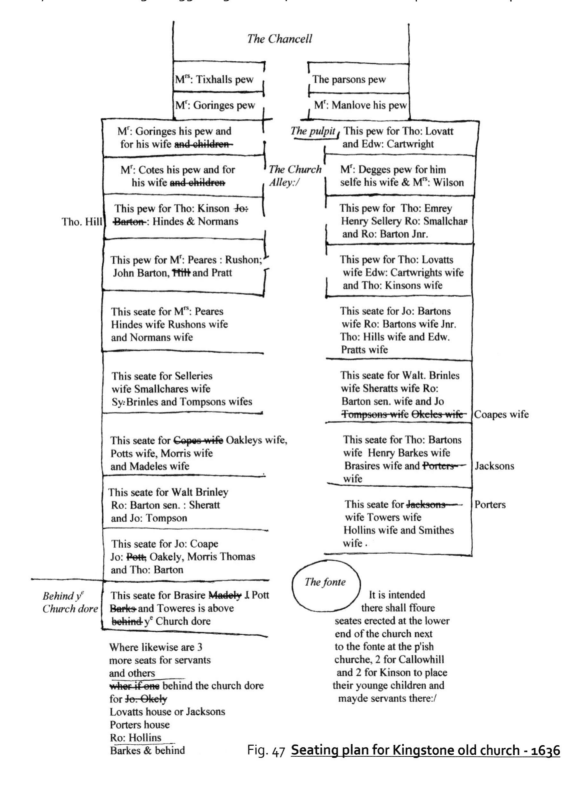

Fig. 47 <u>Seating plan for Kingstone old church - 1636</u>

The seating plan for Kingstone old church, dated 1636, is interesting in a number of ways, including what it reveals about the social hierarchy of the time. It is perhaps because of disputed seating arrangements that this document exists. The plan shows that this church consisted simply of a chancel and nave, having no aisles, and was then without the Degge chapel which would have been added on the north side at a later date.

Box pews (in the chancel, and in the nave nearest the chancel) and other seats were arranged on each side of the central 'church alley'. A circular font is shown. A drawing of the font exist (Plate 7, page 35). Was this the font now sited in the churchyard - the font illustrated is rather elongated by comparison?

Where you sat was most important - you could not sit anywhere. Places were specifically allocated to properties and named individuals living in the parish. The 'best seats' (in the chancel, and in the nave closest to the pulpit) were reserved for the gentry who lived in the major residences such as Leese Hill Manor, Wanfield Hall, Callowhill Hall and Blythe Bridge Hall. Further back in the nave there were places for the yeoman, farmers and tradesmen. The further back you sat, the lower your status. Right at the back were seats for unnamed individuals. These may have been simple benches or forms for house servants and farm workers. Notably, those who sat at the front of the church were usually men. Their wives and children were likely to be further back! Among the gentry, comfortably seated in their box pews were the Tixall family of Lees Hill, and the Manloves of Wanfield Hall.

Mr. Goring lived in Kingstone itself. The Lovatt family lived at Callowhill, as they had done for centuries past. Behind Thomas Lovatt sat Mr. Degge and his wife. This almost certainly refers to the later, Sir Symon Degge, the celebrated lawyer and antiquarian. This is the earliest-known record of his whereabouts after his birth; he would have been a young man of 23 at the time. Mr. Cotes was clearly a gentleman of some importance. John 'Cootes' of Callowhill was High Sheriff of Staffordshire in 1629. He appears to have lived at Upper Callowhill (page 86). Amongst other individuals shown on the plan, and seated prominently in the nave were Thomas Kinson of Callowhill, Edward Cartwright, Robert Barton and Thomas Emery of Kingstone - all were yeoman.

[A yeoman may be defined as a man, below the rank of gentleman who owned a small estate of land which he cultivated himself.]

Plate 35 **An interior view of Kingstone Old church** - from a series of watercolour paintings by Miss. Theodosia Hinckes and Mrs. Rebecca Moore, dated 1857-1861.

Reproduced with the permission of the Lichfield Cathedral

Others who lived in Kingstone would have been tenants, mainly of the Goring family. The seating plan shown is one of two similar versions. The plan copied here shows Mr. Goring seated in the chancel. He was in the same seat which was occupied by Mr. Tixall on the other (evidently earlier) plan (Mr. Tixall having died in 1632). Annotations included with the two plans reveal that the allocation of this seat was contested. One plan may have shown the 'before' i.e. existing arrangement, and the other, the 'after', i.e. the resulting arrangement when the dispute had been resolved, although the presumed 'after' plan illustrated here shows further alterations. According to the notes, Mr. Tixall had taken the seat *'pretending himself to be thick of hearing'*. His own allocated seat was actually the next seat, further up the chancel but it seems he wanted to be nearer the pulpit. [Mrs. Tixall, who died in 1651 is shown to occupy this seat on the plan illustrated.] Additionally, it was noted that Mr. Perry, Mr. Tixall's son-in-law (presumably after Mr. Tixall's death) had been sitting in the seat Mr. Tixall had occupied, and which was claimed by Mr. Goring! This seat, the notes tell us *'about 12 years since did belong to Mr. Goringe's house'*. Mr. and Mrs. Goring were said to be content for Mr. Perry to have the next seat (the one Mr.Tixall had moved from) in exchange for the seat they claimed, subject to the Bishop's approval. Interestingly, the pew in the nave, next to the disputed seat that the Goring family wanted restored, was also allocated to them. According to the notes, Mrs. Goring sat in this seat which *'anciently belongeth to the Mannor house, which is theirs'*. A point of confusion arise here in that Mr. (Henry) Goring's son John married Mr. (William) Tixall's youngest daughter and co-heir, Phelice, and the Gorings are said to have acquired Leese Hill at some point. So is the 'Mannor house' referred to here Leese Hill Manor? The answer to this question is, probably not. Firstly, in 1636, William Tixall's youngest daughter was probably too young and not yet married to John (baptised in 1620) in 1636. (Their first child, Thomas was not born until about 1647.) Phelice Tixall may also not have had access to her inheritance until after 1651, when Mrs. Tixall died (26). Secondly, the seat which *'belongeth to the Mannor house'*, on what appears to be the earlier seating plan is said to have been *'formerly Mr. Aston's'*. Sir Walter Aston, the former owner, had sold the Manor of Kingstone, and the chief farms to Henry Goring in 1625 (page 10), a date consistent with the *'about 12 years since'* statement above. On the other hand, Leese Hill Manor (page 68) seems to have been then owned, not by the Astons but by the Tixall family. Henry Goring, in his will, dated 1650 was said to be 'of Kingstone', suggesting that his family seat, *'the Mannor house'* was in Kingstone. So where was this manor house? There are two main possibilities, including firstly and obviously, Manor Farm, a very old house which must date back to at least the 17$^{th}$ century. However, Kingstone Hall (page 42), recorded as being owned by the Gorings in the 1690s, is perhaps more likely.

In a final twist, annotations on the seating plans further revealed that Mr. Perry did not in fact live in Kingstone parish. It was said that *'Mr. Perry dwelleth in the p'ish of Uttoxeter and in that churche is a seate belonginge to the House. So that here he is an Intruder in that he hath 2 or 3 small tenentes in kingston p'ish and to them competent seates are belonginge in the church which the tennants doe enjoy'*. In other words, Mr. Perry had a seat allocated to him in Uttoxeter church, but not in Kingstone. Mr. Goring appears to have had his way, and got his seat back!

It is interesting to compare the seating plan of 1636 with the interior of the church (Plate 35, page 130). The box pews are shown near the chancel end of the nave and into the chancel. The pulpit is in the same position although a more significant raised feature. The painting also shows the Degge chapel, probably added in about 1696.

## 6. A case of excommunication!

In May 1757, Thomas Wilson (of Blythe Bridge Hall (page 87) or the blacksmith (page 92)?) had been summoned, but failed to appear before the Bishop's Consistory Court to answer charges of non-payment of Church Rates. [Church Rates were levied to maintain the church fabric and to meet its running costs; they were not tithes.] The Court decreed that *'contumaciously absenting himself and still persevering so to do, pronounced him contumacious, and in pain of such his contempt, decreed him to be excommunicated - upon the Sunday next - during the time of divine service - publically denounce and declare the said Thomas Wilson by our Authority to be ex-communicated'*.

Edward Shaw, the curate at Kingstone added a note to the Court's declaration in July 1757, recording that *'the within written excommunication was openly and publically read and pronounced in the parish church of Kingston in the time of divine service there in the face of the congregation there assembled'* (24).

By this date excommunication was not of such consequence, if someone chose not to attend church anyway.

## 7. Some more recent matters

Kingstone church, in the last few years, has undergone major repairs on its spire, but it is interesting to look back (via records kept by churchwardens) at see how the church was been cared for in years past.

An insurance policy document surviving from 1921, recorded that the then vicar (Mr. J. R. Palmer) and churchwardens paid an annual premium of £1- 8s - 6d to insure the church against fire. The church was insured for £2000, which consisted of £1300 for the building, £200 for seats, pulpit, font etc., £175 for the stained glass windows in the chancel, £150 for the organ and £175 for the bells and the clock. This indicates that the present clock, dated to 1932 (page 38) was not the first clock.

Another insurance policy document, dating from 1919 insured church workers. For an annual premium of 5s - 6d the document recorded that the workers insured were one cleaner (annual pay £3), and one organ blower/bell ringer (annual pay £2 -10s -0d). [The organ blower/bell ringer would have been Thomas Wood, page 106.]

The church clock has had regular maintenance by Smiths of Derby, with the records going back to at least 1948. However, in 1966, the clockmaker reported, following his annual visit that the belfry was in an extremely dirty state through the *'depredations of pigeons'*, and that the accumulation of rubbish had almost stopped the clock! In his opinion there was a serious danger that the belfry floor would be rotted. His recommendation that the birds should be excluded from the belfry clearly needed to be acted upon, but there was also the consequence that some individuals were faced with the unenviable task of removing all the 'guano'!

Kingstone church has three bells which were all removed from the old church. In 1975, John Taylor & Co., bell founders of Loughborough re-hung the bells (on the old bell frame), but with stationary fittings. The tenor bell was unfortunately cracked and had to be recast, for the considerable cost of £598-32.

Records dating back to 1955 list fund-raising activities, including dances, raffles and donations in order to provide a replacement organ. Proceeds from the organ fund enabled an organ to be brought from Pattingham, near Wolverhampton in 1958, and to be relocated in Kingstone church. There had clearly been a problem, however during a Sunday service in November 1965, when the organ failed to function. Following the incident, Hawkins and Son, who maintained the organ wrote in reply to a letter from then Vicar, Mr C. T. Upton. Such a problem, they said, had not been encountered before; the manufacturers of the tubing used inside the organ having told them it was inedible. It had been discovered that mice were responsible ; they had eaten through the tubing!

We tend to take the supply of services including electricity and water for granted. In 1945 a licence was obtained to provide a water supply to the church. South Staffordshire Waterworks Co. quoted £12 -12s- 0d for 36 feet of ½ inch lead pipe and a stop tap, linking with the mains in the road, and suggested a local plumber to lay the supply pipe up to the church.

Ward & Godbehere, builders of Uttoxeter carried out repairs to the roof timbers in 1947, and in 1952 carried out internal decoration work. This involved staining and varnishing all the pews, choir-stalls, reading desks and organ, and painting all the walls. In 1956 John Chell of Uttoxeter fitted and painted new guttering and down-pipes.

In 1949, Braithwaite and Co. of Birmingham reported on the state of the spire. The stone work was said to be in good condition, but some tiles were broken or missing, the weathercock needed cleaning and re-gilding, and the lightning conductor was obsolete. Their complete survey and report was supplied at a cost of just £2 -10s- 0d.

In 1961, Furse & Co. of Nottingham carried out an inspection of the spire, described as of the broach type, rising to a height of approximately 90 feet, and *'surmounted by a wrought iron weather vane, which carries a wind indicating bird'*. They reported they were not able to take ladders to the top of the spire because it was not boarded underneath the tiles. The weather vane was said to be leaning due to lead work on the wooden boss below the vane having split. There was corrosion of the iron vane, and with probable rotting of the wooden boss. The weather cock was reported to have a hole in it, probably due to a gunshot (someone shooting the pigeons?), and required repair, cleaning and re-gilding. The small iron vanes on each of the four window openings also required repair or removal. Additionally they reported broken tiles, and that the tiles had been cemented in position, contrary to normal building practice, making repair work more difficult. They could only give a provisional estimate (of £191) for the work, which included scaffolding to cover the entire spire, and his did not include the cost of repairs to the weather vane which could not be accurately assessed.

It would appear that no remedial work was subsequently carried until 1971 when Rafferty Bros & Co. Ltd, steeplejacks of Stoke-on-Trent submitted their estimate to carry out repairs to the spire. Scaffolding was to be erected, enabling the weather vane to be removed and repaired using new timber and lead work. The iron vanes/finials on top of the spire windows were to be removed, the top of the windows covered in lead and the apertures boxed in. They also quoted to replace some timbers at the base of the spire and replace tiles which had fallen away from the broach. The estimate for this work on the spire then? It was £727, significantly less that the cost of repairs to the spire and roof carried out in recent years!

## 8. Kingstone Charities

Reference to the several Kingstone charities associated with Kingstone is made here because although charitable donations have no necessary link to the Church in the present age, traditionally it was the case. Charitable bequests were made in wills, and wills were proved by the Church authorities.
Two stone slabs to the side of, and behind the organ in Kingstone church have inscriptions detailing the conditions of three charities :

On the first slab:

1. Robert Crompton of Elstow in the County of Bedfordshire Esqr. gave 30 shillings (£1 - 50) yearly to be paid at Christmas to the poor of the town and parish of Kingstone for ever. Being a rent charge issuing out of the Manor or Lordship of Cresswell in the County of Stafford.

2. Simon Whithall of Blythbridge Gent. gave a meadow called *Casy Croft* to be given 6 pence ( 2½ p) a week in bread to the poor of the township and parish of Kingstone for ever.

On the second slab:

3. Thos. Byrd of Hixon gave by his will, bearing the date of Nov. 29th 1843, to the widows and orphans resident in the parish of Kingstone the sum of 12s (60p) yearly for ever on the feast of Saint Thomas, out of certain lands called *Ferny's Croft and Paddock* and *Barley Croft* situate in the parish of Kingstone and County of Stafford.

A granite slab attached to the wall of the church to the left of the main door gives the conditions of the Beard charity :
4. Charles Beard of Burton on Trent
By his will dated the 20th January 1891 (26) bequeathed the legacy of £1000 to be invested in Government Securities in the name of the official trustee of Chartered Funds and the dividends arising there from to be paid to the churchwardens for the time being of Kingstone near Uttoxeter in the County of Stafford and to be by them applied half yearly towards the maintenance of three or more indigent persons of the age of 63 years and upwards residing at a distance not exceeding three quarters of a mile from the site of the parish church of Kingstone aforesaid and without distinction of sex or regard to the religious beliefs of such persons.

5. The Stonier Bequest
Ernest Stonier was the owner and occupier of Kingstone Hall Farm, Kingstone. He died in 1933.
By his will dated 19th November 1932 he left the sum of £3000 to the parish of Kingstone. This was to be invested and the annual interest to be used to provide a parish nurse or for the necessities of life for the aged poor, infirm or sick of the parish. This was to be administered by three trustees at their absolute discretion.These persons were to be appointed at the annual parish meeting. However, Mr. Stonier left a life interest in his estate to his spinster sister Mabel Stonier. Thus the money did not become available to the parish until after her death in 1958. In 1955 the parish meeting was replaced by the parish council - the

first trustees being Mr. N.B. Capewell (Chairman), Mr. Alfred Bettson and Mrs. Elsie Cotton. Payments have been paid annually at Christmas or also at Easter e.g. in December 1989. £443 was distributed to 41 people and a further £442 was distributed to 44 people at Easter 1990.

Some comments relating to Kingstone Charities

1. The Crompton Charity can be dated to 1676. Among Stafford Charities a charity called Lovett's Charity arose from a deed of gift of 1676 by Robert Crompton of Elstow, Beds. This gift was in fulfillment of the intention of his grandfather Robert 'Lovett', a London merchant from Callowhill in Kingstone who died at Elstow in 1657, and of Crompton's uncles Richard and Robert Crompton (26)(44). The Crompton family lived at Cresswell, Stafford. The long association of the Lovatt family with Callowhill has already been mentioned. Robert Lovatt, who died in 1657, was the younger brother of Thomas Lovatt of Callowhill (page 84).

2. The Whitehall Charity dates from 1630. Symon Whitehall of Blythe Bridge died leaving a will dated 1630. Sir Symon Degge, the antiquarian was related to this Symon Whitehall (Symon Degge's great grandmother was firstly married to Thomas Degge, and secondly she married William Whitehall, producing a son, Symon Whitehall (page 102)(36). Symon Whitehall and his wife had no children, and Symon Degge became Symon Whitehall's heir, inheriting his estate which is believed to have included Blythe Bridge Hall.
*Casey Croft / Cosy Croft / Kissey Croft /Kessey Croft* is a piece of land totalling approximately 3¾ acres which at the time of the 'in lieu of tithe apportionment' in 1838 was divided between Blythe Bridge Hall {442} and what is now the Blythe Inn {441} (Fig. 38, page 88) (24).

3. Thomas Byrd was a publican and maltster at Hixon, in Colwich parish, who was recorded as living with his wife, Hannah in Pool Street, Stowe by Chartley in 1841. He died in 1844, aged 51 and was buried at Colwich. He was married three times, but appears not to have had any children.
*Ferney Croft* and *Paddock and Barley Croft* (approximately 4½ acres in total) were part of the property of Samuel Durose of Kingstone (pages 43-44) until his death in April 1842 and sold by auction later in that year (2). Thomas Byrd presumably purchased this land in 1842 when it was offered for sale. Thomas Byrd has no known link with Kingstone so why he acquired this land, and then made this charitable provision in his will is a mystery. No rent-charge is now payable as this charity was redeemed in 1976.

4. Charles Beard was baptised in Kingstone in 1817, son of John and Elizabeth Beard. John Beard was publican at the Dog and Partridge Inn. John Beard's son, George succeeded his father at the Dog and Partridge (later called the Shrewsbury Arms) while Charles Beard, his younger brother sought his fortune elsewhere. Charles Beard and his wife Susannah were servants, living in lodgings in Melton Mowbray in 1851, but by 1861 he also had become a publican, being recorded, with his wife, running the Fox and Goose (now the Burton Bridge Inn), in Burton upon Trent (3). By 1871 Charles and Susannah Beard had moved to the Every Arms at Eggington, Derbyshire (more recently, Anoki an Indian restaurant), which was an inn, but also a farm of 110 acres. In 1881 and 1891, Charles Beard (a farmer), and his wife Susannah were retired and living in a property in Derby Road, Horninglow, Burton upon Trent. Charles Beard died in 1895 and Susannah Beard died in 1899, both being buried in Stapenhill Cemetery, Burton upon Trent. It appears that Charles and Susannah Beard had no children. Presumably, in old age, being then reasonably 'well-off', Charles Beard remembered his Kingstone roots, and recalled those he knew in Kingstone in his youth who were not so well provided for. The name of Beard has long associations with Kingstone, which continue to the present day. The name first appears in Kingstone parish registers in 1705 (24).

5. Ernest Stonier was unmarried and had no direct descendants. His property included Kingstone Hall Farm together with Broomy Leasow, and also Kingstone Wood, so he was clearly a man of means. However, £3000 was a considerable sum to leave as a bequest.

# Bibliography

1. *Alumni Cantabrigienses*: A Cambridge Alumni Database
   http://venn.lib.cam.ac.uk venn.lib.cam.ac.uk/Documents/acad/intro.html

2. The British Newspaper Archive   www.britishnewspaperarchive.co.uk
    - Sale of Blythe Bridge Hall estate 1795: Staffordshire Advertiser 28 Nov. 1795
    - Michael Crutchley, gamekeeper- appointed by Earl Talbot: Staffordshire Advertiser 7 Sep. 1805
    - Sale of timber from Kingstone Woods: Staffordshire Advertiser 11 Apr. 1812
    - Sale of bankrupt's estate - James Bakewell the elder and James Bakewell the younger, of Weston on Trent, soap boilers: Staffordshire Advertiser 23 Dec. 1815
    - Sale of timber, Abbot's Wood, Kingstone: Staffordshire Advertiser 10 May 1817
    - Sale of timber in Kingstone Wood: Staffordshire Advertiser 30 Mar. 1822
    - Newly erected mill at Blythe Bridge: Staffordshire Advertiser 10 May 1823
    - Sale at Rugeley of timber growing in Kingstone Woods: Staffordshire Advertiser 26 Oct. 1823
    - Theft of sheep belonging to John Ward of Kingstone: Staffordshire Advertiser 14 Mar. 1829
    - Fowls stolen, including from Ward of Kingstone: Staffordshire Advertiser 13 Feb. 1830
    - Fowl stolen from John Ward of Kingstone: Staffordshire Advertiser 6 Mar. 1830
    - Sale of timber growing in Kingstone Woods: Staffordshire Advertiser 7 Mar. 1835
    - Kingstone and Gratwich clothing club: Staffordshire Advertiser 6 Jan. 1838
    - Sale of three cottages by William Perkin: Staffordshire Advertiser 13 Jan. 1838
    - Auction of farming stock, Mr. Sampson Sharratt of Kingstone Hall: Staffordshire Advertiser 16 March 1839
    - Celebrations marking the birth of the Prince of Wales: Staffordshire Advertiser 19 Feb. 1842
    - Sale of property at Kingstone - as directed under the will of Samuel Durose: Staffordshire Advertiser 17 Sep. 1842
    - Theft of food by Thomas Taylor: Staffordshire Advertiser 18 Mar. 1843
    - Earl Talbot provides funding for a constable: Staffordshire Advertiser 6 Jan. 1844
    - Two fowls stolen from William Upton: Staffordshire Advertiser 13 Apr. 1844
    - Theft of silver watch by Anne Bentley: Wolverhampton Chronicle & Staffordshire Advertiser 23 Oct. 1844
    - Railway instead of canal for transporting timber from Kingstone Wood: Staffordshire Advertiser 18 Oct. 1845
    - Sale of land belonging to Thomas Griffin: Staffordshire Advertiser 3 Apr. 1847
    - Sale of Heathcote's farm: Staffordshire Advertiser 8 May 1847
    - Sale of timber at Kingstone: Staffordshire Advertiser 3 Feb. 1855
    - Two pigs stolen from William Upton: Staffordshire Advertiser 1 Dec. 1855
    - Sale by auction, stock of Thomas Spooner, shopkeeper, Kingstone: Staffordshire Advertiser 26 Jan. 1856
    - Thomas Fernyhough of Kingstone - alleges assault: Staffordshire Advertiser 29 Mar. 1856
    - Sale of timber from Kingstone Wood: Staffordshire Advertiser 10 Apr. 1858
    - Broomy Leasows Farm for sale: Staffordshire Advertiser 3 Dec. 1859
    - Sale of small farm at Blythe Bridge (in occupation of John Green): Staffordshire Advertiser 25 Dec. 1860
    - George Wood convicted of bigamy: Staffordshire Advertiser 5 Jan. 1861
    - Consecration of Kingstone Church: Staffordshire Advertiser 11 Nov. 1861
    - Theft of wood from Kingstone Wood by besom makers: Staffordshire Advertiser 26 Mar. 1864
    - Sale of Blythe bridge Mill (let to Mr. Webb): Staffordshire Advertiser 30 Apr. 1864
    - William Ainsworth, caught fishing in Tad Brook: Staffordshire Advertiser 3 Jun. 1865
    - Sale of Manor Farm: Staffordshire Advertiser 25 Jan. 1868
    - Henry Croxton fined - beer house open after 10 pm: Staffordshire Advertiser 11 Apr. 1868
    - Samuel Taylor - theft of gun from Michael Critchlow: Staffordshire Advertiser 15 May 1869
    - Broomy Leasows Farm for sale: Staffordshire Advertiser 29 May 1869
    - Sale of farm stock by Sutton, Broomy Leasows: Staffordshire Advertiser 9 Oct. 1869
    - Alleged assault of Johnson by Crutchley: Staffordshire Advertiser 14 Aug. 1869
    - 'A Ramble Round Kingstone': Staffordshire Sentinel and Commercial & General Advertiser 14 May 1870
    - Three houses for sale, two houses for sale: Staffordshire Advertiser 26 Feb. 1876 & 4 Nov. 1876.
    - Two cottages for sale, opposite the church, near the new school: Staffordshire Advertiser 29 Sep. 1877
    - Opening of new Kingstone School: Staffordshire Advertiser 24 Nov. 1877

- House and shop, with bakehouse, in Kingstone - to let (C. Bunting): Staffordshire Advertiser 22 Dec. 1877
- Cottages for sale - tenants: Constable Steele, Francis Sherratt, John Fradley: Staffordshire Advertiser 31 Jan. 1891
- Dwelling houses for sale in Kingstone; six cottages at Kingstone sold to Mr. Helmsley for £206: Staffordshire Advertiser 22 Aug. 1891 ; 29 Aug. 1891
- 'Armed Burglars near Uttoxeter': Tamworth Herald 12 Mar. 1892
- Accidental death of Thomas Johnson in Kingstone Wood: Staffordshire Advertiser 2 Sep. 1893
- Clothing distributed to the poor - including at Kingstone: Staffordshire Advertiser 30 Dec. 1893
- County Council grants for technical instruction: Staffordshire Advertiser 11 Jan. 1896
- Henry Johnson charged with deserting his children: Staffordshire Advertiser 10 Jun. 1899
- Farewell dinner for Kingstone volunteers for Boer War: Staffordshire Advertiser 27 Jan. 1900
- Kingstone school closed due to scarlet fever: Staffordshire Advertiser 17 Feb. 1900; 15 Mar. 1900
- Welcome home from Boer War volunteers: Staffordshire Advertiser 22 Jun. 1901
- For sale:- Lot 1 dwelling house at Blythe Bridge bank, outbuildings include malt-house; Lot 2 All six freehold dwelling houses in the centre of Kingstone: Staffordshire Advertiser 5 Jun. 1909
- Sale by auction - The Old Town Farm (occupation of Joseph Gorse): Staffordshire Advertiser 28 May 1910
- The Malt House, Blythe Bridge Bank, for sale: Staffordshire Advertiser 4 May 1912
- Road bridge built at Blythe Bridge: Staffordshire Advertiser 7 Nov. 1914
- Sale of the Blythe Bridge Estate: Staffordshire Advertiser 3 Jul. 1915
- Kingstone School closed due to whooping cough: Staffordshire Advertiser 31 Jul. 1918
- Sale of small holding at Blythe Bridge (in occupation of Mr. Brandrick): Staffordshire Advertiser 24 May 1919
- Sale by auction of Moorfields; sold to Mr. Hawthorn for £825: Staffordshire Advertiser 8 May 1920; 15 May 1920
- Sale of Wanfield Hall and Leese Hill estate ; sale prices: Staffordshire Advertiser 5 Mar. 1921; 26 Mar. 1921
- Third annual Kingstone Show: Staffordshire Advertiser 16 Aug. 1924
- Birches Farm for sale; sold to Mr. T. Bettson: Staffordshire Advertiser 17 Mar. 1926; 27 Mar. 1926
- Death of John Stonier (Kingstone Friendly Society founded by his father): Staffordshire Advertiser 16 Oct. 1926
- Surveyor of Rural District Council reported on Kingstone School sanitary arrangements; cases of diptheria in Kingstone : Staffordshire Advertiser 26 Jan. 1929
- Lych Gate built: Staffordshire Advertiser 8 Jun. 1929
- Kingstone Show - silver cups and prizes total £100: Staffordshire Advertiser 9 Aug. 1930
- Death of Sarah Fradley, postmistress at Kingstone: Staffordshire Advertiser 17 Jan. 1931
- Tenth annual Kingstone Show: Staffordshire Advertiser 8 Aug. 1931
- Public clock installed on tower of Kingstone church: Staffordshire Advertiser 16 Apr. 1932
- Kingstone parish requests for four council houses to be built: Staffordshire Advertiser 10 Jun. 1933
- Nursery rhymes tableau at Kingstone School, organised by Mrs. Beech: Staffordshire Advertiser 24 Apr. 1934
- Retirement of Mrs. Beech, headmistress of Kingstone School: Staffordshire Advertiser 28 Dec. 1935
- Kingstone Friendly Society meal: Staffordshire Advertiser 16 May 1936
- Thomas Wood - 60 years devoted service to be recognised: Staffordshire Advertiser 19 Jun. 1937
- Kingstone School closed due to epidemic of whooping cough: Staffordshire Advertiser 23 Oct. 1937
- Obituary of Thomas Wood: Staffordshire Advertiser 6 Aug. 1938
- Church Fete at Kingstone: Staffordshire Advertiser 16 Aug 1941
- Six new council houses. 8 more houses are to be built at Kingstone: Staffordshire Advertiser 21 Dec. 1946
- Eli Fradley - cut the first sod of the Uttoxeter to Stafford railway: Staffordshire Advertiser 12 Apr. 1947
- 34th birthday party for Kingstone WI: Staffordshire Advertiser 4 Jul. 1952
- Pantomime 'Cinderella' presented at Kingstone: Staffordshire Advertiser 30 Jan. 1953
- Tender submitted for building council houses at Blythe Bridge: Staffordshire Advertiser 30 Jul. 1954
- Miss Guntripp, headmistress of Kingstone school is leaving: Staffordshire Advertiser 20 Aug. 1954

3. History of the Burton Bridge Inn (formerly Fox & Goose), Burton on Trent
   http://www.burtonbridgebrewery.co.uk/Pubs/BridgeInn/BridgeInnHistory.shtml

4. Census records 1841-1911

5. The Chetwynds of Ingestre   www.tixall-ingestre-andrews.me.uk/ingestre/chetwyndt.htm

6. Derbyshire Record Office
    - Papers of the Holden family. Mortgate by William Pott & Humphrey Pott, both of Leafields, parish of Stowe  1705. Ref. D779B/B 7-8
    - Papers of the Holden family. Counter lease by Thomas Croxton to Humphrey Potts, senior of Leafields 1709. Ref. D779B/B 15

7. Domesday Book  A Complete Translation  Editors: Dr. Ann Williams & Professor G. H. Martin Penguin Classics 2003.  ISBN 0-141-43994-7

8. Drabble, P., 1948 Staffordshire (The County Book Series) (Robert Hale Ltd).

9. Ekwall, E. , 1960 The Concise Oxford Dictionary of English Place Names. (Oxford).

10. Erdeswicke, Sampson  A Survey of Staffordshire, with a description of Beeston-Castle in Cheshire. To which are added some observations upon the possessors of monastery-lands in Staffordshire, c. 1600. By Sir S. Degge. Collated with MS. copies, and with additions and corrections, by Wyrley [and others] by Rev. T. Harwood. 1844

11. Eyton, Rev. R. W, 1881 Domesday Studies : An Analysis and Digest of the Staffordshire Survey, Trubner & Co..

12. Furse & Co. (London), 1961 Kingstone Church - An inspection of the spire.

13. Gallimore, J. F. , Kingstone memorials and epitaphs 2010

14. Gallimore, J. F. , Sir Symon Degge: his Family and their World 2016
    Amazon Books  ISBN 9781535465830

15. Hall, D. , 1982 Medieval Fields, Shire Public. Ltd..

16. Hutchinson, Rev. S.W. , 1893 The Archdeaconry of Stoke - on - Trent. Historical notes on N. Staffs. Abbeys, Churches, Chapels and Parishes, Bemrose & Sons Ltd.

17. Illustrated London News, Dec. 28 1861 The erection of the new church ; St. John's Church, Kingstone, Staffs.

18. The Inner Temple Admissions Database. http://www.innertemple.org.uk

19. Kerby, Graham (on behalf of Kingstone Church) <u>Lest We Forget</u> - First World War 1914-1918.

20. King. P.W. , Wealdon Ironmasters in the Midlands - an article from Wealdon Iron: Bulletin of the Wealdon Iron Research Group Second series No. 21 2001.  http://www.wealdeniron.org.uk/BullSer2/Vol2-21.pdf

21. Kingstone Women's Institute: Kingstone in the Year 2000 Stowefields Publications,  Stafford ISBN 095191102 8 o

22. Leicestershire Record Office
    - Summons to attend 26 July 1865 to hear plaintiff's application that purchase of lands at Kingstone (and other properties) co. Staffs from the trustees of the Duke and Duchess of Sforza Ceserini, to be approved. 22 July 1865.  Ref 25D60/407
    - Consent to the purchase - freehold estate at Blithe Bridge, Kingstone (and other properties) co. Staffs. 1 Aug. 1865.  Ref 25D60/408

23. Lichfield Cathedral, Deanery watercolours
    - St John's church, Kingstone, (exterior), watercolour 1857
    - St John's church, Kingstone (interior), watercolour 1857

24. Lichfield Record Office  [Note - now closed, all documents are at:  39. Staffordshire Record Office]
- Bishops' Transcripts ; parish of Kingstone 1679 - 1868. Ref. B/V/7
- Case type: Non-payment of church levies/Excommunication 1757 - Kingston: Thomas Wilson. Ref. B/C/5/1757/6
- Petitions for registration of Protestant meeting houses 1798-1849. Ref B/A/12ii/17
- Prenuptial marriage settlement John Mott & Henrietta Oakley 1814. Ref. D546/5/3/2
- Kingstone, Staffordshire - Tithe Award 1838. Ref. B/A/15/547
- Kingstone, Staffordshire -Tithe Map 1838. Ref. B/A/15/177
- Nomination of parish clerk - Kingston: William Stonier 1823. Ref. B/A/11/4/98/2
- Sale of freehold farm - Little Callow Hill 1888. Ref. LD/18/8/1-3

Probate records- wills and inventories
- Robert Norman - Lees Hyll, Uttoxeter 1538
- Ellen Wright - Kynston  1543
- William Lovatt - Callowhill, Kingston 1564/5
- John Tyxall - Lees hill, Uttoxeter 1550
- Arthur Nedham, yeoman - Kynson 1570/1
- Thomas Holt - Kinston 1577/78
- John Shelley, husbandman - Kinston 1588/9
- Ralph Browne - Kinston 1601
- Hugh Netam - Kingston 1601
- Roger Brindley, husbandman - Kyngston 1613/4
- Henry Crompton - Kingston 1613/4
- William Whythall - Blithbridge 1616
- Symon Whitehall - Kingston 1630
- William Tixall, gent. - Lees hill 1632
- Robert Barton, yeoman - Kingston, 1637
- Richard Tooth, yeoman - Blyth Bridge, Kinson 1666
- John Emsworth, yeoman - Leeshill, Uttoxeter 1664
- Anne Goring, widow - Callowhill 1681
- William Barton, yeoman - Kingston 1682
- Humphrey Pott, yeoman - Leayfeildes, Stowe 1684
- William Sherratt, yeoman - Kinston 1687
- Joyce Goreng, spinster - Callowhill, Kingston 1688
- Alexander Manlove, gent.- Leeshill, Kingstone 1688
- William Norman, gent. - Caverswall 1693
- Richard Boulton, yeoman - Kinston,  1701
- Rowland Manlove, gent. - Leese Hill, Kingstone 1714
- Ellin Allen, widow - Loxley 1717
- Robert Hitchcock, husbandman - Woodcocks Heath, Kinston 1719
- Katherine Boulton, widow - Kinston  1725
- Mary Manlove, widow - Leeshill, Kinston 1725
- Mary Jenkinson - Wanfield Green, Kingston 1728
- Johis Holt, yeoman - Stow 1729
- William Martin, yeoman - Blythe Bridge 1731
- John Shelley - Callowhill, Kingston 1731
- Simon Brindley - Kingston 1742
- Elizabeth Willot - Broome Lesows, Kingston 1746
- John Vernon, gentleman - Abbots Bromley 1756
- John Bakewell, yeoman - Kingston 1765
- Mary Wakelin, widow - CallowHill 1765
- Ellen Vernon - Abbot's Bromley 1781
- Thomas Adams, yeoman - Loxley, Uttoxeter 1798
- Jacob Wolliscroft, farmer - Broom Leasow, Kingston-upon-Toad-Brook 1800
- William Atkins, gent. - Newton in Blithfield 1804
- Edward Shelley, farmer - Callowhill, Kingston 1808

- Richard Stonier, miller - Blythebridge Mill, Kingston 1809
- John Elsmoor, farmer - Callowhill, Kingstone 1818
- Joseph Sherrat, publican - Stone 1818
- William Durose, farmer - Loxley, Uttoxeter 1820
- Elizabeth Johnson, widow - Stoke upon Trent 1829
- Joseph Hubbard, builder - Kingstone 1831
- Thomas Wilson, senior, blacksmith - Blythe Bridge 1832
- Samuel Durose, bricklayer - Kingstone 1842
- Sarah Hubbard, widow - Kingstone 1856

25. Lynam, Charles, The Church Bells of the County of Stafford, 1889.

26. National Archives

    National Archives: Wills 1384-1858
    http://www.nationalarchives.gov.uk/help-with-your-research/research-guides/wills-1384-1858
    - Sir Edward Aston - Tixall, Staffordshire 1598
    - Thomas Ridgley, Esqr. - Hawkesyard, Armitage, Staffordshire 1598
    - Henry Goreing, Gentleman - Kingston, Staffordshire 1650
    - John Garenge - Kingston, Staffordshire 1654
    - Joyce Goringe, widow - Bluntshall, Staffordshire 1654
    - Elizabeth Tixall, widow - Lees hill, Uttoxeter 1651
    - Rowland Manlove, Gentleman - Wanfield 1656
    - William Goreng, Gentleman - Bauld, Staffordshire 1656
    - Robert Lovett - Elstow, Bedfordshire 1658
    - John Goring - Callow Hill, Staffordshire 1696
    - Lovet Goring, of the Inner Temple, Esqr., Common Cryer and Sergeant at Arms of the City of London, 1697
    - Sir Symon Degge - Derby, Derbyshire 1702/03
    - Isaac Hawkins - Burton upon Trent, Staffordshire 1713
    - Edward Vernon, Doctor of Physic - Abbots Bromley 1780
    - Rev. Thomas Lawrence - Albrighton, Staffordshire 1812
    - Ellen Lawrence, widow - Winfield Hall, Kingston, Staffordshire 1824
    - Earl Ferrers, the Right Honorable Robert 1827
    - Charles Beard, Gentleman - Burton on Trent 1895

27. The Shorter Oxford English Dictionary on Historical Principles. Third Edition (Revised) (Oxford), 1978.

28. Palliser, D.M. The Staffordshire Landscape, Hodder & Stoughton 1976

29. Post Office Directories
    - Directory of Staffordshire 1818.
    - White's Directory of Staffordshire 1834
    - White's Directory of Staffordshire 1851
    - Postal and Commercial Directory of Staffordshire 1870, J. G. Harrod & Co.
    - Directory of Staffordshire 1876.
    - Kelly's Directory of Staffordshire 1896
    - Kelly's Directory of Staffordshire 1912
    - Kelly's Directory of Staffordshire 1928

30. The History of Parliament. http://www.historyofparliamentonline.org/
    - Sir Walter Leveson MP [1551-1602]
    - Sir Richard Leveson MP [c1570-1605]
    - Walter Chetwynd MP - Stafford [1678-1736] Ist Viscount Chetwynd
    - Walter Chetwynd MP - Lichfield [1688-1732]

31. Pitt, William  A topographical History of Staffordshire  1817

32. Primitive Methodist circuit plans.  http://www.myprimitivemethodists.org.uk/

33. Redfern, Francis,  History and Antiquities of the Town and Neighbourhood of Uttoxeter. Second Edition. Simpkins, Marshall & Co. 1886

34. Rice, A. , Abbot's Bromley , Wilding & Son Ltd. 1939.

35. Caroline Shirley, Duchess Sforza Cesarini.  https://en.wikipedia.org/wiki/Caroline_Shirley,_Duchess_Sforza_Cesarini

36. <u>William Salt Library, Stafford</u>
    - Foeffment  4 Jan.1355  Callowhill (Kalewehul).  Ref. SD Salt/10
    - Domesday Loxley - William Salt Arch. Soc. Collections for a History of Staffordshire Vol. I 1880.
    - Obligatory Knighthood; Staffordshire gentlemen fined for not accepting knighthood from Charles I in 1625/6 - William Salt Arch. Soc. Collections for a History of Staffordshire  Vol. II 1881 Part II.
    - Subsidy Roll of 1327 - William Salt Arch. Soc. Collections for a History of Staffordshire Vol. VII 1886 Part I.
    - Sale of Kingstone by Sir Thomas Gresley to Sir Edward Aston 1593 - William Salt Arch. Soc. Collections for a History of Staffordshire Vol. XVI 1895
    - The Gresleys of Drakelowe - William Salt Arch. Soc. Collections for a History of Staffordshire. 1898
    - Thomas, son of John Lovatt of Callowhill 1619 - William Salt Arch. Soc. Collections for a History of Staffordshire Vol. VI 1903 Part I.
    - Keepers and Justices of the Peace - new Commission listed in 1647 - William Salt Arch. Soc. Collections for a History of Staffordshire 1912.
    - Staffordshire Incumbents and Parochial Records - William Salt Arch. Soc. Collections for a History of Staffordshire 1915.
    - Note on the early history of the parish of Blithfield - William Salt Arch. Soc. Collections for a History of Staffordshire 1919.
    - Articles of agreement between Sir Walter Chetwynd (of Ingestre) and Rowland Menlove, gent. of Perton for Chetwynd's sale of lands in King[ston] and Loxley. Bargain & Sale  12 Aug. 1614.  Ref. S.MS. 565/14
    - Plan and description of the arrangement of pews in Kingston church 1636. Ref. M.837
    - William Salt Arch. Soc.1925 Historical Collections of Staffordshire (Totmonslow Hundred) Hearth Tax for Kingstone Constablewicke 1666.
    - Suicide of John Goring of Callowhill 1696. Letters and manuscripts re. Dr. Richard Wilkes. Ref. S. MS.342/2/1-20.
    - South East view of Kingstone Church, sepia drawing : 1839. Ref. SV V65a
    - Font in Kinston Church, sepia drawing: 1839. Ref. SV V65b
    - Kingstone Church, water colour painting. A north view, from the road by a bridge and cottage. nd [c.1830-40]. Ref. SV V66a.
    - Sale Catalogue - sale by auction of farms and lands 5 Jan. 1860, including Broomy Leasows Farm.  Ref. Sc. F/1/48
    - St. John's Church, Kingstone, Staffordshire: Detailed geophysical (Resistance) Survey 2005, Grantham Archaeology Group   David Charles Hibbit.  Ref. Misc 1071.

37. Stebbing Shaw, Rev. , The History and Antiquities of the County of Stafford.

38. County Museum, Shugborough  McCann photograph collection c.1900 - 1966. Ref. P76.041. Kingstone School 1910-1912

39. <u>Staffordshire Record Office</u>
    - Chetwynd family documents - include references to inheritance of Rugeley family from Richard Norman of the Bold (Booth) 1418-1628.  Ref. D1798/HMChetwynd/30
    - Manor of Kingston (tenants names) Thomas Gresley of Drakelowe/ Sir Edward Aston of Tixall, bart. Bargain & Sale 1593. (Also with a list of Thomas Gresley's tenants) Ref. D1798/HM ASTON/8/1.
    - Kinston: Mortgage of manor 1609  Sir Walter Aston, Thomas Crompton of Stone. Ref. D1798/HM ASTON/21/4
    - Title deeds to manor of Kingstone, capital messuage at Callow Hill and lands in parishes of Kingstone and Uttoxeter
    - 28 May 1625  Sir Walter Aston - Manor of Kingston to Henry Goring and his heirs. Descent of title: Aston/Goring/Chetwynd Talbot. 1625-1803. (Also with a list of Walter Aston's tenants)  Ref. D240/B/1/77

- Title deeds to Birchwood Park estate p. Leigh, and lands in Leigh, Kingstone, Milwich and Uttoxeter 1626-1788 Descent of title: Aston/ King/Goring/ Chetwynd/Talbot. Ref. D240/B/1/87 includes reference to marriage settlements of William Goring with Anne Lovatt 1646, Thomas Goring with Elizabeth Floyer 1668, and John Goring with Barbara Fleetwood 1690.
- Uttoxeter, Lees Hill Farm and a cottage. Deed of partition amongst co-heirs of Elizabeth Tixall, deceased (Perrie, Ensor, Manlove, Goring) 1641/2. Ref. D1798/HM ASTON/10/31
- Marriage settlement of William Gorenge and Anne Lovatt 3 April 1646. Ref. 7560/1
- Staffordshire Pedigrees 1664 - 1700 (Harleian Society Vol. LXiii ) 1907 - Degge, Goring, Manlove
- Conveyance of premises in High St., Uttoxeter: Alexander Manlove of Leeshill, gent., son and heir of Rowland Manlove of Wanfield, gent., deceased to Nicholas Mynors of Uttoxeter, gent. 8 April 1667. Ref. D786/14/1
- Title Deeds to Blithe Bridge Estate, including the marriage settlement of Degge/Williams 1696, and bargain and sale of the Bowden and Fenny Bentley estates, Co. Derbyshire. 1696-1796. Ref. D240/B/1/78.
- Release of Manor of Kingstone and Birchwood Park and Callow Hill Estates p. Kingstone; cottages and market tolls in Uttoxeter 1716. Parties: Walter Chetwynd of Grendon and Barbara his wife née Goring to John Chetwynd of Meere. Ref. D240/A/1/7
- A Survey of the Mannor of Kingstone together with the Farmes of Byrchen Bower, Lady Newlands and belonging to the Hon'ble John Chetwynd - by William Godson c.1717 - 1720 Ref. D240/E(A)/2/157 (for map only) & Ref. D240/E/S/1/25 (for accompanying survey schedule)
- Re. Frances Chetwynd A moiety of the manor of Kingston etc. 1786. Ref. D240/B/1/77/14-20
- Valuation of Mr. Mott's estate Little Callowhill 1795. Ref. D240/E/V/1/24-26
- In-letters to Thomas Mills including letter expressing regret at failure to purchase Blythe Bridge Hall Farm, p. Kingstone, all from Colonel Talbot. 1795-1796. Ref. D240/E/C/1/46/1-19
- Survey of manor of Kingstone and Gratwich and Birchwood Park, p. Leigh. Surveyor: Samuel Botham 1801 Ref. D240/E/S/1/20/1-2 & Ref. D240/E/S/1/21
- Valuation of Heathcote's estate 2 Aug. 1800. Ref. D240/E/V/1/24-26
- Petitions for certificates for briefs. Petition from minister, churchwardens and inhabitants of Kingstone for certificate for a brief to gather funds to take down and rebuild Kingstone church. Oct. 1803. Ref. Q/SB 1803 M/234-237
- Copy will of Edward Shelley, farmer - Callowhill, Kingston 1804, with settlement re. Blythe Bridge estate 1827. Ref. D877/207/2
- Shrewsbury Estate - Tenancy agreements 1838-1910 (including letters to the Earl's agent from tenants - Hobbis in 1882, & Fernyhough in 1902). Ref. D240/D/14
- Conveyance of two cottages at Kingstone. Parties - Guardians of the Poor/ Earl of Shrewsbury and Talbot 16 Feb. 1859. Ref. D240/B/3/10
- Release of land for road widening where a toll gate house lately stood 1878. Ref. D240/B/3/30.
- Shrewsbury Estate : 1918 Catalogue of Sale - Plan and Particulars of the Gratwich, Kingstone and Birchwood Park Estates (W.S. Bagshaw & Sons). Ref. D240/K/18a-d.
- Parish Registers - Kingstone, Staffs. 1755 - (Marriages). 1813 - (all records); and other parishes

40. Staffordshire County Council: Historic Environmental Record

41. Staffordshire Record Society. Edited by Kettle Ann J. A List of Families in the Archdeaconry of Stafford 1532-3. Reprinted by Staffordshire and Stoke on Trent Archive Service 2008.

42. John Taylor & Co., The Bell Foundry, Loughborough. Report: The Bells of the Church of St. John the Baptist, Kingstone.

43. Population of Kingstone - Victoria History of the Counties of England : Staffordshire Vol. I (Oxford).

44. Crompton Charity - Victoria History of the Counties of England : Staffordshire Vol. VI (Oxford).

45. Wood, Goldstraw & Yorath, Stoke - on - Trent 1960 Report : Inspection of the condition of Kingstone Church.

46. Woolley, P, 1995 Seven Studies in the Economic and Social History of Uttoxeter and its adjacent parishes. 1530 - 1830.

## Surname Index

Adams 20 48 49 50
Ainsworth (Hainsworth) 45 47 57 66 78
Allen (Allin) 18 50 64 66 70
Aspinall 86
Aston 9 10 12 91 97 131
Atkins 90
Babb 45
Bagot 7 13 14 19 64 84 117
Bakewell 43 84 94 95 104 105 117 119
Ball 59
Barks 18 19 22 24 72
Barlow 57
Barton 18 19 40 41 70 130
Bassett 119
Bathew 38 69 96 97 98 100 101 106 110 122 123
Beard 20 41 43 44 45 47 51 57 59 62 78 87 96 121 133 134
Bebbington 55 115
Beech 38 55
Bennett 78 84
Bentley 24 57 58 96
Bettson 43 46 54 55 57 59 63 66 71 74 106 113 116 119 120 122
Blackshaw 47
Blithfield (de Blifeld) 9 125 127
Bloor /Blore 86 113
Bond 41
Boole 46
Botham 24
Boulton 22 30 41 47 76 77
Brandrick 63 90 94
Brooks 74
Brough 84 86
Brown(e) 58 60 70 74 78 80 81 122
Bridgwood 95 105
Brindley 18 19 56 57
Brinkler 84 113
Buckley 70
Bull 61
Bunting 45 48 121
Buxton 58
Byrd 43 133 134
Cadwallader 44 46
Campion 46 67 81 121
Capewell 58 96 110 111 112 113 134
Cartmail 70
Cartwright 91 129 130
Causer 113
Charles 81
Chell 70
Cheney 80
Chetwynd 12 13 14 15 16 21 22 24 40 41 42 47 48 51 57 58 60 65 74 75 77 79 82 84 85 86 92 96 97 98 127
Chetwynd Talbot / Earl of Shrewsbury and Talbot 14 15 16 24 25 37 42 46 47 57 58 80 107 117 120 121 127
Chilton 112
Clarke 91 92
Clews 45
Clowes 69
Cole 114 116
Collier 62
Cooke 80
Cope (Cowappe, Coop) 18 41 57 69 92 123
Cotes 85 86 130

Cotterell (Cottrell) / Cotterill 38 42 106 113 116 120
Cotton 54 134
Cresswell 50
Crompton 10 50 84 91 102 133 134
Croxton (Croxdon) 20 41 43 48 51 58 80
Crutchley 62 67 78 81
Dakin 70
Dawson 69
Day 57 62
Deacon 115
Deakin 78 86 91
Degge 12 22 30 33 35 76 77 84 87 89 101 102 103 117 119 130 134
Derry 49 54 59 111 113 114 116
Deaville / Deville 46 48 55 59 62 67 113 123
Dicken 80
Doughty 62 113 116
Durant 59
Durose 43 44 46 73 78 120 134
Dyche 114
Elsmore 18 41 42 51 81 86 95 105
Emery 120 130
Emsworth 60 68
Evans 71 113
Felthouse 58 66
Fearn 71
Fernyhough 40 41 45 49 61 62 79 121
Finnemore 48 51 58 78 81
Fisher 44 92
Fleetwood 12 13
Fletcher 74 98
Foster 73
Fox 94 105
Fradley 43 44 45 46 50 54 57 62 63 70 78 93 96 119 121 122
Gallimore 44 54 59 63 65 74 110 111 114 115 116 119
Gaunt 19 23 73 92
Gilbert 12 13 44 50
Ginders 57
Goodall 92
Goodwin / Godwin (Gorwin) 74 88 98
Goring 10 11 12 13 18 19 22 42 60 68 80 84 86 99 130 131
Gorse 71
Gough 70 84
Gould 70
Green 48 70 93 94
Gresley 9 10 69 91 97 125 127
Griffin 65 69 73 74 104 105
Grimes 66
Guntripp 55 112 113
Harper 70 91
Harrison 78 122
Hathaway 70 119
Hartshorne 69 99 100
Harvey 46
Hawkins 79 80
Hawthorn 79
Hayford 116
Heath 86
Heathcote 94 95
Hilditch 36 60
Hitchcock 18 19 65
Hine 114
Hobbis 55 57

142

Holland 42 121
Hollins 12 13 19 62 63
Holt 18 64 72 76 78
Horobin 55 74
Hubbard 20 70 71
Jackson 18 54 92 110 113 114 116 122
James 116
Jenkinson 19 57 98
Jessop 98
Johnson 20 38 40 41 42 43 44 45 46 56 57 62 63 67 77 78 79 80 89 91 96 121
Jones 54 55
Kinson 130
Kynnersley (Kenersley) / Sneyd Kynnersley 16 22 24 25 72 74
Land 74
Launder 42
Lawrence 24 67 69 96 98 99 100 101 117 119
Leadbetter 86
Leese 78
Leigh 98
Locker 49 89 106
Lovatt 11 12 13 18 48 54 55 80 84 101 110 130 134
Lowe 112 114 116
Lymer / Limer 77 95 96
Manlove 13 16 18 22 64 68 69 96 97 98 99 100 119 130
Martin 18 54 62 88 92 94 98 120
Meakin 69
Mellor 58 84 89 90 120
Meverell 85
Morris 59
Moss 54 55 67 92
Mott 86
Motteram (Mottram) 18 19 84 86 87
Mould 93 111
Nash 71
Neaum 113
Needham (Netum/Neidtam/ Nedham) 24 39 40 46 118
Noakes 43 79
Norman 18 60 67 68 85
Orme (Armes) 96
Orrell 12 102
Osbourne (Osbern / Osbarn) 24 70 128
Pakeman 49 50 122
Palmer 123 132
Pearce / Pierce 19
Peill 63
Perkin 51 56 57 67 74
Perry 68 131
Phillips 96
Pickering 37 46
Plant 90 91 113
Poole 48 60 113
Potts / Pott 41 45 57 58 60 61
Pountain 96
Preston 49
Prince 98 122
Probyn 114 116
Raynes 92
Rees 113
Reynolds 43 61
Richardson 54

Riley 73
Roberts 93
Sanders 12 80
Rugeley (Ridgeley) 85
Rushton 73
Sargeant 54 61 78 116 122
Severn 70 74
Sforza, Duchess 92
Shaw 40 49 57 71 86 131
Shenton 41 45
Shelley 84 86 94 105
Shepherd 73
Sherratt / Sharratt 18 19 35 41 42 43 44 63 67 71 73 80 81 91 121
Shirley / Earl Ferrers 92
Shipley 71
Slater 45
Smith 30 45 64 67 70 72 73 76 79 92 114
Smyth 19 102
Somerville 55 114 116
Spooner 43 44 58 69 84 86
Steele 18 19 43 44 121
Stephens 74
Stevenson 45 46
Stonier 20 38 43 46 47 49 58 59 60 71 74 87 91 92 96 103 110 117 118 120 123 133 134
Sutton 74
Talbot / Earl Talbot 14 15 24 40 41 42 47 51 58 59 61 62 63 66 74 77 78 79 80 81 84 86 89 91 92 94 95 96 107 117 127
Tams 81
Taylor 55 57 61 62 110 119 120 123
Titley 95 96
Titterton 81 120
Tixall (Tyxall) 12 13 18 67 68 99 130 131
Tompson 18 19 30 40 41 88
Tooth 18 19 87
Turner 114
Upton 38 59 73 115 132
Vernon 69 99 100
Wakelin (Wateling) 72 76 84
Walthall 80
Ward 20 45 50 58 59 69 77
Watson 110 115
Webb 62 79 92
Webster 96
West 43 46 55 57
Weston 74
Wheat 46
Willart (Willot) / Willan 40 43 74 95
Williams 49 77 117 118
Wilks / Wilkes 96 99 100 123
Wilson 20 24 45 46 54 61 62 66 81 87 89 92 93 94 120 131
Whieldon 71 74
Whitehall (Whythall) 19 66 67 78 83 84 101 102 103 133 134
Whittaker 54 55 113 115
Wood 20 41 42 43 45 46 47 49 58 59 67 71 90 96 106 117 123 132
Woodcock (Wodcok) 18 65
Woodings 48 49 60 73 74
Woolley 20 40 62 70 87
Woolliscroft (Wollescroft) 48 57 58 74 90
Worsey 71
Wright 18 39 90

Note: Complete surname lists from pages 17-19, 125, Table 3, page 126 and Fig 47, page 129 are excluded. Similarly excluded are names given on page 53 for Plate 11, page 109 for Plate 23 & page 112 for Plate 25.

## Place Index

Abbot's Wood  (Abbott's Wood) 23 24 57 75 76 77 96
Alder Carr Coppice (Migery Bank Coppy) 75 76 77
Alton Towers 15 16
Ashcroft  Wood or Coppice (Ashton Coppy) 23 24 63 121
Ashcroft Farm 27 63 121
Barley Croft 43 78 133 134
Barley Mow 27 33 43 51 56 67 107
Barn Croft 58
Barn Farm 48 59 60
Barn Ground 24 48 59 110 121
Barn Yard & Orchard 56 57
Barracks / School View 28 45 46 51 54 55 96 106
Birches Farm & 'Birches Corner' 23 47 60 71
Birchwood Park 11 13 16 24 42 84
Black Pits (Pitts) & the 'Black Pool' 22 27 33 50 51 57 61 62 63 70
Blakeley sich / Blakly syche 23 61 62 67
Blithfield 7 9 17 105 125 127
Blount's Hall  (Blunt's Hall) 8 13 96 100 109
Blythe Bridge Bank 27 51 61 63 75 78 86 87 92 94 95 96 105 106
Blythe Bridge 8 19 21 23 25 83 84 87 - 94 101 102 103 112
Blythe Bridge, Butcher's shop / Wheelwrights shop 16 28 94
Blythe Bridge Hall 19 28 77 80 84 86 87 88 89 90 91 92 94 102 103 117 130 131 134
Blythe Bridge Mill 8 10 27 87 88 89 91 92 94 95 96 103 110 122
Blythe Bridge smithy 16 24 27 46 50 61 87 92 93 94 120 131
Blythe Bridge Cottage 91
Blythe Inn 28 90 91 94 134
Bolton Coppice (Katherine Boulton's Coppy) 76 77
Booth (Bold / Bould / Bauld) 8 11 13 83 84 85 87 89 93 120
Brick Leasow Coppy 75 77
Brickhill Leasow & Brickhill 'poole' 24 57
Broomy Croft 43 44
Broomy Leasows 16 23 24 27 41 42 43 60 69 70 71 73 74 123 134
Brough's Farm 84 86
Brown's Rough 77
Burndhurst Mill 8 92 109 120
Callowhill 8 9 10 11 12 13 19 22 23 28 78 79 80 82 83 84 85 86 94 95 101 102 105 120 129 130 134
Casey (Cosy/ Kissey/ Kessey) Croft 87 89 91 133 134
Caverswall (at Lower Loxley) 60 67 68 85 109 120
Chapel, Primitive Methodist 50 70 113 121
Chapel Bank / Chapel Hill 46
Chapel Field / Chapel Meadow 111 113 114 115 116
Chartley 7 8 11 15 60 92
Church Cottage 22 27 33 43 44 121 122
Church Farm (Church House) 16 23 24 25 27 33 35 36 41 47 50 55 58 59 66 69 71 73 119 120 121 122
Church View 28 43 44 45 46 50 67 71 81 95 121
Cocksey Nook (Cookey Nook / Cook hey / Le Cochayes) 23 24
Cottage (in Wood Lane) 41
Cuckold's Haven (Gate) & Tollgate Cottage 8 70 73 74 118 119
Degge chapel 33 36 101 103 117 118 119 124 130 131
Degg's Wood (Mr. Degg's Coppy) 30 75 77 88
Dowry(Dowery) Farm 16 28 75 76 78 79 80 81 83 86 95
Drakelow 9 10 97
Ferney's Croft & Paddock 43 133 134
Four Acres 76 77
Galleytree (Gallow's Tree) Cottage 24 27 69 70
Glasshouse Bank (Glasshouse Coppy) 75 76 77
Gratwich 7 8 9 15 16 17 24 92 93 107 110 111 113 115 118 120 127
Great High Wood 75 76 77

Grindley 8 10 11 12 21 92 117 118 120 122
Heathcote's Farm / Gravelly Bank 94 95
Hitchcock's Rough (Oldfield Coppy) 22 65
Hollydene (Old Town / Old Town Farm)  27 47 70 71 74
Hollyhays (Holly Hay Farm) 28 60 73 74 93
Holly Lane (Cuckold's Haven Lane)  8 70 72 73 74 93 118 119
Holly Trees 95
Ingestre 13 14 15 16 51 56 107
Institute & Village Hall 34 57 58 110 111 112 113
In Town Meadows 22 24 30 31 33 40 41 49 72 73
Johnny Field Coppice (Johnney Field Coppy) 30 31 64 65 77 105
Leafields 8 60
Leese Hill (Lea's Hill) (Lee's Hill) (Loxley Lees) 7 8 13 22 24 27 60 64 65 67 68 69 83 87 94 96 97 98 99 100 104 109 130 131
Leese Hill well 22 64 65
Little High Wood 75 77
Loxley / Loxley Hall/ Loxley Park 7 8 9 16 22 24 25 69 70 71 74 96
Kingstone church 37 38 39 104 106 113 119 123 127 132 133
Kingstone old church 1 2 9 27 32 33 34 35 36 37 39 60 101 103 104 117 119 124 125 128 129 130 132
Kingstone Hall Farm 12 16 23 28 32 38 42 43 49 71 74 106 117 118 119 121 131 133 134
Kingstone Post Office (& Shop) 45 46 50 93 121
Kingstone School 16 38 50 51 52 53 54 55 56 57 120
Kingstone spring 25 44 56
Kingstone Wood 8 41 42 75 76 77 78 79 81 94
Maer (Mere / Meere) 13 14 15 22
Magpie Hall 27 67
Malt house / Malt House Farm 27 43 51 86 95 96 105
Manor Farm 16 23 24 25 27 33 41 47 48 49 50 77 117 118 122 131
Mill Coppice (Millpool Coppy) 75 77
moat / Moats Meadow (near Moss Farm) 22 24 41
Moisty Lane (Musty Lane) 22 30 33 43
Moorfields (Wood Farm) 16 28 40 75 76 77 78 79 83
Moss Farm (Moss House Farm) 24 25 27 33 40 41 49 79 109 121
Moss Lane 22 30 75 76
Mosses, The 16 27 48 78 91 96 121
Motteram's tenement 84 86
Mount Pleasant 27 33 43 60 61 70 93 122
Nene House (School House) 27 50 55 56 57 113 119
Old Field 22 65
Old School 33 37 46 50 67 121
Policeman's House / Police Office 43 44 121
Poor House, The 27 57 58 61
Potts' Lane 27 33 51 58 60 61 62 63 65 70 93
Shrewsbury Arms (Dog & Partridge) 16 24 28 33 45 46 47 48 59 60 71 78 107 108 109 110 118 119 121 134
Stalk Bank Farm (Stalk bank orbalk, Staulk Baulk) 23 59 71
Rocester Abbey 7 9 75 127
Rose Cottage 28 61 69 70 119
Rosevale 27 66 67
Shoul's Wood (Sroul's Coppy, Shroulds /Shrouds) 22 24 75 76 77
Tad Brook 2 4 8 22 47 57 74 76 82 117 118
Villa, The 28 38 43 54 67 73 76 82
Walnuts Farm  (Walnut Tree House) 28 41 46 47 49 50 59 121
Wanfield (Windfield) (Windy) Hall 16 19 21 22 23 24 27 30 31 38 66 68 69 77 83 87 88 94 96 97 98 99 100 106 109 122 130
Watery Lane  (Park Lane) 8 23 64 65 69 70 73 119
Woodcock Heath 22 24 27 59 65 66 67 77 78 81 83 94 106 119 122
Woodside Cottage 27 96
Yew Tree Cottage 27 96 106

Printed by Amazon Italia Logistica S.r.l.
Torrazza Piemonte (TO), Italy